Frommer's®

Los Angeles
day BY day®

2nd Edition

by Garth Mueller

Contents

Published by:

Wiley Publishing, Inc.

111 River St.
Hoboken, NJ 07030-5774

ISBN 978-0-470-92611-6 (paper); 978-1-118-01332-8 (ebk); 978-1-118-01333-5 (ebk); 978-1-118-01334-2 (ebk)

Editor: Stephen Bassman
Production Editor: Eric T. Schroeder
Photo Editor: Richard Fox
Cartographer: Roberta Stockwell
Production by Wiley Indianapolis Composition Services

Front cover photos, left to right: © Bob Torrez / Getty Images; © Taylor / Souls-Veer / Corbis; © Sylvain Grandadam / Robert Harding Picture Library Ltd / Alamy Images

For information on our other products and services or to obtain technical support, please contact our Customer Care Department within the U.S. at 877/762-2974, outside the U.S. at 317/572-3993 or fax 317/572-4002.

Wiley also publishes its books in a variety of electronic formats. Some content that appears in print may not be available in electronic formats.

Manufactured in China

5   4   3   2   1

A Note from the Editorial Director

Organizing your time. That's what this guide is all about.

Other guides give you long lists of things to see and do and then expect you to fit the pieces together. The Day by Day guides are different. These guides tell you the best of everything, and then they show you how to see it in the smartest, most time-efficient way. Our authors have designed detailed itineraries organized by time, neighborhood, or special interest. And each tour comes with a bulleted map that takes you from stop to stop.

Hoping to tour Hollywood's famous sights, stroll Venice Beach, or shop your way through all of L.A.? Planning a walk through Downtown, or plotting a day of fun-filled activities with the kids? Whatever your interest or schedule, the Day by Days give you the smartest routes to follow. Not only we take you to the top attractions, hotels, and restaurants, but we also help you access those special moments that locals get to experience—those "finds" that turn tourists into travelers.

The Day by Days are also your top choice if you're looking for one complete guide for all your travel needs. The best hotels and restaurants for every budget, the greatest shopping values, the wildest nightlife—it's all here.

Why should you trust our judgment? Because our authors personally visit each place they write about. They're an independent lot who say what they think and would never include places they wouldn't recommend to their best friends. They're also open to suggestions from readers. If you'd like to contact them, please send your comments our way at feedback@frommers.com, and we'll pass them on.

Enjoy your Day by Day guide—the most helpful travel companion you can buy. And have the trip of a lifetime.

Warm regards,

Kelly Regan

Kelly Regan, Editorial Director
Frommer's Travel Guides

About the Author

Garth Mueller is a writer who lives in Los Angeles with his wife, Barb, and their young sons, Miles and Benjamin. He has a B.A. in English from Emory University and an M.F.A. in film production from Florida State University. He is the co-author of *Frommer's California Day by Day*.

Acknowledgments

For my extraordinary wife, Barb Crawford—home is wherever you are.

Loads of thanks to my editor, Stephen Bassman, and to Cate Latting, for the opportunity to rediscover my city.

An Additional Note

Please be advised that travel information is subject to change at any time— and this is especially true of prices. We therefore suggest that you write or call ahead for confirmation when making your travel plans. The authors, editors, and publisher cannot be held responsible for the experiences of readers while traveling. Your safety is important to us, however, so we encourage you to stay alert and be aware of your surroundings.

Star Ratings, Icons & Abbreviations

Every hotel, restaurant, and attraction listing in this guide has been ranked for quality, value, service, amenities, and special features using a star-rating system. Hotels, restaurants, attractions, shopping, and nightlife are rated on a scale of zero stars (recommended) to three stars (exceptional). In addition to the **star-rating system,** we also use a **kids icon** to point out the best bets for families. Within each tour, we recommend cafes, bars, or restaurants where you can take a break. Each of these stops appears in a shaded box marked with a coffee-cup-shaped bullet ☕.

The following **abbreviations** are used for credit cards:

AE	American Express	DISC	Discover	V	Visa
DC	Diners Club	MC	MasterCard		

Frommers.com

Now that you have this guidebook to help you plan a great trip, visit our website at **www.frommers.com** for additional travel information on more than 4,000 destinations. We update features regularly to give you instant access to the most current trip-planning information available. At Frommers.com, you'll find scoops on the best airfares, lodging rates, and car rental bargains. You can even book your travel online through our reliable travel booking partners. Other popular features include:

- Online updates of our most popular guidebooks
- Vacation sweepstakes and contest giveaways
- Newsletters highlighting the hottest travel trends
- Online travel message boards with featured travel discussions

A Note on Prices

In the "Take a Break" and "Best Bets" sections of this book, we have used a system of dollar signs to show a range of costs for 1 night in a hotel (the price of a double-occupancy room) or the cost of an entree at a restaurant. Use the following table to decipher the dollar signs:

Cost	Hotels	Restaurants
$	under $100	under $10
$$	$100–$200	$10–$20
$$$	$200–$300	$20–$30
$$$$	$300–$400	$30–$40
$$$$$	over $400	over $40

An Invitation to the Reader

In researching this book, we discovered many wonderful places—hotels, restaurants, shops, and more. We're sure you'll find others. Please tell us about them, so we can share the information with your fellow travelers in upcoming editions. If you were disappointed with a recommendation, we'd love to know that, too. Please write to:

Frommer's Los Angeles Day by Day, 2nd Edition
Wiley Publishing, Inc. • 111 River St. • Hoboken, NJ 07030-5774
frommersfeedback@wiley.com

16 **Favorite Moments**

16 Favorite **Moments**

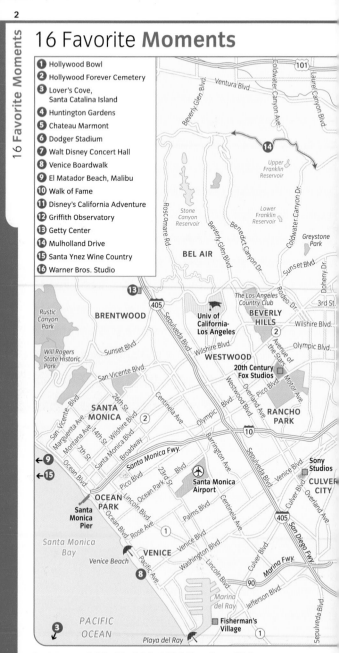

Previous page: Architect Frank Gehry's Walt Disney Concert Hall.

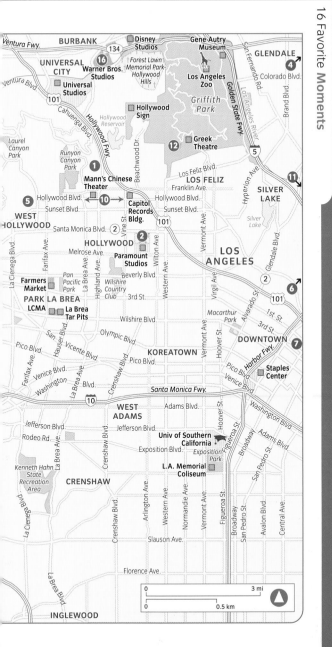

Constantly adapting to new identities, Los Angeles is a great actor, impossible to pin down. I love the way that, within a single block, the city can switch from gritty to glitzy, capable of embodying both the American Dream of endless opportunity ("Go west, young man") and the American Nightmare of not being cool enough ("You're not on the guest list, man"). Here's a highlight reel of some of L.A.'s best roles, from star-making turns to bit parts.

❶ Pack a picnic for the Hollywood Bowl. The nation's largest natural amphitheater is a lovely place to enjoy dinner with a bottle of wine under the stars. Summer home to the L.A. Philharmonic and its ebullient and energizing conductor Gustavo Dudamel, the Bowl also hosts touring heavyweights like Willie Nelson and Radiohead. *See p 126.*

❷ Catch a flick at the Hollywood Forever Cemetery. Join Rudolph Valentino, Douglas Fairbanks, and the other unemployed actors here any Saturday night in summer. Spread your blanket on the grass in front of a marble mausoleum wall (the screen), pop a bottle of vino, and enjoy the show. The schedule shuffles between the classic and creepy: *All About Eve, Vertigo, A Clockwork Orange.* And feel free to scream, or laugh, your head off— you won't wake anybody. *See p 20.*

The tearoom overlooks the Rose Garden at the Huntington Botanical Gardens.

❸ Snorkel in Lover's Cove. This pristine marine preserve on Santa Catalina Island is only 22 miles from the mainland. If you're looking to escape the urban bustle, this should float your boat. The water is calm, blue, and dotted with colorful schools of small fish such as calico bass, blue perch, and the neon-orange garibaldi, California's protected state fish. *See p 155.*

❹ Stop and smell the roses in the Huntington Botanical Gardens. The Rose Garden is the crowd favorite among these 150 green acres, which manage to appear both manicured and sprawling. Applaud nature's sense of humor in some of the strange, ballooning succulents of the Desert Garden, or Zen out in the quiet retreat of the Japanese Garden. *See p 93.*

❺ Soak up some Old Hollywood glamour with your highball. The lobby of the infamous Château Marmont may be a costly place for a cocktail, but it buys you a chance to stargaze on the sly. This legendary hideaway prides itself on its exclusivity; to gain entry, you'll need either a globally recognized face or a hard-won reservation at the hotel or restaurant. *See p 140.*

❻ Down a Dodger Dog. Dodger Stadium welcomed the boys from Brooklyn back in 1962. While newer sports stadiums strain to manufacture a vintage vibe, Dodger Stadium is a SoCal classic, sunny and laidback, with swaying palm trees framing panoramic views of the San

An in-line skater draws a crowd on the Venice Boardwalk.

Gabriel Mountains and downtown. *See p 22.*

⑦ Experience the majesty of the Walt Disney Concert Hall. This is the other home of the L.A. Philharmonic (those lucky dogs). Frank Gehry's audacious exterior looks gift-wrapped by God in curvilinear steel, a stunning catalyst for the revitalization of Downtown. But the hall is no hollow shell—the acoustics within are flawless. A must-see and a must-hear. *See p 56.*

⑧ Rollerblade up Venice Boardwalk. C'mon, there's no shame in trying. Matter of fact, there's no shame in anything on this kitschy stretch of street performers, leathery-skinned exhibitionists, tacky trinket peddlers, break dancers, soothsayers, and doomsdayers. If you've got a freak flag, this is the spot to fly it. *See p 59.*

⑨ Tiptoe in the tide pools. Pick the right time—early on weekdays, off-season—to explore the rocky coves of El Matador Beach, a remote enclave backed against the cliffs of Malibu, and, with a little luck, you'll get what many locals hold so dear: a little privacy. *See p 81.*

⑩ Walk the Walk of Fame. The front of Grauman's Chinese Theatre may look like a zoo of tacky tourism, but don't let that fool you—this is some of Hollywood's most hallowed ground. Snap a couple of shots of the celebrity impersonators—say a sweaty Charlie Chaplin or an ill-tempered Marilyn Monroe—and try to imagine the flashbulbs a-popping on their real-life counterparts walking the red carpet all those years ago. *See p 10.*

⑪ Light up the night at Disney's California Adventure. After 5 years of planning and $75 million, Disney's newest nighttime spectacle, *World*

Famous film stars leave their marks outside Grauman's Chinese Theatre.

The Griffith Observatory reopened in 2006 after a $93-million renovation.

of Color, is a jaw-dropper. Water and fire whip around the sky, and images from Disney and Pixar classics—*Fantasia, The Little Mermaid, Finding Nemo, WALL-E*—are painted with light onto a 380-by-50-foot water canvas. *See p 151.*

⑫ **Celebrate some lesser-known stars.** At the recently renovated Griffith Observatory, it's easy to get caught up in the scientific exhibits, the planetarium, or the spectacular views of the city and the HOLLYWOOD sign, but don't forget to use the free public telescopes and direct some of that wonder skyward. *See p 21.*

⑬ **Get sketchy at the Getty Center.** Feast your eyes on Monet's Impressionistic gems or on *Irises* by Vincent van Gogh, and once you're sufficiently inspired, head over to the sketching gallery, where you can try your hand at mimicking the masters. *See p 11.*

⑭ **Cruise Mulholland Drive.** A great way to get the lay of the land is to drive the winding ridgeline of the Santa Monica Mountains, which separate the city from the valley. Pull off onto one of the many overlooks for stunning panoramas. *See p 13.*

⑮ **Head Sideways to the wine country.** Sample the chardonnays and world-class pinot noirs at one of many wineries nestled among the rolling hills of vineyards in the low-key Santa Ynez Valley north of Santa Barbara. *See p 163.*

⑯ **Peek behind the curtain.** Take a tour of a working movie studio. On the Warner Bros. Studios VIP tour, you can see where Bogie bid farewell to Bacall in *Casablanca,* or sit on the couch where the cast of *Friends* traded zingers (Chandler Bing not included). *See p 9.* ●

Van Gogh's Irises *is one of the Getty Center's main attractions.*

1 The Best **Full-Day Tours**

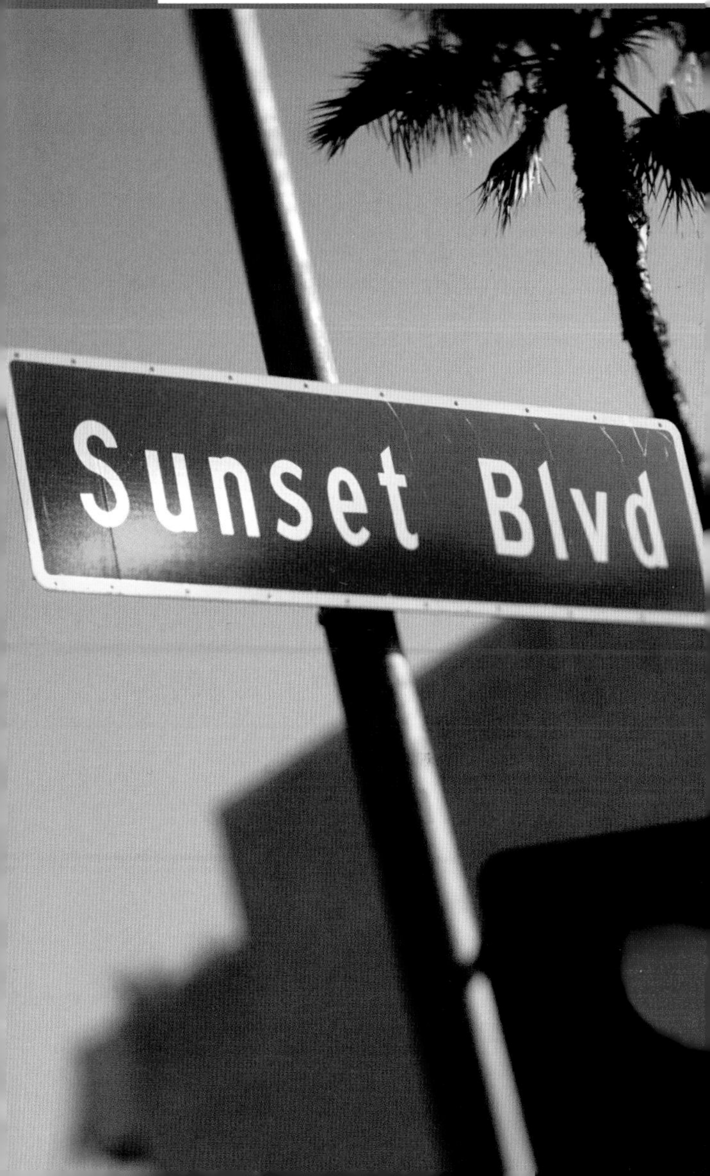

The Best in **One Day**

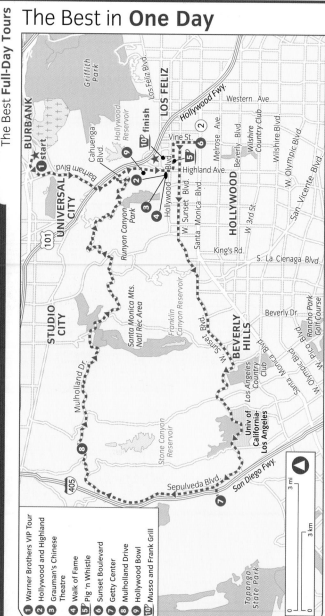

1 Warner Brothers VIP Tour
2 Hollywood and Highland
3 Grauman's Chinese Theatre
4 Walk of Fame
5 Pig 'n Whistle
6 Sunset Boulevard
7 Getty Center
8 Mulholland Drive
9 Hollywood Bowl
10 Musso and Frank Grill

Previous page: All first-time visitors to L.A. should take a drive on Sunset Boulevard.

Seeing the country's largest city in a single day takes preparation. It's best to secure reservations in advance for the Warner Bros. Studios VIP tour, your first stop, as well as tickets to the Hollywood Bowl for the day's finale. In between, you'll see landmarks in pop culture, experience the majestic Getty Center, and wind along a couple of the city's most scenic and historical roads. START: **From Riverside Dr., take Avon St. south to Warner Blvd. Go left and follow the signs to VIP Tour parking.**

① ★★ **Warner Bros. Studios VIP Tour.** Start the day early in Burbank because that's how the ghost of studio chief Jack Warner would want it. Warner Bros., the third-oldest movie studio (founded in 1918), took over 110 acres from First National Pictures in 1928 with the payout from betting big on the first "talkie," *The Jazz Singer.* The 2½-hour tour takes you behind the scenes of the working lot, and with roughly 35 soundstages and outdoor sets, there's a lot of work going on. The hit television show *ER* was shot here, as were *The Dukes of Hazzard, The West Wing,* and *Friends.* These days the sets of *The Mentalist, Ellen,* and *Two and Half Men* fill the soundstages. But it's the studio's film history that boggles the mind—*My Fair Lady, Rebel Without a Cause,* and *Bonnie and Clyde* were all made here. Children 7 and under are not admitted. Reservations are

Take a guided tour of the Warner Bros. lot.

recommended and can be made online. ⏱ *2–3 hr. 3400 Riverside Dr., Burbank.* ☎ *818/972-8687. www.wbstudiotour.com. VIP tour $48 per person. Mon–Fri continuously 8:20am–4pm (extended hours in spring & summer).*

Coming from Riverside Dr., head left on Olive Ave., continue on Barham Blvd., turn left at Cahuenga Blvd., continue on Highland Ave., and park in the parking structure on your right after you pass Franklin Ave.

② ★ **Hollywood & Highland.** After languishing for years as flypaper for runaways and hustlers, Hollywood Boulevard has Times Squared itself in the past decade and is now a polished link to Tinseltown's heyday. The centerpiece of the area's revitalization is the retail and entertainment behemoth at Hollywood & Highland, which includes the grand Kodak Theatre, the first permanent home of the Academy Awards. Explore the multitiered Babylonian-style courtyard, inspired by D. W. Griffith's silent film epic *Intolerance,* and you'll find photo-ready views of the HOLLYWOOD sign perched atop Mount Lee in the distance. ⏱ *30 min. 6801 Hollywood Blvd., at Highland Ave.* ☎ *323/817-0200. www.hollywoodandhighland.com. Mon–Sat 10am–10pm; Sun 10am–7pm.*

You can leave your car in the Hollywood & Highland parking complex; the next stops are walkable.

3 ★★ Grauman's Chinese Theatre. "Over the top" would be an understatement. The bronze pagoda roof, garish columns, leering gargoyles, and fiery dragons—for mad impresario Sid Grauman, these were only half the fun. According to the apocryphal story, silent-film star Norma Talmadge accidentally stepped in a patch of wet cement at the theater's opening (the 1927 premiere of Cecil B. DeMille's *The King of Kings*) and the great imprinting tradition was born. A less dramatic version says Grauman got the idea when he observed his chief mason signing his work (look for "J.W.K."). Today, the Forecourt of the Stars is cemented in history, crammed with the handprints and footprints of more than 200 movie legends. ⏱ *45 min. 6925 Hollywood Blvd.* ☎ *323/464-8111. www.mann theatres.com. Free admission to forecourt. Daily 24 hr.*

4 ★ Walk of Fame. On 18 blocks of pink terrazzo stars, you can find more than 2,000 names—some unforgettable, some already forgotten, and others perhaps less than deserving (sorry, I just don't think Godzilla is much of an actor). Joanne Woodward received the first star in 1960, and Gene Autry received the most, one for each of the five categories: film, television, music, radio, and theater. Immortality doesn't come cheap; the honoree must fork over $25,000 (a "sponsorship fee") to cover installation and maintenance. Be sure to poke your head up every once in a while as you shuffle along, or you could miss other landmarks: the immaculate El Capitan Theatre (6838 Hollywood Blvd.), which premiered *Citizen Kane* in 1941; the Hollywood Roosevelt (7000 Hollywood Blvd.), where the first Academy Awards were held; and another Sid Grauman inspiration, the Egyptian Theatre (6712 Hollywood Blvd.), now home to the American Cinematheque. ⏱ *30 min.; best times are weekday mornings. Hollywood Blvd. from La Brea Ave. to Gower St. & down Vine St. from Yucca St. to Sunset Blvd.*

5 Pig 'n Whistle. Food options abound at the Hollywood & Highland Center, but if you're looking for old-school ambience, try the slightly upscale pub fare at this renovated landmark. In the Forties, customers like Shirley Temple and Judy Garland downed ice-cream sodas. *6714 Hollywood Blvd.* ☎ *323/463-0000. Soups, salads, sandwiches $7–$15.*

John Travolta's star on the Walk of Fame.

The gardens at the Getty Center are as impressive as the architecture.

Back in your car: From Hollywood & Highland, head east to Vine St. and take a right. At Sunset Blvd., take another right.

⑥ ★★ **Sunset Boulevard.** If you have to choose only one road by which to see the city of Los Angeles, this is the one. Beginning near El Pueblo, the historic core of downtown, and stretching nearly 25 miles west to the Pacific Ocean, Sunset links working-class ethnic communities (Hispanic, Armenian, Thai), bohemian Silver Lake, historic Hollywood, the rockin' Sunset Strip, exclusive Beverly Hills and Bel Air, UCLA, and the Pacific Palisades. For an abbreviated tour, start in Hollywood at Sunset and Vine and head west. You can't miss the Cinerama Dome (6360 Sunset Blvd.), which anchors the ArcLight Cinemas complex, where serious cineastes get their fix. When you hit Crescent Heights, you're officially on the world-famous Sunset Strip. Keep your eyes peeled—the names are going to jump out at you hard and fast: Chateau Marmont (no. 8221),

the Sunset Tower (no. 8358), the Viper Room (no. 8852), and Whisky a Go Go (no. 8901), to name just a few. By the time you reach the pink palace of the Beverly Hills Hotel (no. 9641), you're loving the lushness of Beverly Hills. Continue on past the gates of Bel Air and the UCLA campus until you reach Sepulveda Boulevard. 🕐 *45 min.*

Head west on Sunset Blvd., take a right at Sepulveda Blvd., and follow the signs for the Getty Center.

⑦ ★★★ kids **Getty Center.** Money can't buy happiness, but J. Paul Getty's $1.2 billion bought plenty of world-class art (works by van Gogh, Monet, and Man Ray, among others) and an architectural marvel in which to display it—that makes you a little happy, right? Ascend the acropolis and admire the way Richard Meier ballasts his modern, airy design with textured travertine blocks. But don't forget about the art on the inside. Grab a GettyGuide ($5), your own personal digital docent, and go.

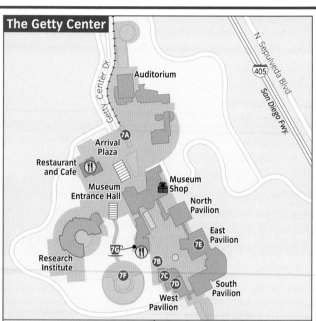

The Getty Center

A 5-minute **7A** tram ride transports you from the parking area up the hill to the museum and provides the first of many excellent views; for now, just pity those poor saps on the 405 freeway. Head across the courtyard to the West Pavilion, where the **7B** Fran and Ray Stark Sculpture Terrace presents modern outdoor sculptures by some of the greatest sculptors of the Twentieth Century, such as Henry Moore and Alexander Calder. Inside the West Pavilion, the **7C** Center for Photographs traces the history of the medium and includes many prints by Walker Evans (1903–1975), and Man Ray (1890–1976), including his famous *Tears*. Take the elevator two floors to the upper level to **7D** paintings (after 1800). On your right are a couple of

Impressionist gems by Claude Monet (1840–1926): *Wheatstacks, Snow Effect, Morning,* and *The Portal of Rouen Cathedral in Morning Light*. Screaming at you from the next wall is the room's rock star, *Irises* by Vincent van Gogh (1853–1890), who created the painting in a Saint-Rémy asylum the year before he died. If your creative juices are flowing, make for the **7E** sketching gallery in the upper level of the East Pavilion. Afterward, take a stroll through the delightful and ever-evolving **7F** Central Garden, created by artist Robert Irwin. Then relax at the **7G** Garden Terrace Café. 🕐 *2 hr. 1200 Getty Center Dr. 📞 310/440-7300. www.getty. edu. Free admission. Tues–Fri & Sun 10am–5:30pm; Sat 10am–9pm. Closed major holidays. Parking $15.*

Head north on the 405, exit at Mulholland Dr., and head east.

⑧ ★ Mulholland Drive. Rolling east along the ridge of the Santa Monica Mountains and away from the setting sun, you can watch the canyons pooling with diffuse golden light. It can be hard to keep your eyes on the road, so pull off into one of the many overlooks to take in vistas of the Los Angeles basin to the south and the San Fernando Valley to the north. Repeat as necessary, because an overload of these curves (or worse, tailgating cars) can be as disorienting as watching David Lynch's *Mulholland Drive.* ⏱ 45 min.

From Mulholland Dr., take a right at Cahuenga Blvd., and continue on Highland Ave.

⑨ ★★★ Hollywood Bowl. Fantastic music, a cool summer evening, a lush green hillside, and an arresting venue steeped in entertainment history—a night at the Hollywood Bowl is a consummate Los Angeles experience. The Bowl derives its name not from its famous backdrop of concentric arches, but from the way Mother Nature cups her hands into a 60-acre canyon once known as Daisy Dell. One of the world's largest natural amphitheaters, the Bowl was built in 1922 and holds nearly 18,000 people. The bleachers can be a blast, but if you decide to splurge on box seats, you won't regret it. You can even have a multicourse meal brought right to your box (buy tickets well in advance and order your dinner the day before by 4pm). A diverse schedule—from classical concerts with the L.A. Philharmonic, to jazz and world music festivals, to Tom Petty—makes it easy to pick the right night for you. Be sure to come early to check out the Bowl Museum, take a self-guided Bowl Walk, or just relax with a bottle of wine. ⏱ 2–3 hr. 2301 N. Highland Ave. ☎ 323/850-2000. www.hollywoodbowl.com. Tickets $1–$105. June–Sept.

⑩ ★★ Musso and Frank Grill. Need a nightcap? The town's oldest restaurant (established in 1919) was once a workday watering hole for such writers as F. Scott Fitzgerald, William Faulkner, Dorothy Parker, and Raymond Chandler, whom they say wrote *The Big Sleep* while boozing in a red-leather booth in the back. Plop onto a seat at the counter, order one of their mean martinis, and let yourself slowly drift back in time. When you start calling the bartender "doll face," he'll let you know it's time to go. 6667 Hollywood Blvd. ☎ 323/467-7788. Martinis start at $8.50.

A stiff drink at the Musso and Frank Grill will do you right.

The Best in **Two Days**

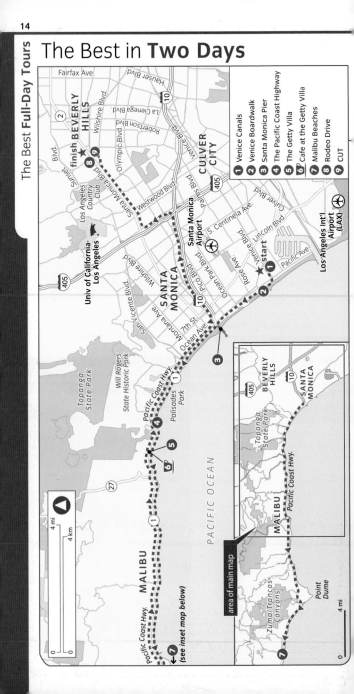

1 Venice Canals
2 Venice Boardwalk
3 Santa Monica Pier
4 The Pacific Coast Highway
5 The Getty Villa
6 Cafe at the Getty Villa
7 Malibu Beaches
8 Rodeo Drive
9 CUT

If you made it through Day 1, you've earned a few hours at the beach. Catch the buzz of bustling Venice Boardwalk, then drift up the Pacific Coast Highway past Santa Monica, and splash in the waves of Malibu. Finish up with some shopping, or at least the window kind, on Beverly Hills's hoity-toity Rodeo Drive, then treat yourself to a fabulous dinner among the beautiful people. START: **Venice Blvd. and Ocean Ave.**

Head south 3 blocks to Linnie Ave. and take a right. Cross the bridge over Eastern Canal.

1 ★ Venice Canals. Today only a handful of canals and bridges remain of Abbot Kinney's elaborate quest to build a fantastic European-style resort on the coast of California. Cute, decades-old bungalows and modernist McMansions flank the canals, which are dotted with ducks and small boats. The perfect setting for a peaceful morning stroll. ⏲ *30 min. Venice Blvd. (btwn Pacific & Ocean aves.), Venice. Start at the Grand Canal & follow the bridges.*

Leave the canals by heading northwest on Dell Ave. At Venice Blvd., take a left and head west to Ocean Front Walk. Take a left and head a few blocks south.

2 ★★★ Venice Boardwalk. When I say it's a "complete freak show," I mean that lovingly. L.A. has a rich history of people who require a lot of attention, and the Venice Boardwalk is where exhibitionists come to

out-exhibit each other: messiahs in Reeboks; amateur acrobats; jewelry-bedecked pit bulls; and a ubiquitous rollerblading, electric guitar–playing dude who seems to be everywhere at once. Join a drum circle, get a henna tattoo, join a political movement you've never heard of, help the skate rats make a YouTube video, or even join the grunts of the Muscle Beachheads. Or take a front-row seat at the **Sidewalk Café** (1401 Ocean Front Walk) and watch it all through a pair of cheap sunglasses that you'll lose by the end of your trip. ⏲ *1–2 hr. Ocean Front Walk (btwn Venice Blvd. & Rose Ave.), Venice.*

Take Pacific Ave. north, continue on Ocean Ave., and take a left at Colorado Ave.

3 ★★ kids Santa Monica Pier. This century-old slice of Americana is considered the end of the line of the legendary Route 66. If you're catching a Coney Island vibe, that might be because it was designed by amusement-park pioneer Charles Looff, the man who carved the first

Houses run alongside the canals in Venice Beach.

wooden carousel at Coney Island. Today the pier's gorgeous Looff Hippodrome Carousel building, which houses a vintage 1922-built merry-go-round, is a National Historic Landmark (and not just for its plum roles in film and television, such as *The Sting* or the opening credits of *Three's Company*). For a great panorama of the entire Santa Monica Bay, head to the far end of the pier or, even better, climb nine stories above the water on the world's first solar-powered Ferris wheel, one of the many rides at the Pacific Park amusement park. On Thursday evenings during summer, the Pier hosts wine tastings and free music concerts (check website for schedule). 🕐 *30 min. Colorado Ave. at Ocean Ave., Santa Monica.* ☎ *310/458-8900. www.santamonicapier.org.*

From the pier, turn right (south) on Ocean Ave., then turn right on the Hwy. 1/PCH ramp. Go north on the Pacific Coast Hwy. (PCH).

Greek, Roman, and Etruscan artifacts are on display at the Getty Villa.

❹ ★ **The Pacific Coast Highway (PCH).** If you haven't dropped the top of your convertible, now might be a good time. The PCH hugs the dramatic California coastline all the way to the San Francisco Bay area and beyond. But you don't need to go that far to get the picture. The ocean shimmers to the west, the warm wind whips your hair, and you finally find a song you dig on the

The entrance to the Santa Monica Pier.

radio—it's little moments like this that keep Angelenos addicted to their cars. 🕐 *30 min. Pacific Coast Hwy.*

❺ ★★ **kids** **The Getty Villa.** Little (but older) sibling of the Getty Center, the Getty Villa is entirely dedicated to ancient Greek, Roman, and Etruscan art. In 1974, when J. Paul Getty's art collection overran his Malibu ranch home (don't you hate it when that happens?), he had a museum built next door and modeled it after the Roman Villa dei Papiri in Herculaneum. The collection grew and, in 1997, moved into bigger digs: the celebrated Getty Center a few miles away in Brentwood. Reopened in 2006 after a 9-year, $275-million makeover, the Villa displays roughly 1,200 artifacts from 6500 B.C. to A.D. 400 (from a total collection of 44,000 items). Admire the *Statue of the Victorious Youth,* one of only a few extant life-size Greek bronzes. Wander the lavish grounds, including the sun-drenched formal gardens of the Outer Peristyle, where you can soak in the magnificent Pacific views. To maximize your visit, grab a $5 GettyGuide, a portable multimedia player that illuminates the museum's highlights. 🕐 *1 hr. 17985 Pacific Coast Hwy. (1 mile north of Sunset Blvd.), Malibu.* ☎ *310/440-7300. www.getty. edu. Advance, timed tickets required for admission. Free admission. Wed– Mon 10am–5pm. Parking $15.*

❻ ★ **Cafe at the Getty Villa.** The Mediterranean-inspired lunch fare is simple, but it's made tastier by an outdoor patio with a killer view. Lunch entrees $7–$14.

Designer stores line famed Rodeo Drive.

Head west along the PCH.

7 ★★★ **Malibu Beaches.** Malibu has several great beach options depending on what floats your boat. The most popular and most accessible choice is **Zuma Beach,** a wide, family-friendly stretch with plenty of activities, snack shacks, and restrooms. Just south is my favorite beach, **Point Dume,** which lacks the Zuma amenities, but also its crowds. The **Robert H. Meyer Memorial State Beach** is a few miles north and is actually three minibeaches: **El Matador, La Piedra,** and **El Pescador.** Each of these rocky coves has little parking and no facilities, and can be reached only by trails and tricky stairways. Set against the Malibu cliffs, these beaches are both cozy and rugged. Choose among splashing in the waves, climbing the rocks, or exploring the tide pools. ⏱ *2 hr. Point Dume: 7103 Westward Rd., Malibu. Zuma Beach: 30000 Pacific Coast Hwy., Malibu. Robert H. Meyer Memorial State Beach: 32900, 32700 & 32350 Pacific Coast Hwy. Daily sunrise–sunset.*

Head back (east) on the PCH to Sunset Blvd. Head east to Rodeo Dr., and then take a right.

8 ★★ **Rodeo Drive.** If the beach doesn't have the cure for what ails you, perhaps some serious retail therapy is in order. In the "Golden Triangle" of Beverly Hills (Santa Monica Blvd., Wilshire Blvd., and Crescent Dr.), the doctor is in, though his rates are sky-high. No street says "beautiful-things-I-can't-afford" quite like fabled Rodeo Drive. Gucci, Versace, Cartier, and Tiffany—all the biggest names in fashion and jewelry design are here. The most popular spot for "look, I was there" snapshots is the "Spanish Steps" that descend from the pedestrian-only cobblestone path, Via Rodeo, to Wilshire Boulevard. Directly across the street stands the Beverly Wilshire, where the *Pretty Woman* was swept off her feet. ⏱ *30 min. 200–500 Rodeo Dr. (at Wilshire Blvd.), Beverly Hills. www.rodeodrive-bh.com. Most shops Mon–Sat 10am–6pm; Sun noon–5pm. Several public parking lots free for 2 hr.*

9 ★★ **CUT.** If you haven't blown your nest egg shopping along Rodeo Drive, splurge on dinner at Wolfgang Puck's sleek steakhouse, a favorite among celebrities and power-players, and one of the best dining experiences in Los Angeles. *See p 103.*

The Best in **Three Days**

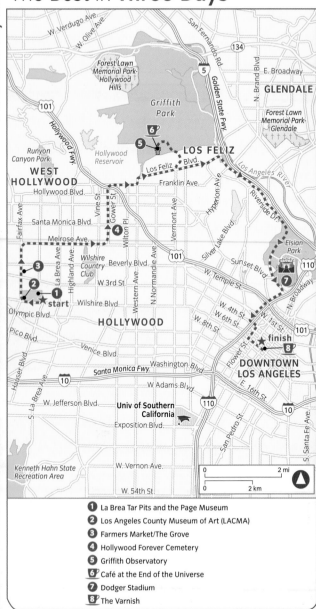

1. La Brea Tar Pits and the Page Museum
2. Los Angeles County Museum of Art (LACMA)
3. Farmers Market/The Grove
4. Hollywood Forever Cemetery
5. Griffith Observatory
6. Café at the End of the Universe
7. Dodger Stadium
8. The Varnish

After 2 jampacked days, it's time to stop and smell the hydrogen sulfide (bubbling up from the La Brea Tar Pits). Then you'll sample the city's most extensive collection of art at the Los Angeles County Museum of Art, have lunch at the Farmers Market, and scope out the sparkling Griffith Observatory. Cap your 3 days with a blast downtown at Dodger Stadium. START: **Near Wilshire Blvd. and Fairfax Ave.**

① ★ kids The La Brea Tar Pits and the Page Museum. Ready for some stinky pools of tar? Well, actually, it's asphalt, and it's been seeping out of the ground here on 23 acres of Hancock Park for the last 40,000 years. In the last Ice Age, animals roaming the Los Angeles basin would get trapped by the sticky pools and sucked into the ground where the asphalt would eventually fossilize the remains. Today the collection at the Page Museum holds around a million bones from more than 200 species of vertebrates, including the long-extinct Columbian mammoth and saber-toothed cat. The first excavations occurred in 1906, and the search for fossils continues. Currently, excavators are busy recovering fossils deposits, including a nearly intact mammoth skeleton, discovered when construction began on an underground parking garage next door for LACMA. ⏱ *1 hr. 5801 Wilshire Blvd.* ☎ *323/934-7243. www.tarpits.org. Admission $7 adults, $4.50 seniors & students, $2 kids 5–12, free for kids 4 & under. Daily 9:30am–5pm.*

② ★★★ Los Angeles County Museum of Art (LACMA). The city's largest collection of art—around 110,000 pieces spread across 7 buildings in a 20-acre complex—offers way more than one could possibly hope to absorb in a day. Heck, you can run out of breath attempting to catalog it all: American (John Singer Sargent, Mary Cassatt), Latin American (Diego Rivera), European, Islamic, Japanese (with its own Asian–meets–*The Jetsons* pavilion), modern (Picasso, Chagall, Matisse, Kandinsky), photography (Weston, Evans, Arbus), and several more. One piece of particular interest is David Hockney's exuberant *Mulholland Drive, The Road to the*

A woolly mammoth rises from the tar at the La Brea Tar Pits.

The Grove, an outdoor shopping mall.

Studio. The offerings are too diverse to simply follow your nose—grab a guide and make a game plan. ⏱ *1–2 hr. See p 42.*

From LACMA, head west on Wilshire Blvd. and take a right on Fairfax Ave.

❸ ★ kids Farmers Market/The Grove. In 1934 during the Great Depression, on a dirt parking lot at the corner of Third Street and Fairfax Avenue, local farmers began selling their fresh produce out of the backs of their trucks. Folks poured in and, before long, a maze of wooden stalls sprung up, with butcher shops, bakeries, and restaurants adding to the mix. Surprisingly, the market today manages to retain its folksy charms (as well as its clock tower from 1941). Sure, there are plenty of tourists, but there are even more locals—power players on a lunch break, Russian retirees playing chess, mommies pushing strollers, and solitary artsy types contemplating big ideas. Favorite eateries include the Gumbo Pot for (you guessed it) Cajun-style gumbo, Loteria! Grill for authentic Mexican food, and since 1938 Du-Par's Restaurant & Bakery. You can

ride the Disney-like trolley a few hundred feet to your next stop, the Grove, an elaborate outdoor mall that's been hugely popular since its debut in 2002. With its faux-European architecture and water fountain that mesmerizes kids, the experience is equal parts fab and prefab. ⏱ *1 hr. Farmers Market, 6333 W. Third St.* ☎ *323/933-9211. www.farmersmarketla.com. Mon–Fri 9am–9pm; Sat 9am–8pm; Sun 10am–7pm. The Grove, 189 The Grove Dr.* ☎ *323/900-8080. www. thegrovela.com. Mon–Thurs 10am–9pm; Fri–Sat 10am–10pm; Sun 11am–8pm.*

Exit on Fairfax Ave. and head north. Take a right on Melrose Ave. and head east to Gower St. and take a left. Head north and take a right on Santa Monica Blvd.

❹ ★★ Hollywood Forever Cemetery. This cemetery, the oldest in Los Angeles, was established in 1899, and by the 1930s, it was *the* hot resting spot for Hollywood's movers and shakers. In 1926 when Rudolph Valentino's casket was carried into the mausoleum, 80,000 fans jammed the grounds to get a

An adoring fan visits the memorial of Johnny Ramone at the Hollywood Forever Cemetery.

JOHNNY RAMONE
RAMONES

For unbeatable views of the city, head to the Griffith Observatory.

glimpse of the fallen idol. Other residents include Douglas Fairbanks, Sr.; Cecil B. DeMille; Benjamin "Bugsy" Siegel; Jayne Mansfield; "Alfalfa" and "Darla" from *The Little Rascals*; and Mel Blanc, whose famous epitaph reads "That's all, folks." My favorite memorial is the larger-than-life bronze statue of Johnny Ramone rocking out. ⏱ *45 min. 6000 Santa Monica Blvd., at Gower St.* ☎ *323/469-1181. www. hollywoodforever.com. Daily 7am–7pm.*

Heading back (west) on Santa Monica Blvd., take a right on Gower St. Take a right on Franklin Ave., a left on Western Ave., then a left on Vermont Ave. Follow the signs to the observatory.

5 ★★ kids Griffith Observatory. Like so many iconic beauties in Los Angeles, the Griffith Observatory had a teensy amount of work done—about 4 years' and $93

million's worth, finally completed in 2006. Architectural details were spit-shined to their original 1930s grandeur; a 40,000-square-foot expansion added slick, but accessible, exhibits like the *Edge of Space,* which displays Martian and lunar meteorites, and the 200-seat Leonard Nimoy Event Horizon multimedia theater for presentations, films, and lectures; the Samuel Oschin Planetarium underwent a massive overhaul (sorry, no more Pink Floyd laser shows). One of the most popular features, and part of the original building in 1935, is the Foucault Pendulum, a 240-pound brass ball that hangs in the Central Rotunda and demonstrates Earth's rotation. Entrance to the observatory is free; planetarium tickets are available on-site and often sell out. Before you step inside, circle the grounds and admire the building's beautiful Art Deco architecture and the stellar views of the city stretched out

Treat yourself to America's favorite pastime with an outing to Dodger Stadium. See below.

below. Parking is very limited at the top of the hill in front of the observatory; you may have to park along the road and then walk uphill.

🕐 *1–2 hr. 2800 E. Observatory Rd.* 📞 *213/473-0800. www.griffith observatory.org. Free admission. Planetarium tickets $7 adults, $5 seniors & students, $3 kids 5–11. Tues–Fri noon–10pm; Sat–Sun 10am–10pm.*

☕ Café at the End of the Universe. The views may trump the menu, but you can't go wrong snacking it up on this sunny terrace catered by Wolfgang Puck. *In the Griffith Observatory. Entrees $7–$12.*

Head east on Los Feliz Blvd., then south on Riverside Dr., and bear right on Stadium Way.

❼ ★★ kids Dodger Stadium. Don't underestimate the simple pleasure of taking in a baseball game in Southern California on a spring or summer evening. Since 1962 Angelenos have rooted on the Dodgers at classic Dodger Stadium,

the third-oldest stadium in the league. Kick back with a Dodger Dog in cushy box seats, or whoop it up with the die-hards in the bleachers. If it's not baseball season, check out what's scheduled at the Walt Disney Concert Hall (p 126). *1000 Elysian Park Ave.* 📞 *866/DODGERS (363-4377). www.dodgers.com. Tickets $10–$225. Most night games 7:10pm; most day games 1:10pm. Check the schedule on the website for specific dates & times.*

Head south on I-110. Exit Sixth St. toward downtown. Head east on Sixth St.

❽ ★ The Varnish. The speakeasy vibe may strike some sourpusses as a load of flimflam, but no one can argue with the artistry of these cocktails. Tipple while a jazz pianist fills the room with a jaunty ragtime tune. *Look for the unmarked door in the back of Cole's. 118 E. Sixth St. (at Main St.).* 📞 *213/622-9999. www.thevarnishbar.com. Cocktails $12–$15.* ●

The Best Special-Interest Tours

L.A. for **Movie Buffs**

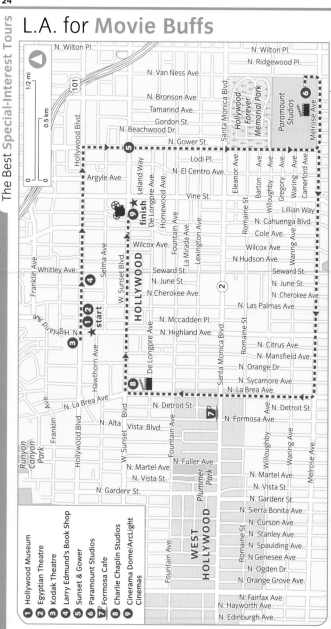

1 Hollywood Museum
2 Egyptian Theatre
3 Kodak Theatre
4 Larry Edmund's Book Shop
5 Sunset & Gower
6 Paramount Studios
7 Formosa Cafe
8 Charlie Chaplin Studios
9 Cinerama Dome/ArcLight Cinemas

Previous page: Celebrity impersonators line the Hollywood Walk of Fame.

Have you done your homework by watching hundreds and hundreds of Hollywood films? Bravo! Then let's go find out where they came from. You'll need to start early and finish strong to cram the following tour into a single blockbuster day. Aaaand action! START: **Park in the Hollywood & Highland complex and walk the first four stops.**

1 Hollywood Museum. Don't make the mistake of lumping this in with tourist traps like the Hollywood Wax or Ripley's Believe It or Not! museums. This museum—occupying the historic Max Factor building, restored to its full Art Deco loveliness—traces the history of film with 5,000 displays of rare Hollywood memorabilia, including Hannibal Lecter's cell block, Indiana Jones's whip, Rita Hayworth's makeup case, Cary Grant's Rolls-Royce, and the earliest film cameras. ⏲ *30 min. 1660 N. Highland Ave. (at Hollywood Blvd.).* ☎ *323/464-7776. www.the hollywoodmuseum.com. Admission $15 adults, $12 seniors & kids 11 & under. Parking $2 w/validation. Thurs–Sun 10am–5pm.*

The courtyard of Sid Grauman's famed Egyptian Theatre.

2 ★ Egyptian Theatre. In 1922, as the hunt closed in on King Tut's tomb, Sid Grauman unveiled the Egyptian Theatre, the second of his spectacular, themed movie palaces. After a multimillion-dollar restoration in 1998, the theater became the home of the nonprofit American Cinematheque, which caters to serious film enthusiasts. It offers fresh, 70mm prints of classics *(Lawrence of Arabia, The Sound of Music)*; programs of national cinema (classic Italian, Russian fantastik, and British new wave); director retrospectives (Douglas Sirk, Orson Welles); and in-person tributes to actors and filmmakers (Terry Gilliam, Mel Brooks). If you're lucky, you can catch the monthly screening of *Forever Hollywood,* an excellent, hour-long look at a century of cinema. ⏲ *15 min., with screening 1 hr. 6712*

Hollywood Blvd. ☎ *323/466-FILM (3456). www.egyptiantheatre.com. Forever Hollywood $7 adults, $5 seniors & students.*

3 ★ Kodak Theatre. If you're the type to host an Oscar party at home with your own printed ballots, a 30-minute walking tour of the Kodak Theatre is a must You'll see the grand entrance (now imagine the red carpet), a few Oscar statuettes, the 3,300-seat auditorium inspired by a European opera house, and the backstage VIP area. ⏲ *30 min. 6801 Hollywood Blvd. (at Highland Ave.).* ☎ *323/308-6300. www.kodaktheatre.com. Admission $15 adults, $10 seniors & kids 3 & up, free for kids 2 & under. June–Aug Mon–Sun 10:30am–4pm; Sept–May Mon–Sun 10:30am–2:30pm.*

An Oscar® statue outside the Kodak Theatre.

The Kodak Theatre on its biggest night of the year.

④ ★ Larry Edmund's Bookshop. This Hollywood mainstay and Quentin Tarantino favorite is a film geek's paradise with stacks of books on the craft and history of filmmaking, thousands of vintage movie posters, and a bottomless well of movie stills, lobby cards, and publicity shots. ⏱ *15 min. 6644 Hollywood Blvd. (at Cherokee Ave.).* ☎ *323/463-3273. www.larryedmunds.com. Mon–Fri 10am–5:30pm; Sat 10am–6pm; Sun noon–5:30pm.*

Head east on Hollywood Blvd., then south on Gower St.

⑤ Sunset & Gower. In an old tavern on the northwest corner of Sunset and Gower, the Nestor Company launched the first film studio in Hollywood in 1911. Using natural California sunshine and a small wooden stage, several one-reelers were shot each week: one Western, one drama, one comedy. In 1912 Nestor merged with Carl Laemmle's Universal Film Company. The original building was razed in 1936 to make room for the CBS Columbia Square radio studio, which can be seen today. On the southeast corner of the same intersection sits the Sunset-Gower studios, formerly the home of Columbia Pictures Studios (1921–72), which produced countless gems such as *It Happened One Night, From Here to Eternity, Dr. Strangelove,* and *Funny Girl.* On the southwest corner known as Gower Gulch, cowboy extras used to loiter in hopes of gaining work on the many Westerns filming nearby. ⏱ *10 min.*

Head south on Gower St. to Melrose Ave. and take a left.

⑥ ★★ Paramount Studios. Paramount Studios traces its origins to a rented horse barn near Sunset and Vine in 1913. Thirteen years later, it moved to its current location and never left, unlike the rest of the major studios in Hollywood. The back lot eventually gobbled up neighboring R.K.O. Pictures, and the distinctive globe is still visible in the southwest corner. Book tickets in advance for a 2-hour golf-cart tour, which scoots you through the "living history" of the film and television soundstages. This is where the stars punch the clock, so keep your eyes peeled for sightings. Don't get so caught up gawking that you forget whose footsteps you're walking in: Rudolph Valentino, Mary Pickford, W. C. Fields, Alfred Hitchcock, the Marx Brothers, and many more. Before leaving, make sure to get a photo of yourself in front of the famous Bronson Gate, the arched gateway you may remember Gloria Swanson driving through in *Sunset*

Cinespia

No one with a pulse can resist a classic movie projected on a mausoleum wall. Classic and campy, creepy and cool—Cinespia is a summer screening series set on the tomb-strewn grounds of the Hollywood Forever Cemetery. With rabid word-of-mouth and national press coverage (*Vanity Fair, USA Today,* and *NPR*), the scene at this boneyard is anything but underground. Pack a picnic basket and get there early to claim a choice spot (or is it plot?) on the grass and enjoy a glass of wine as the sun sets and the DJ spins. Parking and entrance can be a slog, but the crowd's enthusiasm—cheering a crackling line from Cary Grant, Bette Davis, or Jack Nicholson—is downright refreshing. *6000 Santa Monica Blvd., at Gower St. www.cinespia.org. Sat in the summer, gates open at 7:30pm; film begins at 9pm. Admission $10.*

Boulevard. ⏱ 2 hr. 5555 Melrose Ave. ☎ 323/956-1777. www.paramount. com. Tours $40 per person. Kids 11 & under not admitted. Mon–Fri 10 & 11am, 1 & 2pm.

Head west on Melrose Ave. Take a right on La Brea Ave. Head north to Santa Monica Blvd. and take a left.

7 ★★ Formosa Cafe. The shiny, strip-mall surroundings may throw you, but trust me: This is a vintage Hollywood watering hole. Formosa Cafe has always attracted celebrity lunch-timers and late-nighters. Marilyn Monroe and Clark Gable shared a red-leather booth while taking a break from shooting *The Misfits.* Bogie, Sinatra, Brando, Elvis and Bono have all sidled up to the bar, and the walls display hundreds of signed photos of its celebrity fans. The food is nothing special, but the atmosphere you can eat with a spoon. *7156 Santa Monica Blvd. (at Formosa Ave.). ☎ 323/850-9050. Entrees $12–$19.*

Take Santa Monica Blvd. east to La Brea Ave., and then head north.

8 Charlie Chaplin Studios. In 1917, on acres of orange groves at Sunset and La Brea, Charlie Chaplin built himself a studio, a row of English-style cottages (perhaps trying to evoke a happier, sunnier version of his childhood). Chaplin shot many of his classics here, such as *The Gold Rush, City Lights,* and *Modern Times.* Today Jim Henson Productions occupies the building, which features a statue of Kermit the Frog donning The Little Tramp's familiar bowler hat, cane, and tails. ⏱ 10 min. 1416 N. La Brea Ave.

Go north on La Brea Ave., and then east on Sunset Blvd.

9 ★★ Cinerama Dome/ ArcLight Cinemas. Built in 1963 to showcase the widescreen format, the landmark Cinerama Dome now belongs to the state-of-the-art ArcLight Complex of 14 theaters. The Dome is the coolest, with its curving, immersive screen. ⏱ 2 hr. 6160 W. Sunset Blvd. (btwn Vine St. & Ivar Ave.). ☎ 323/464-1478. www. arclightcinemas.com. Tickets $7.75–$15. Parking $2 for 4 hr. w/validation.

L.A. for **Kids**

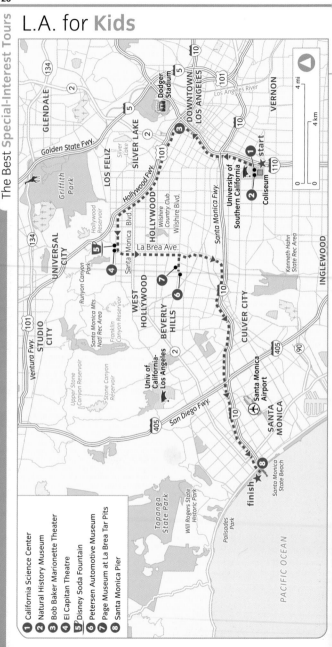

1 California Science Center
2 Natural History Museum
3 Bob Baker Marionette Theater
4 El Capitan Theatre
5 Disney Soda Fountain
6 Petersen Automotive Museum
7 Page Museum at La Brea Tar Pits
8 Santa Monica Pier

Let's be honest: Kids' moods can be as unpredictable as Los Angeles traffic. By no means do I recommend trying to hit *every* stop on this list. Let your kid be the guide. START: **Downtown in Exposition Park at 39th and Figueroa sts.**

❶ ★ kids **California Science Center.** This interactive museum about science and technology never fails to dazzle kids of all ages. Watch an IMAX movie in 3-D on L.A.'s biggest screen (seven stories high!), or investigate exhibits such as *Ecosystems and Timescapes: California from the Air.* Take a spin on a high-wire bicycle, or strap into the Millennium Falcon flight simulator. Tess, a 50-foot woman with a see-through body, teaches kids about homeostasis, how the body keeps its system in balance. There are also hands-on areas for younger kids. Check the website for current exhibits and IMAX movies. ⏲ *1–2 hr. 39th & Figueroa sts.* ☎ *323/724-3623. www.californiasciencecenter.org. Free admission. IMAX movie $4.75– $8. Parking $8. Daily 10am–5pm.*

❷ ★★ kids **Natural History Museum.** Opened in 1913, this museum is the largest of its kind in the western United States. A scrapbook documenting the history of Mother Earth and her inhabitants,

Tess, the 50-foot-tall model at the California Science Center.

the museum holds 33 million specimens and artifacts. The dinosaur skeletons, the perennial favorites, are currently being cleaned (watch scientists work in the Dino Lab) and new specimens are being added in preparation for a roaring new exhibition in 2011 called *Dinosaur Mysteries.* Another ambitious new exhibit, *Age of Mammals,* outlines the 65-million-year evolution of mammals using 248 specimens, many that were found in Los Angeles and surrounding counties. ⏲ *1 hr. 900 Exposition Blvd., Exposition Park.* ☎ *213/763-DINO (3466). www.nhm. org. Admission $9 adults; $6.50 seniors, students, & kids 13–17; $2 kids 5–12; free for kids 4 & under. Free for everyone 1st Tues of the month. Daily 9:30am–5pm.*

Head east on Exposition Blvd. Take 110 north, exit Third St., and go west. Go right at Lucas St.; the theater is under the bridge.

❸ kids **Bob Baker Marionette Theater.** With all the high-tech wizardry out there competing for kids' attention, sometimes it's nice to enjoy the good, old-fashioned fun of watching wooden puppets spring to life with string. Founded in 1963 by puppeteer pioneer Bob Baker, this children's theater company is the oldest in Los Angeles. You'll have to forgive its less-than-pristine exterior; this labor of love is the real deal. Handmade puppets are for sale. ⏲ *1 hr. 1345 W. First St.* ☎ *213/250-9995. www.bobbaker marionettes.com. Shows Tues–Fri 10:30am, Sat–Sun 2:30pm. Reservations required. Tickets $20 adults & children, free for kids under 3.*

Bob Baker has worked with many Hollywood legends, including Elvis Presley, The Three Stooges, and Judy Garland (pictured here).

Head northwest on Beverly Blvd., then take a right on Alvarado St. Get on the U.S. 101 heading north. Exit at Hollywood Blvd. and head west.

④ ★★ kids **El Capitan Theatre.** This is *the* spot to catch the latest summer blockbuster from Disney/Pixar. Debuting in 1926 as "Hollywood's First Home of Spoken Drama," the theater has been fully restored to its original grandeur by the Walt Disney Company. It boasts a Spanish colonial facade; a lively, East Indian–influenced interior; and a 2,500-piped organ from the 1920s called the "Mighty Wurlitzer." Get there early for the preshow song-and-dance numbers by costumed characters. ⏱ *2 hr. 6838 Hollywood Blvd.* ☎ *800/347-6396. Tickets $13 adults, $10 seniors & kids. $2 discount on adult tickets for matinees.*

⑤ kids **Disney Soda Fountain.** Your kids are going to beg you for a milkshake or a movie-themed sundae at the old-fashioned ice-cream parlor next door to El Capitan Theatre. *6834 Hollywood Blvd.* ☎ *323/939-9024. Shakes & sundaes $4–$9.*

Head west on Hollywood Blvd. Take a left at Fairfax Ave. and head south to Wilshire Blvd.

⑥ ★ kids **Petersen Automotive Museum.** Los Angeles is the ideal place for a museum about the automobile and how it's shaped American culture. An ongoing exhibition of Hollywood star cars includes the original 1966 Batmobile and a 1942 Cadillac that Clark Gable gave to his wife, Carole Lombard. Kids flock to the Discovery Center, where they can learn about how a car works with Professor Lugnut or hop on a police motorcycle in the Vroom Room. ⏱ *1 hr. 6060 Wilshire Blvd., at Fairfax Ave.* ☎ *323/930-CARS (2277). www.petersen.org. Admission $10 adults, $5 seniors & students, $3 children 5–12, free for kids 4 & under. Parking $5. Tues–Sun 10am–6pm.*

⑦ ★ kids **Page Museum at La Brea Tar Pits.** At the glass-walled "Fishbowl Lab," kids can watch scientists and volunteers excavating, polishing, and cataloguing bones. The gift shop has great toys for budding paleontologists. ⏱ *1 hr. See p 19.*

Take Fairfax Ave. south. Get on I-10 heading west. Exit Fourth/Fifth St., go north on Fifth St. to Colorado Ave., and then take a left.

⑧ kids **Santa Monica Pier.** The rides at **Pacific Park** might not match those of Disneyland, but hey, you're on the water and the park does a swell job hearkening back to the turn-of-the-century amusement piers of yesteryear. The Ferris wheel is the high point, literally and figuratively. At the 1916-built **Looff Hippodrome,** hop aboard the vintage carousel, a spinning spectacle of lights, hand-carved ponies, and brightly colored chariots. Beneath the carousel is the **Santa Monica Pier Aquarium,** a small, interactive aquarium with three touch tanks where kids can handle marine species common to the Californian

Universal Studios Hollywood

Although this high-tech theme park may not have the same magical allure as Disneyland, it is close to Hollywood, and it packs an entertaining, if sanitized, hour-long tour of its moviemaking facilities. In 1915, Carl Laemmle bought hundreds of acres of farmland just north of Hollywood and built the world's largest motion-picture production facility, Universal City Studios. In the early years, the studio, figuring the burgeoning film industry needed all the publicity it could get, happily opened its doors to all spectators; today the tradition continues (albeit at a much higher price).

Popular thrill rides and attractions include the new *King Kong 360 3D,* billed as the world's largest 3-D experience; the *Simpsons Ride,* a "virtual roller-coaster" where you sail through Krustyland with Homer and the gang; an actual roller-coaster, *Revenge of the Mummy; Backdraft,* a simulated warehouse fire; and—my favorite for a hot summer day—the water-soaked *Jurassic Park* river ride.

Lines can get long; consider splurging on a "Front of the Line" pass ($139), which eliminates the wait for any ride, or a VIP pass ($199), which combines the "Front of the Line" pass with a private studio tour and gourmet lunch. Multiday discounts are available online. *100 Universal City Plaza (off the 101 Hollywood Fwy.).* ☎ *818/662-3801. www.universalstudioshollywood.com. Admission $69 for adults, $59 for children under 48 inches, & free for kids 2 & under. Call for hours.*

shores, such as sea stars and sea urchins. Other creatures are in observation-only tanks: the two-spotted octopus, flower-like anemones, and best of all, horn sharks and swell sharks, which draw crowds for feeding time (3:30pm) on Shark Sundays. 🕐 *1 hr. Colorado Ave. at Ocean Ave. Pacific Park:* ☎ *310/260-8744. www.pacpark.com. Free admission; cost varies per ride. Summer Sun–Thurs 11am–11pm; Fri–Sat 11am–12:30am. Carousel:* ☎ *310/394-8042. www.santamonicapier.org. Rides $1 adults, 50¢ kids. Mon–Thurs 11am–5pm; Fri–Sun 11am–7pm.* 🕐 *30 min. Aquarium: 1600 Ocean Front Walk.* ☎ *310/393-6149. www.healthebay.org. Summer Tues–Fri 2–6pm; Sat–Sun 12:30–6pm. $2–$5 adults, free for children under 13 with adult. Check websites for off-season hours.*

Enjoy the view of the beach from the Ferris wheel at Pacific Park.

The Best Special-Interest Tours

L.A. for **Architecture Fans**

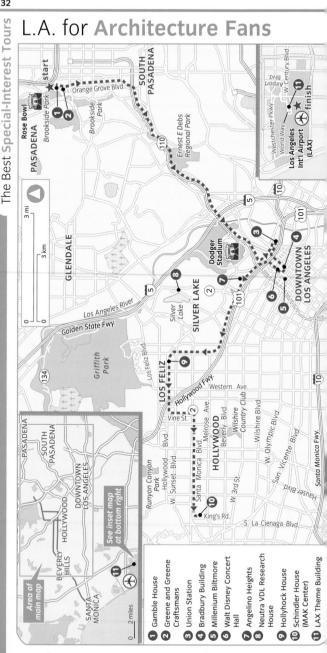

1 Gamble House
2 Greene and Greene Craftsmans
3 Union Station
4 Bradbury Building
5 Millenium Biltmore
6 Walt Disney Concert Hall
7 Angelino Heights
8 Neutra VDL Research House
9 Hollyhock House
10 Schindler House (MAK Center)
11 LAX Theme Building

Area of main map

See inset map at bottom right

I't's wrongheaded to dismiss the cityscape of Los Angeles as nothing but freeways and strip malls. This tour will give you plenty of architecture to digest: Pasadena's Craftsman bungalows, Downtown's mix of old and new classics, well-preserved 19th-century Victorians, prime examples of Californian modernism from Schindler and Neutra, and innovative work from America's greatest architect, Frank Lloyd Wright. START: **Pasadena.**

Take Hwy. 134 east, exit at Orange Grove, and head north. Turn left on Westmoreland Place.

① ★★ Gamble House. This 1908 masterpiece in the American Arts and Crafts style was designed by Charles and Henry Greene, masters of the Craftsman bungalow. Commissioned by David and Mary Gamble (of Proctor and Gamble) to be their winter residence in California, the house is a National Historic Landmark. The exterior uses Japanese-style proportions, low and horizontal, in an open, California setting. The interior is especially impressive, with stained-glass doors and windows and intricately crafted woodwork. In the home's original garage structure, the bookstore (Tues–Sat 10am–5pm; Sun 11:30am–5pm) carries a fantastic selection of architectural books and guides (in fact, pick up a walking-tour map for **②**). ⌚ *1 hr. 4 Westmoreland Place, Pasadena.* ☎ *626/793-3334. www.gamblehouse.org. Tours $10 adults, $7 seniors & students, free for kids 11 & under. Thurs–Sun noon–3pm.*

② ★ Greene & Greene Craftsmans. Several excellent examples of the Greene and Greene architectural firm dot the streets of Arroyo Terrace and Grand Avenue (within walking distance of the Gamble House). Start at 2 Westmoreland Place with the Cole House, which is distinguishable by the river-rock pillars of the carriage porch. Head south to Arroyo Terrace and check out nos. 440, 408, 400, and 370, and Charles Sumner Greene's own house at 368 Arroyo Terrace. Follow the road west to Grand Avenue and head south to find my favorite, the Duncan-Irwin House at 240 N. Grand Ave., and continue on to nos. 235 and 90. ⌚ *30 min. Arroyo Terrace & Grand Ave., Pasadena. Maps available from Gamble House bookstore. Note: None of these houses is open to the public.*

Go south on Orange Grove Blvd., and then southwest on 110; exit Cesar E. Chavez Ave. Head southeast to Alameda St.

③ ★ Union Station. The trouble with being an architectural highlight

The Gamble House in Pasadena is a National Historic Landmark.

in Los Angeles since 1939 is the risk of overexposure in film and television. You've seen Union Station in *Speed, The Italian Job, Bugsy*, and more recently in the series *24*. This grand building combines elements of California Mission style with Streamline Moderne, and its cathedral-size interior is lavishly detailed with colorful tiles, ornate wood paneling, retro leather chairs, and exposed roof beams. 🕐 *20 min. 800 N. Alameda St.* ☎ *213/683-6979. Open 24 hr.*

Head south on Alameda St. Take a right at Arcadia St. Take a left at Spring St. and head south, passing City Hall, once the tallest building downtown. Take a right at Third St. and go 1 block.

4 ★★ Bradbury Building. The ordinary brick facade of this 1893 structure masks one of the most striking interior spaces you'll ever find. A peaked glass ceiling makes for a dramatic dance of sunlight and shadow in the five-story atrium, which has two open-cage elevators, suspended mail chutes, marble staircases, and spidery, wrought-iron railings. When the original architect was fired for boring his backer, the job was handed to an inexperienced draftsman, George Wyman, who took more inspiration from science fiction than from formal architectural training. 🕐 *10 min. 304 S. Broadway.* ☎ *213/626-1893. Mon–Fri 9am–6pm; Sat–Sun 9am–5pm.*

Head south on Broadway and turn right at Fifth St. Go west 3 blocks to Grand Ave.

5 ★★ Millenium Biltmore. Considered to be one of the grand hotels of the Jazz Age, this landmark building from 1923 is ideal for an elegant afternoon tea, served in the magnificent Rendezvous Court. For a more robust refreshment, slip into the Gallery Bar for a Manhattan.

506 S. Grand Ave. (at W. Fifth St.). ☎ *213/624-1011. www.millennium hotels.com. Afternoon tea Wed–Sun 2–5pm. $22–$45.*

Head north on Grand Ave.

6 ★★★ Walt Disney Concert Hall. Frank Gehry's instant classic may have taken 30,000 architectural drawings and double the original budget to realize, but 22 million pounds of steel has probably never looked this fluid and graceful. The audio tour is a great primer, but you'll have to come back for a show to experience the auditorium and its stunning acoustics. 🕐 *1 hr. 111 S. Grand Ave.* ☎ *323/850-2000. www.laphil.com. Free self-guided audio tours most days 10am–2pm; free guided tours Thurs–Sun 10am–1pm (times vary).*

Head north on Grand Ave. Take a left at Temple St. Take a right at Edgeware Rd. and head to Carroll Ave.

7 ★ Angelino Heights. With blocks of elegant Victorian homes erected during the residential boom of the 1880s, this hilly area west of downtown is considered to be one of the city's first suburbs. The best preserved Queen Anne and Eastlake Victorians can be found on Carroll Ave. 🕐 *20 min tour. 1300 Carroll Ave. Note: None of these houses is open to the public.*

Take Carroll Ave. west and take a right on Douglas St. Take a left on Sunset Blvd. Take a right on Silver Lake Blvd.

8 ★ Neutra VDL Research House. Modernist master Richard Neutra set up shop in Silver Lake and designed several residences along the Silver Lake Reservoir, including his own, which is available for tours. A block south at the intersection with

A peak inside Frank Lloyd Wright's Hollyhock House.

Earl Street is "Neutra Colony," a clutch of Neutra designs: 2226, 2232, 2238, 2242, and 2250 Silver Lake Blvd. and 2218, 2210, and 2200 Neutra Place. 🕐 *30 min tour. 2300 Silver Lake Blvd. www.neutra-vdl.org. Admission $10. Sat 11am–3pm.*

Return to Sunset Blvd. and take a right. At Virgil/Hillhurst Ave., continue onto Hollywood Blvd.

⑨ ★ Hollyhock House. The exalted Frank Lloyd Wright designed this private residence for oil heiress Aline Barnsdall, who envisioned it as the centerpiece of a large arts complex. The hilltop structure is modeled after a Mayan temple, with exterior walls tilting back slightly, and a roofline with symmetrical reliefs based on a geometric abstraction of the owner's favorite flower, the hollyhock. 🕐 *1 hr. 4800 Hollywood Blvd.* ☎ *323/644-6269. www.hollyhockhouse.net. Tours $7 adults, $3 students & seniors, free for kids 11 & under. Wed–Sun 12:30, 1:30, 2:30 & 3:30pm.*

Head west on Hollywood Blvd. Take a left on Fairfax Ave. Take a right on Santa Monica Blvd. Take a left on King's Rd.

⑩ ★ Schindler House (MAK Center). An Austrian architect who worked under Frank Lloyd Wright,

Rudolph Schindler came west to work on the Hollyhock House before launching his own practice with the design of his home in 1922. Modern and modular, with interlocking L shapes, the innovative house was conceptualized as shared living and work space for multiple households. 🕐 *30 min. 835 N. King's Rd.* ☎ *323/ 651-1510. www.makcenter.org. Admission $7 adults, $6 seniors & students, free for kids 11 & under. Wed–Sun 11am–6pm. Free tours Sat–Sun.*

Heading south on King's Rd., take a right at Melrose Ave. Take a left at La Cienega Blvd. Take a right at La Tijera Blvd., and then a left on Airport Blvd. Take a right on Century Blvd.

⑪ ★ LAX Theme Building. If you're flying in or out of LAX, look for the shiny white flying saucer that seems to have landed in the center of the airport. With its bold and futuristic, yet whimsical design, this iconic building is one of the most famous examples of Googie architecture. Inside at the Encounter Restaurant, a space-age theme is played to the hilt, with lava lamps and cocktails like the Milky Way. 🕐 *15 min. Los Angeles International Airport. Observation Deck open Sat– Sun 8am–5pm.*

Rockin' L.A.

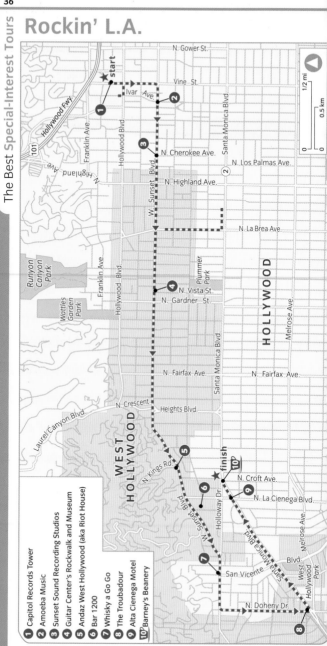

1 Capitol Records Tower
2 Amoeba Music
3 Sunset Sound Recording Studios
4 Guitar Center's Rockwalk and Museum
5 Andaz West Hollywood (aka Riot House)
6 Bar 1200
7 Whisky a Go Go
8 The Troubadour
9 Alta Cienega Motel
10 Barney's Beanery

This tour will take you through the heart & history of the Los Angeles music scene—the good, the bad, and the ugly. Let the city become your musical mix: "Good Vibrations" by The Beach Boys, "L.A. Woman" by The Doors, "Hotel California" by The Eagles, "Los Angeles" by X, "I Love L.A." by Randy Newman, "Valley Girl" by Frank and Moon Zappa, "Walking in L.A." by the Missing Persons, "Welcome to the Jungle" by Guns N' Roses, "Straight Outta Compton" by N.W.A., and Beck's "Que Onda Guero?" To experience Silver Lake's music scene when it's cranked up to eleven, come in August for the annual **Sunset Junction Street Fair** (www.sunsetjunction.org)—now over 30 years old—a 2-day barnburner of music, food, and people-watching that takes over Sunset Boulevard.
START: **Hollywood Blvd. and Vine St.**

❶ ★ Capitol Records Tower.
Two blocks north of the world-famous corner of Hollywood and Vine is the landmark that Hollywood loves to demolish—at least in its disaster movies *(Earthquake, The Day After Tomorrow)*. The 13-story structure might look like a gigantic stack of vinyl 45 records on a turntable (a heap of MP3s doesn't have the same magic, does it?), but it was actually designed by Modernist architect Welton Becket as the world's first circular building when it debuted in 1956. Frank Sinatra banged out 19 albums in these hallowed studios, which also recorded the likes of Nat King Cole, Ella Fitzgerald, Dean Martin, and The Beach Boys. The first record company based on the West Coast, Capitol Records also imported British acts such as Pink Floyd, Duran Duran, Radiohead, and The Beatles. On the sidewalk in front of the building's lobby, you can find John Lennon's Hollywood star, still decorated by fans every December 8 to commemorate the anniversary of his death. 🕐 *20 min. 1750 Vine St.* ☎ *323/462-6252.*

Head south on Vine St., and then go west on Sunset Blvd.

❷ ★ Amoeba Music. A mecca for music lovers, this independently owned store spans an entire block of Sunset and offers the biggest and

Amoeba Music is L.A.'s best independent record store.

baddest selection of tunes in town. It's also an intimate live venue; recently featured was an unannounced set by an up-and-comer named Sir Paul McCartney. 🕐 *1 hr. 6400 Sunset Blvd.* ☎ *323/245-6400. www.amoeba.com. Mon–Sat 10:30am–11pm; Sun 11am–9pm.*

❸ Sunset Sound Recording Studios. It may be impossible to find a recording studio that's got more musical mojo than Sunset Sound: It's turned out 200 gold records, including some of the most revered rock albums of all time: *Led Zeppelin II* and *IV*, Michael Jackson's *Thriller*, The Beach Boys' *Pet Sounds*,

Blondie solidifies its place in history at Hollywood's Rockwalk.

the Stones' *Exile on Main Street,* as well as classics by Dylan, Van Halen, and Fleetwood Mac. ⏱ *10 min. 6650 Sunset Blvd.* ☎ *323/469-1186. www. sunsetsound.com.*

❹ **Guitar Center's Rockwalk and Museum.** The Rockwalk, the sidewalk in front of the Guitar Center, is the rock equivalent of the forecourt of Grauman's Chinese Theatre. The concrete has been high-fived by the talented hands of Chuck Berry, Jerry Lee Lewis, Jimmy Page, Eddie Van Halen, and more. There's also an awesome display of memorabilia such as Eddie's homemade red Kramer guitar, Stevie Ray Vaughn's denim jacket, Keith Moon's drum kit, and platform boots from KISS. Oh yeah, you can buy a guitar here, too. ⏱ *15 min. 7425 Sunset Blvd.* ☎ *323/874-1060. www.rockwalk. com. Mon–Fri 10am–9pm; Sat 10am–8pm; Sun 11am–8pm.*

❺ **Andaz West Hollywood (aka Riot House).** This monument to mayhem began life innocently enough in 1958 as the Gene Autry Hotel. By the mid-'60s, the name had changed to the Continental Hyatt,

and the hotel became the stomping grounds (literally) of rock-'n'-rollers who came to play nearby clubs on the Strip. Over the years the Riot House, as it came to be called, became a sort of bad-boy finishing school; members of Led Zeppelin careened down the hallways on Harleys, and, on separate occasions, Keith Richards of The Rolling Stones and Keith Moon of The Who hurled televisions out of 10th-floor windows. If you opt to stay here, ask for the hallowed room 905, known as the Robert Plant Suite. ⏱ *10 min. 8401 Sunset Blvd.* ☎ *323/656-1234.*

❻ **Bar 1200 at the Sunset Marquis.** With a state-of-the-art recording studio on the property, this small, dark lounge has long been famous for its rocker clientele—Anthony Kiedis, Billy Gibbons, Courtney Love. It's also famous for being tough to get into—arrive early, dressed like you've got a couple gold records. *At the Sunset Marquis Hotel, 1200 Alta Loma Rd.* ☎ *310/657-1333. www.sunsetmarquishotel. com. 8pm–2am.*

7 ★ Whisky a Go Go. Aside from its footnote as the birthplace of go-go dancing, the Whisky was the epicenter of the Los Angeles rock scene for 3 decades since opening in 1964. The later 1960s saw The Doors, The Byrds, Love, and Buffalo Springfield. The 1970s imported Led Zeppelin, The Who, and Roxy Music. The lineup in the later '70s edged toward the home-grown punk rock of The Germs, The Runaways, and X. Then came the pop metal of Van Halen, followed by Mötley Crüe, and Guns N' Roses in the '80s. In 2007 the reunited Police polished their chops at the revered venue before embarking on their worldwide tour. 🕐 *10 min. 8901 W. Sunset Blvd., at Clark St.* ☎ *310/ 652-4202. www.whiskyagogo.com.*

Head west on Sunset Blvd., and then go south on Doheny Dr. to Santa Monica Blvd.

8 ★ The Troubadour. In the 1960s the Troubadour was a hotbed for folkies such as Bob Dylan and Joni Mitchell. Over the years, the small club helped launch the careers of other singer-songwriters: James Taylor, Elton John, Randy Newman, and Tom Waits. And in 1985, during

George Harrison, Jayne Mansfield, and John Lennon at Whisky a Go Go in 1964.

the heyday of heavy metal, Guns N' Roses made its debut on this stage and caught the eye of a Geffen A&R rep. My favorite "wish-I-was-there" moment happened in 1974, when John Lennon (on his 18-month-long "lost weekend" in Los Angeles) and Harry Nilsson were tossed out for getting drunk and heckling the Smothers Brothers. 🕐 *10 min. 9081 Santa Monica Blvd.* ☎ *310/276-6168. www.troubadour.com.*

Take Santa Monica Blvd. east to La Cienega Blvd.

9 Alta Cienega Motel. From 1968 to 1970, Jim Morrison made room no. 32 his crash pad. Today its walls are graffitied with messages from adoring fans who rent a piece of history for a night or two. Wondering why a rock star would bed down at this dump? It was stumbling distance from The Doors' recording studios across the street at 8512 Santa Monica Blvd. A restaurant occupies the space now, but you can still see the men's room on the lower level where Jim laid down the vocal track for "L.A. Woman." 🕐 *10 min. 1005 N. La Cienega Blvd.* ☎ *310/652-5797. www.altacienegamotel.com.*

Continue 2 blocks east on Santa Monica Blvd.

10 Barney's Beanery. In the late '60s and early '70s, this restaurant and bar drew local rockers with its roadhouse loosey-gooseness. With The Doors' offices and studio practically next door, it was one of Jim Morrison's favorite spots to eat, drink, and hold court. Regular Janis Joplin preferred booth 34, where she knocked back a couple screwdrivers on the night she died. *8447 Santa Monica Blvd.* ☎ *323/654-2287. www.barneysbeanery.com. $.*

L.A. for **Art Lovers**

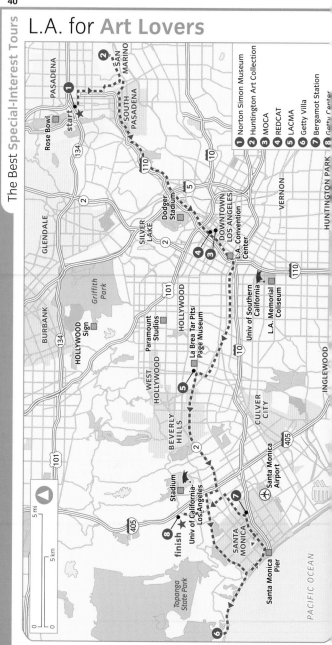

1 Norton Simon Museum
2 Huntington Art Collection
3 MOCA
4 REDCAT
5 LACMA
6 Getty Villa
7 Bergamot Station
8 Getty Center

The city isn't just red-carpet flashbulbs & bad Botox jobs. A day (or even two) at the following museums and galleries will shatter the myth that "Los Angeles culture" is an oxymoron. START: **In Pasadena at Colorado Blvd. and Orange Grove Ave.**

1 ★★ **Norton Simon Museum.** This museum displays excellent collections of European, American, and Asian art, and boasts major pieces by Picasso, Matisse, Diego Rivera, van Gogh, and Rembrandt. The museum holds a significant collection of works by Impressionists, including Monet and Renoir, and over 100 works by Edgar Degas. A stroll around the charming courtyard reveals sculptures by Auguste Rodin and Henry Moore. ⏲ *1 hr. 411 W. Colorado Blvd.* ☎ *626/449-6840. www.nortonsimon.org. Admission $8 adults; $4 seniors; free for students & kids 17 & under; free for everyone 1st Fri of the month 6–9pm. Mon, Wed–Thurs & Sat–Sun noon–6pm; Fri noon–9pm; Closed Tues.*

Head east on Colorado Blvd. Turn right at Allen Ave. Turn left at Orlando Rd., and then right onto Oxford Rd.

2 ★ **Huntington Art Collections.** Check out this fine collection of European art, elegantly displayed in the Huntington Art Gallery, Huntington's former residence, a lovely Italianate mansion. Thomas Gainsborough's *The Blue Boy* and Thomas Lawrence's *Pinkie* are its most celebrated paintings. In the recently expanded Virginia Steel Scott Galleries, the emphasis is on American art, such as Mary Cassat's *Breakfast in Bed* and Edward Hopper's *The Last Leg*. Lovers of the Arts and Crafts movement should check out the permanent exhibition on furniture design and the decorative arts by the renowned Pasadena architects, Charles and Henry Greene (see Huntington tour on p 93).

Tour the Huntington Art Gallery as well as the estate's gorgeous Botanical Gardens.

⏲ *1 hr. 1151 Oxford Rd., San Marino.* ☎ *626/405-2100. www.huntington. org. Mon–Fri noon–4:30pm; Sat–Sun 10:30am–4:30pm. Closed Tues. Admission (Mon–Fri/Sat–Sun)$15/$20 adults; $12/$15 seniors 65 & up, $10 students & kids 12 & up, $6 kids 5–11; free for kids under 5. Free for everyone the 1st Thurs of the month.*

Return to Allen Ave. and head north. Turn left at California Blvd. Turn left at Arroo Parkway, which turns into Hwy. 110; head south. Exit at Fourth St. Follow Fourth St. to Hope St. and take a left. Turn right on Third St. and left on Grand Ave.

3 ★★ **Museum of Contemporary Art (MOCA).** Dedicated to art from 1940 to the present, MOCA's permanent collection contains seminal works of abstract expressionism and pop art, including work by Andy Warhol, Jackson Pollock, Mark Rothko, Jasper Johns, and Cindy Sherman. The museum's

At the Museum of Contemporary Art (MOCA).

superb reputation derives from its sparkling temporary exhibitions such as recent retrospectives of Warhol and Basquiat. MOCA has another branch in Little Tokyo called the Geffen Contemporary (152 N. Central Ave.), which is known for more experimental fare. It made a splash in 2010 when, following the death of actor and artist Dennis Hopper, it presented a compelling exhibit of his photography and paintings that was curated by Julian Schnabel. ⏱ *45 min. 250 S. Grand Ave.* ☎ *213/626-6222. www.moca. org. Admission $10 adults, $5 seniors & students, free for children 11 & under; free for all Thurs 5–8pm. Mon & Fri 11am–5pm; Thurs 11am–8pm; Sat–Sun 11am–6pm.*

Head north on Grand Ave., then take a left on Second St.

④ ★ **REDCAT.** Tucked away in the southwest corner of the Walt Disney Concert Hall, REDCAT (the Roy and Edna Disney/CalArts Theater) is devoted to the visual, performing, and media arts, and has earned a reputation as a hotbed of the avant-garde. Gallery exhibits range from a multimedia video presentation on the social and political changes in contemporary China to the colorful, wry wall installations of Barry McGee. ⏱ *30 min. 631 W. Second St.* ☎ *213/237-2800. www.redcat. org. Gallery hours: Tues–Sun noon–6pm. Check website for performance events.*

Head south on Grand Ave. Take a right at Fifth St. Continue onto Sixth St.

⑤ ★★ **Los Angeles County Museum of Art (LACMA).** LACMA is nearing the completion of a multi-year, multi-stage transformation meant to redefine its campus, spearheaded by internationally acclaimed architect Renzo Piano. Recently opened is another Piano-designed building with a saw-tooth roofline, the single-story Resnick Exhibition Pavilion, which will host special exhibitions. There's also talk of a wild installation from Jeff Koons called *Train*—a 160-foot crane dangling a 70-foot replica of a 1940s locomotive over the piazza near the entrance pavilion.

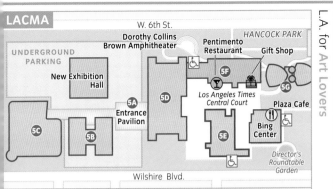

You'll begin at the **5A BP Grand Entrance,** an open-air pavilion that's designed to unify the sprawling complex of buildings. Take note of the oddly alluring installation piece on the south piazza (along Wilshire Blvd.), Chris Burden's *Urban Lights,* a regimented platoon of antique lampposts that amateur photogs find irresistible. Head to the **5B Broad Contemporary Art Museum (BCAM),** a new 60,000-square-foot space that is home to the Contemporary Art collection, including works by Jeff Koons, Jasper Johns, Barbara Kruger, and Richard Diebenkorn. If you're with kids, head next door to the **5C LACMA West** (in the 1939 Art Deco building that was formerly the May Company department store) to play in the Boone Children's Gallery, where kids can make art of their own. Head back to the entrance pavilion, then on to the **5D Ahmanson Building,** where you can meander for days through an astounding array of galleries: Modern Art (Picasso, Matisse, Magritte), Textiles, Decorative Arts, Islamic, South and Southeast Asian, European Painting (Cezanne, Degas), German Expressionism, Greek, and Roman. East of the Ahmanson on the south

side of the courtyard is the **5E Art of the Americas Building,** which contains the American and extensive Latin American collections; here you'll find work by David Hockney (*Mulholland Drive*), Winslow Homer (*The Cotton Pickers*), Mary Cassatt (*Mother About to Wash Her Sleepy Child*), and Diego Rivera. The **5F Hammer Building,** just north across the courtyard, houses Chinese and Korean art, as well as an excellent photography collection, which includes work by Ansel Adams, Alfred Stieglitz, and Edward Weston. Next-door to the east, the serene **5G Japanese Pavilion** displays Buddhist and Shinto sculpture, woodblock prints, Edo paintings, and intricately carved sculptures called netsuke. Time your visit to catch the free **Friday Night Jazz** series, which features Californian jazz artists playing in the Central Court (Apr–Nov Fri 6–8pm). ⏱ *2 hr. 5905 Wilshire Blvd. (parking lot off Sixth St.).* ☎ *323/857-6000. www.lacma. org. Admission $12 adults, $8 seniors & students, free for kids 17 & under; free for all after 5pm & all day the 2nd Tues of the month. Parking $5–$8. Mon–Tues & Thurs noon–8pm; Fri noon–9pm; Sat–Sun 11am–8pm.*

A detail from Camille Pissarro's Place du Théâtre Francais *(1898)*, at LACMA.

Head south on Fairfax Ave. Head west on I-10. Bear right onto Hwy. 1 (PCH).

6 ★★ **The Getty Villa.** You enter the lavish grounds from an elevated walkway, as if stumbling across an archaeological dig, appropriate since here you'll find one of the world's finest collections of Greek, Roman, and Etruscan antiquities. Be sure to see the *Lansdowne Herakles*, a Greek marble statue from A.D. 125; the striking Getty *kouros;* and the *Statue of the Victorious Youth*, a rare life-size Greek bronze. 🕑 *1 hr.* See p 16.

Downtown Art Walk

On the second Tuesday night of the month from 7 to 11pm, local artists of all ages, gadabouts, students, and scenesters gather in downtown's Historic Core to stroll through the 45 or so participating galleries along Gallery Row. Five years ago, the first event drew less than 100 folks; the most recent art walk drew over 10,000. If your feet start to flag before your sense of fun does, hop on the Hippodrome, a shuttle bus (although the driver prefers "floating salon featuring live music and art happenings") that loops along the row. The action takes place on Main and Springs streets, between Second and Ninth streets. For more information, see www.downtownartwalk.com.

Watt's Towers

It may be a bit out of the way, but if you're seeking artistic inspiration, you won't do any better than this. For over 30 years, from 1921 to 1955, an Italian immigrant named Simon Rodia toiled away in his yard on a series of steel and concrete structures, decorating them with found objects like broken glass, tiles, seashells, and pottery shards. Upon completion he gave the property to a neighbor and left. Today the series of soaring, Gaudi-esque sculptures is a National Historic Landmark (one of only four in Los Angeles) and thought to be the largest piece of folk art ever created by a single person. As Rodia put it, "I had in my mind to do something big. And I did it." *1765 E. 107 St.* ☎ *213/847-4646. Fri–Sat 11am–3pm; Sun 12:30–3:30pm. Admission $7 adults, $3 seniors & teens, free for kids 12 & under.*

Head east on I-10. Exit 1B for 20th St. and take a left at 20th St. Take a right at Olympic Blvd. Take a right at Cloverfield Blvd., then left at Michigan Ave.

⑦ ★ **Bergamot Station.** Go gallery hopping at this complex featuring around three dozen independent art galleries. You may stumble across a name or two you recognize—Robert Crumb, Yoko Ono—but for the most part, you'll never know what you'll find, and that's precisely the beauty of it. And who knows, maybe you'll find a few pieces to collect. ⏱ *1 hr. 2525 Michigan Ave., Santa Monica.* ☎ *310/586-6488. www.bergamotstation.com. Tues–Sat 10am–6pm. Free admission.*

Head east on Olympic Blvd. Take a left at Bundy Dr. Take a right at Sunset Blvd. Take a left at Sepulveda Blvd.

A detail of Van Gogh's Irises, at the Getty Center.

⑧ ★★★ **Getty Center.** Finish your day at the art acropolis overlooking the city. In the late afternoon the crowds thin out a bit, and if you're visiting on a Saturday when it stays open until 9pm, then even better—the Getty at nighttime is especially lovely. Upcoming exhibitions include looks at Rococo Paris and fashion in the Middle Ages. ⏱ *1 hr. See the minitour on p 11.*

L.A.'s Shops & Spas

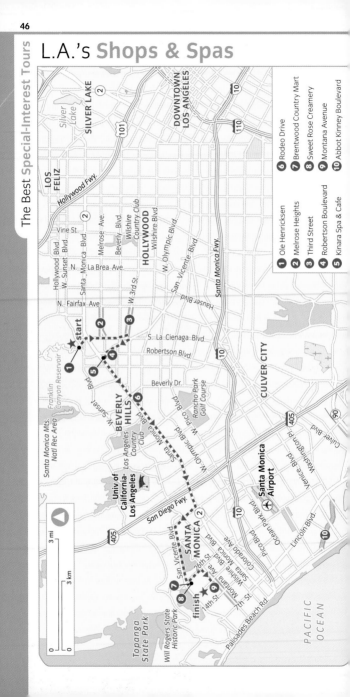

1 Ole Henricksen
2 Melrose Heights
3 Third Street
4 Robertson Boulevard
5 Kinara Spa & Cafe
6 Rodeo Drive
7 Brentwood Country Mart
8 Sweet Rose Creamery
9 Montana Avenue
10 Abbot Kinney Boulevard

For the serious shopper, a stroll through the malls like the Grove, the Beverly Center, and Third Street Promenade (as solid as they may be) is a bit, shall we say, pedestrian. In that case try the following hotspots on for size. And because all that browsing can be so taxing, be sure to hit a few spas along the way (book beforehand).
START: **Sunset Plaza, Sunset Blvd. & Alta Loma Rd.**

❶ ★★ Ole Henriksen. Start your day with a facial at the Facialist to the Stars, Ole Henriksen, whose eight-step complexion treatments have made many a pretty face even prettier. Afterwards, you'll definitely want to take some of the amazing skin products home. Fans include Justin Timberlake and Renee Zellweger. *8622 W. Sunset Blvd., west of Alta Loma Rd.* ☎ *310/854-7700. www.olehenriksen.com.*

Head east on Sunset Blvd. to La Cienega Blvd., and take a right. Take a left at Melrose Ave.

❷ ★★★ Melrose Heights. This is the spiffier part of Melrose, west of Fairfax, that competes with the high-end designers on Robertson. The area is anchored by the legendary Maxfield's and Fred Segal—both are must-stops. You'll also find the snappy Paul Smith, the splashy Betsey Johnson, Diane von Furstenberg, and Alexander McQueen. Divas should inspect Cameron Silver's Decades for vintage couture, or Agent Provocateur for something even slinkier. Big names line fancy **Melrose Place:** Marc Jacobs, Monique Lhuillier, Carolina Herrera, and Oscar de la Renta. Also, be sure to sniff out Santa Maria Novella, a darling Florentine perfumery. *Melrose Ave. (from La Cienega Blvd. to Fairfax Ave.) & Melrose Place.*

Head south on Fairfax Ave. to Third St. and take a right.

❸ ★★★ Third Street. In contrast to the antiseptic malls (the Beverly Center and the Grove) that bookend it, Third Street offers a refreshing stretch of independently owned and independently minded boutiques. Smart, stylish, eccentric—these shops specialize in the "I had no idea I needed that" experience: fashion boutiques like Satine, Noodle Stories, Sigerson Morrison, and the playful Trina Turk, as well as Douglas Fir for men; vintage wear at Polka Dots & Moonbeams; design-heavy gifts at O.K. and Plastica. *W. Third St. (btwn La Cienega Blvd. & Fairfax Ave.).*

Head east on Third St. to Robertson Blvd.

❹ ★★ Robertson Boulevard. The is *the* shopping destination for young starlets on the glam. Strolling these über-trendy shops, you can sometimes find yourself in the middle of a flashbulb-popping frenzy: Is Paris Hilton doing an in-store promo at Kitson? Is one of the Kardashian girls being Kardashian at Intermix? Or is it the power-broker powwow over at the Ivy? Robertson specializes in chic boutiques for

Kitson, on Robertson Boulevard, attracts the fabulous and the flashbulbs that follow them.

chicks: Curve, Vionnet, Nanette Lepore, Lisa Kline, and Alice + Olivia. There are also old reliables like Chanel, Dolce & Gabbana, and Armani. Looking for the perfect pair of jeans? Slip into Paige Premium Denim, 7 For All Mankind, or True Religion. A few blocks north, near Melrose, men can try Logan Riese, Jay Wolff, and John Varvatos. *Robertson Blvd. (btwn Beverly Blvd. & Third St).*

5 ★★ **Kinara Spa & Cafe.** If all those shopping bags are starting to weigh you down, it must mean you're due for a body wrap and a massage, right? Head to this trendy spot where A-listers like Halle Berry, Naomi Watts, and Jennifer Garner go to get red-carpet ready. This place offers it all: a variety of massages and body treatments, facials, hairstyling, waxing, nails. They also have a small cafe with tasty, healthy eats. *656 N. Robertson Blvd. (btwn Melrose Ave. & Beverly Blvd.).* ☎ 310/657-9188. www.kinaraspa.com.

Head north on Robertson Blvd. to Santa Monica Blvd. and take a left. At Rodeo Dr., take a left.

6 ★ **Rodeo Drive.** This bastion of conspicuous consumption encourages you to catch a glimpse of an alternative reality of yourself, a shinier version bedecked in diamonds and wearing a gown that costs a teacher's salary. After sauntering by Prada, Bvlgari, Hermes, Louis Vuitton, Harry Winston, and all the dizzying names, slowly bring yourself back to reality. *200–500 Rodeo Dr. (at Wilshire Blvd.), Beverly Hills.* www.rodeodrivebh.com. *Most shops Mon–Sat 10am–6pm; Sun noon–5pm. Several public parking lots free for 2 hr.*

Head west on Wilshire Blvd. Turn right at San Vicente Blvd. Turn left at 26th St.

7 ★ **Brentwood Country Mart.** A neighborhood (albeit a ritzy neighborhood) staple since 1948, the Mart

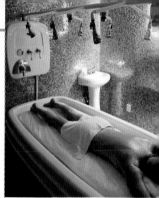

Enjoy a massage treatment at Kinara spa.

relaunched in 2006 with a fresh collection of high-end retailers to go along with its charming, kitschy redbarn theme. Yesteryear regulars included Gregory Peck, Joan Crawford, and Elizabeth Taylor; these days you might see Reese Witherspoon or Tom Hanks. Women can find casual dresses and more at Calypso, Jigsaw, and Malia Mills; men can peruse Apartment 9, and the comfortable clothes of Los Angeles designer James Perse. Or pick up some chocolates from Edelweiss Chocolates, an outpost of the 65-year-old Beverly Hills institution, and wander through the Diesel bookstore. Marie Mason Apothecary offers upscale beauty supplies. *225 26th St., just off San Vicente Blvd., Brentwood.* ☎ 310/451-9877. www.brentwoodcountrymart.com. *Free parking.*

8 ★★ **Sweet Rose Creamery.** Finish your day with a scoop or two of small-batch, organic ice cream at this new old-school-style ice-cream parlor. The fresh mint with homemade chocolate chips is heavenly. *Brentwood Country Mart.* ☎ 310/260-CONE. www.sweetrosecreamery.com. *$3.50 per scoop; $5 for 2.*

Head south on 26th St. Take a right at Montana Ave.

Best Hotel Spas

The Fairmont Miramar has the supremely serene Exhale Mind & Body Spa; the **Peninsula** (see p 145) has the Peninsula Spa, which offers crazy-luxurious body treatments with Shiffa precious-gem oil; **Shutters on the Beach** (see p 145) has ONE the Spa, which uses Ole Henriksen products (see p 47); the **W Hotels** in Westwood (see p 146) and Hollywood pamper guests at the sassy Bliss Spa, which caters to the young with treatments like the hangover detoxifying package.

9 ★ **Montana Avenue.** Next to a lovely Santa Monica neighborhood, this lovely stretch of shops is all about maintaining the good life. There's Kiehl's and Dermologica for skincare; Bellacures for nails; Jonathan Adler's playful home furnishings; Shabby Chic's newly revamped brand of home linens, Shabby Chic Couture; precious duds for kids at Janie & Jack and Peek Aren't You Curious; Every Picture Tells a Story, a marvelous gallery for children's-book illustrations; the Blues Jean Bar with an incredible selection of jeans; Andrew's Cheese Shop; and plenty of high-end clothing boutiques like French Lessons. *Montana Ave. (btwn 7th & 17th sts.).*

Take Montana Ave. west. Take a left at Ocean Ave. Continue on Pacific Way. Take a left at Brooks Ave.

10 ★★ **Abbot Kinney.** This is the antithesis of Rodeo Drive. An eclectic mix of funky art, health-conscious eats, and beach-chic decor—these shops are born of Venice's bohemian roots. Find unique home furnishings at A + R, Tortoise General Store, French 50s-60s, and the supercool Surfing Cowboys. Have your own custom scent made for you at Strange Invisible Perfume, or visit Urbanic Paper Boutique, which has stationery so stylin' that you almost wish you had thank-you notes to write. A Steven Alan Annex and a new Jack Spade shop stock smart, well-made clothes for men, while the Stronghold is a corral of denim Americana.

Abbot Kinney Boulevard is known for its funky stores and eateries.

L.A. for Foodies

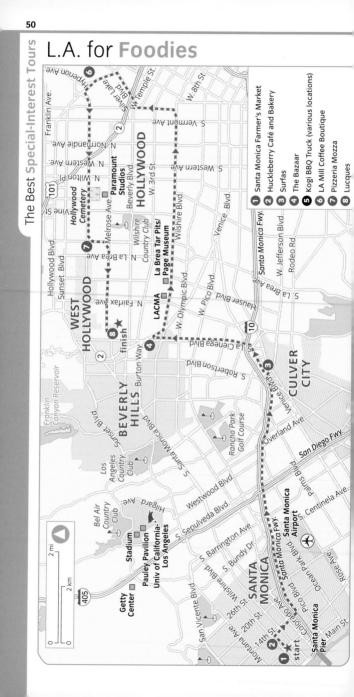

1 Santa Monica Farmer's Market
2 Huckleberry Cafe and Bakery
3 Surfas
4 The Bazaar
5 Kogi BBQ Truck (various locations)
6 LA Mill Coffee Boutique
7 Pizzeria Mozza
8 Lucques

The vibrancy of the Los Angeles food scene isn't just defined by its food makers—celebrity chefs like Nancy Silverton, Suzanne Feniger, Mark Peel, Suzanne Goin, and the ubiquitous Wolfgang Puck—but also by its sophisticated eaters who pore over blogs and queue up for restaurant openings. If you cook it, they will come. Especially when the food is as delicious as the following stops on this 2-day tour. *Tip:* Follow Jonathan Gold, L.A.'s high priest of foodie culture, at LA Weekly (www.laweekly.com). START: **Santa Monica.**

Day 1

1 ★★ Santa Monica Farmers Market. Don't be surprised if you find yourself picking over seasonal organic fruit alongside some of the city's best chefs like Neal Fraser and Suzanne Goin. *Arizona Ave. & Second St., Santa Monica. www.smgov. net. Wed & Sat 8:30am–1:30pm. Free admission.*

Head north on Second St. and take a right at Wilshire Blvd.

2 ★★ Huckleberry Café and Bakery. Need something to wash down all that farmers market healthiness? Then how about a maple-bacon biscuit or cinnamon-sugar doughnut baked by Zoe Nathan, who's being heralded as the best young pastry chef in town? The brunch menu and the takeaway rustic sandwiches are also terrific. *1014 Wilshire Blvd., Santa Monica.* ☎ *310/451-2311. www. huckleberrycafe.com. Tues–Fri 8am– 7pm; Sat–Sun 8am–5pm. AE, MC, V.*

Head east on I-10. Exit 7A for La Cienega Blvd. and stay right. Take a right at Washington Blvd.

3 ★ Surfas. Local foodies and chefs flock to this cooking- and restaurant-supply store for kitchen tools, commercial bakeware, stainless steel work tables, and specialty ingredients like Russian caviar, almond pistachio paste, or Indian curry spices. *8777 W. Washington Blvd., at National Blvd., Culver City.* ☎ *310/559-4770. www. surfaslosangeles.com. Mon–Sat 9am– 6pm; Sun 11am–5pm.*

A tart from Huckleberry Café with almonds, figs, and raspberries.

Return to La Cienega Blvd. and head north.

4 ★★★ The Bazaar. With an open kitchen, three dining rooms (one casual, one formal, one private), a craft-cocktail bar, patisserie, and gift shop, the aptly named Bazaar is a feast of the senses and the playground of Jose Andres, the Spanish chef and molecular gastronomist. With a modern tapas menu that includes cotton candy–wrapped *foie gras* and rainbow-colored caviar presented like an ice-cream cone, the Bazaar is truly a singular dining experience. *465 S. La Cienega Blvd., in SLS Hotel.* ☎ *310/246-5555. Tapas $5–$36. AE, DC, DISC, MC, V. Sun 11am–10pm; Mon–Wed 6pm–10pm; Thurs–Fri 6pm–11pm; Sat 11am– 11pm. Map p 50.*

Check kogibbq.com or twitter. com/KOGIBBQ for the current location of the:

5 ★★ Kogi BBQ Truck. Roy Choi takes the humble taco, the everyman of Mexican street food,

Cotton candy foie gras at Jose Andres' The Bazaar.

and gives it a Korean barbecue twist. If you're still hungry, visit www.findlafoodtrucks.com for more gourmet truck options. *See p 105.*

Day 2

From the Hollywood area, head east on Sunset Blvd. Turn left at Parkman Ave., and then left at Silver Lake Blvd.

6 ★★ LAMILL Coffee Boutique. Order one of the tabletop services, such as the elaborate Siphon Brew, which resembles a small lab experiment, and you may even learn how and why the coffee you're sipping is so damn good. *1636 Silver Lake Blvd., Silver Lake. ☎ 323/663-4441. www.lamillcoffee. com. Coffee $8–$12 for table service for 2, hot chocolate $3. Sun–Thurs 7am–10pm; Fri–Sat 7am–11pm.*

Head south on Silver Lake Blvd. Stay right and continue onto Beverly Blvd. Take a right at Highland Ave. Head north to Melrose Ave.

7 ★★★ Pizzeria Mozza. Take Mario Batali's expertise in Italian cooking and toss in La Brea Bakery

founder Nancy Silverton's bread skills, and you get one seriously gourmet pizzeria that took Los Angeles by storm when it opened in 2006. Your best choice for pizza is the bacon, salami, fennel sausage, and *guanciale* (cured pork cheek). Save room for dessert: made-from-scratch gelato or butterscotch pudding with sea salt. *Tip:* Get schooled at the restaurant's **Scuola di Pizza** ($150 for a 3-hr. class) taught by Silverton and executive chef Matt Molina. *See p 107.*

Head west on Melrose Ave.

8 ★★★ Lucques. For dinner, enjoy the French-inspired take on California cuisine from Los Angeles native and James Beard Award winner for the best chef in California, Suzanne Goin, who is also the chef-owner of the popular wine bar A.O.C. Tavern, and along with her husband, the Hungry Cat. There's always going to be flashy new restaurants riding the latest trends (gourmet burgers!), but Lucques has consistently remained one of the city's best for over a dozen years. First Lady Michelle Obama recently enjoyed the slow-roasted lamb. *See p 105.* ●

Pizza and vino at Pizzeria Mozza.

Downtown

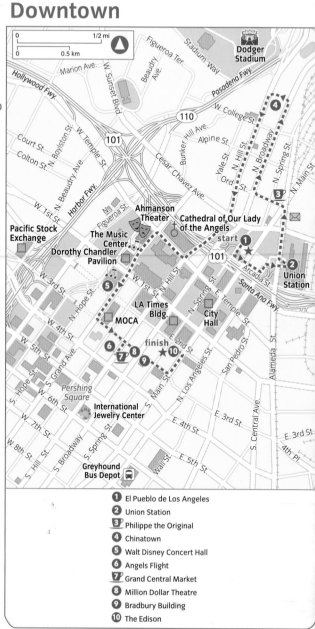

1. El Pueblo de Los Angeles
2. Union Station
3. Philippe the Original
4. Chinatown
5. Walt Disney Concert Hall
6. Angels Flight
7. Grand Central Market
8. Million Dollar Theatre
9. Bradbury Building
10. The Edison

Previous page: In-line skaters liven up the crowds at Venice Beach.

Downtown Los Angeles has seen a remarkable res
in recent years. Old architectural marvels (City Hall, th
Orpheum, and the Eastern Columbia) have been gussied up, wri.
new marvels (Walt Disney Concert Hall and Cathedral of Our Lady of
Angels) have been added. Even an economic downturn and a precip-
itous drop in California real estate have not slowed the steady influx
of überhip bars (the Edison, the Varnish) and scene-stealing restaurants (Rivera, Church and State, Bottega Louie). A good resource for
walking tours is the Los Angeles Conservancy (☎ 213/623-2489;
www.laconservancy.org.) START: **N. Main St. and Caesar Chavez Ave. If
you don't wish to drive downtown, take the Metro Red Line from Hol-
lywood/Highland to Union Station.**

**1 ★★ El Pueblo de Los Ange-
les.** As the birthplace of Los Angeles, this makes an *excelente* start to a
downtown tour. Forty-four Mexican
settlers founded a pueblo in 1781 on
the orders of Carlos III of Spain, who
needed food for the troops guarding
Alta California, this faraway Spanish
province. The 44-acre historical park
contains the city's oldest house,
Avila Adobe (1818); the city's oldest
church, **Old Plaza Church** (1822);
and the city's first fire station, **Old
Plaza Firehouse** (1884). Wander
the brick path of **Olvera Street**, a
pedestrian marketplace bursting like
a piñata with Mexican knickknacks.
Keep an eye out for the **Pelanconi
House** (1855), the first brick building
in Los Angeles, and home to the popular **La Golondrina** restaurant since

*Olvera Street is teeming with colorful
souvenirs.*

1930. The visitor center is located in
a Victorian building from 1887 called
the **Sepulveda House,** where tours,
maps, brochures, and gifts are available, as well as a free screening of a
short film, *Pueblo of Promise. Visitor
center, 622 N. Main St. ☎ 213/628-
1274. www.elpueblo.lacity.org. Park
Mon–Sat 10am–3pm. Most historic
buildings Mon–Sat 10am–3pm.
Olvera St. market daily 10am–7pm.
La Golondrina restaurant daily
9am–9pm.*

2 ★ Union Station. Considered to
be the last great railway station built
in America, this 1939 terminal used to
see 7,000 folks a day, coming and
going on three different railroads.
Although still a vital transportation
hub (subway, light rail, Metrolink, and
Amtrak all stop here), today the station is better known as a time capsule
of the golden age of train travel. A
quiet seat in the glamorous waiting
room—with a cathedral ceiling, twinkling chandeliers, and marble and tile
finishes—is a trip back in time. *800 N.
Alameda St. ☎ 213/683-6979. Daily
24 hr.*

3 ★ Philippe the Original. Since
this legendary eatery opened its
doors a century ago, the big seller
has been the French dipped sand-
wich, which the restaurant claims to

have invented (after taking a bite, you're not going to question it). With sawdust floors and dirt-cheap prices, this is an everyman's paradise. And just to prove that they're keeping it real, a cup of joe is a dime—you heard right: 10¢. *1001 N. Alameda St. (at Ord St.).* ☎ *213/628-3781. www.philippes.com. Daily 6am–10pm. Sandwiches $5–$7.*

Head west on Ord St. past the Jade Pavilion, and turn right on Broadway. Head north to Central Plaza at 947 N. Broadway.

④ ★ **Chinatown.** Lacking the scope and vibrancy of the Chinese communities in San Francisco and New York, the "new" Chinatown—sadly, the "old" Chinatown was razed to make way for Union Station—juxtaposes a reverence for ancient traditions with an appreciation for the vanguard, such as the experimental art galleries blossoming on Chung King Road. Poke through the tiny shops in Central Plaza and look for my favorite building, the Hop Louie Restaurant, a 1941 structure with a five-tier pagoda roof. Serenity seekers can visit the lovely new Buddhist temple,

Cam Au, a few blocks away at 750 Yale St. *www.chinatownla.com.*

Just east of the intersection of Broadway and Ord St. is a DASH bus stop. For 25¢, Route B (or, on weekends, the DD) will take you to Grand Ave. and First St.

⑤ ★★★ **Walt Disney Concert Hall.** Frank Gehry's masterpiece is often credited with revitalizing Downtown L.A., but it didn't happen overnight. Lillian Disney, Walt's widow, got the ball rolling in 1987 with a gift of $50 million. Groundbreaking finally took place in 1999, and the building was completed 4 years later, at a final cost of $275 million. *111 S. Grand Ave.* ☎ *323/850-2000. www.laphil. com. 45- to 60-min. audio tours most days 10am–2pm. 45- to 60-min. guided tours Sat–Sun; times vary, 10am–1pm. Free admission.*

Head south to California Plaza Watercourt at 350 S. Grand Ave.

⑥ ★ **Angels Flight.** The "shortest railway in the world" (actually a two-car funicular) was built in 1901 so that the wealthy residents of the Victorian mansions of Bunker Hill could take a penny ride down to the town's main shopping district. Eventually the

Union Station in Downtown Los Angeles.

Spices, grains, produce, and unusual ingredients of all kinds are on offer at the Grand Central Market.

well-heeled split for the 'burbs and the Bunker Hill enclave degenerated into slums; by 1969, the cars were put into storage. In 1996, after a 27-year hiatus, the city landmark was restored and reopened; unfortunately, a fatal accident in 2001 shut it down once again. But as of spring 2010, Angels Flight is finally back on track; a one-way, 1-minute jaunt costs only 25¢. *Connects 350 S. Grand Ave. to 351 S. Hill St. www. angelsflight.com. Daily 6:45am–10pm.*

Ride down to Hill St.

7 ★ **Grand Central Market.** Since 1917 this open-air market has been a lively place to pick up coffee, ice cream, or tasty ethnic grub on the cheap—Hawaiian barbecue, Cuban sandwiches, Persian kabobs, pupusas (deep-fried pastries filled with meat, beans, and cheese), and empanadas. *317 S. Broadway (entrance on Hill St.).* ☎ *213/624-2378. www.grandcentralsquare. com. Most items $3–$9.*

8 ★★ **Million Dollar Theater.** Built for (gasp!) $1 million, Sid Grauman's first take on a movie palace opened in 1918 with a lavish interior meant to evoke a Mexican cathedral; in fact, for many years a Spanish-speaking church held services here. The surrounding blocks are known as the Broadway Historic Theatre District, the highest concentration of movie palaces in the world, and the street once glowed with the neon lights of a dozen marquees. There you'd find a medley of architectural styles: Beaux Arts, Zigzag Moderne, Spanish Baroque, and so forth. Other spectacular theaters still on their feet are the Los Angeles Theatre (615 S. Broadway), the Palace (630 S. Broadway), and the 1926-built Orpheum Theatre (842 S. Broadway; www.la orpheum.com). *307 S. Broadway. www.milliondollartheater.com.*

9 ★★ **Bradbury Building.** The city's oldest commercial building (built in 1893) contains an awe-inspiring courtyard, which has starred in numerous films, most memorably *Blade Runner.* *304 S. Broadway.* ☎ *213/626-1893. Mon–Fri 9am–6pm; Sat–Sun 9am–5pm.*

Heading north on Broadway, take a right at Second St.

10 ★★ **The Edison.** Descend into the bowels of the city's first private power plant, now a swank lounge where you can enjoy expertly mixed cocktails like its namesake The Edison (Woodford Reserve bourbon with pear cognac and honey). *108 W. Second St., at Main St.* ☎ *213/613-2000. www.edisondowntown.com. Wed–Fri 5pm–2am; Sat 8pm–2am. Dress code: no shorts, athletic gear, or sandals.*

Venice

1. Venice Canals
2. Norton House
3. Venice Boardwalk
4. Jody Maroni's Sausage Kingdom
5. Muscle Beach
6. Venice Art Walls
7. Venice Beach State Park
8. Venice Murals by Rip Cronk
9. Abbot Kinney
10. Jin Patisserie

No area of the sprawling Los Angeles metropolis has as colorful a history as Venice. Before it was a place, it was a grand concept: first the "Coney Island of the Pacific," then "Venice of America." At the end of the 1920s, it was an oil boomtown; a few years later, it was a ghost town. The '50s brought the Beatniks; the '60s, the hippies; the '70s, the surfers and skateboarders. In recent years, as the canals cleaned up, gourmet restaurants moved in, and real estate soared, Venice has somehow managed to maintain its bohemian edge. START: **Venice Blvd. and Ocean Ave.**

Head south 3 blocks to Linnie Ave. and take a right. Cross the bridge over Eastern Canal.

① ★ **Venice Canals.** The image of these canals, like the HOLLYWOOD sign, is a Los Angeles icon born of a busted real-estate venture. In the early 1900s, entrepreneur Abbot Kinney dreamt up "Venice of America," 16 miles of canals connecting piers, theaters, restaurants, and hotels; he even imported a couple dozen gondoliers from Italy. Cars or gondolas: Guess which won out in the long run? Only 6 canals remain of Kinney's original 16; most were paved over in 1929 to make room for automobiles, while the few remaining canals were neglected for half a century. In 1994 the city dredged the canals and added small bridges and sidewalks. Tossing a few crumbs to the ducks in the placid water, you might wonder whether Kinney's vision was so crazy after all. Wander along Howland Canal and Carroll Canal and take in the eclectic homes that line the water.

Leave the canals by heading northwest on Dell Ave. At Venice Blvd., take a left and head west to Ocean Front Walk. Take a left and head a few blocks south.

② ★ **Norton House.** This residential design by Frank Gehry fascinates me, mainly because of its awfulness, as if a 9-year-old boy replaced the blueprints with his crayon sketch of a treehouse. If, however, you side with

The eye-catching Norton House.

the architect's opinion that "buildings under construction look nicer than buildings finished," you'll love this. *2509 Ocean Front Walk.*

Head back north on Ocean Front Walk.

③ ★★★ **Venice Boardwalk.** In most places, it's not polite to stare, but on the boardwalk, it's the highest compliment you can pay a performer (without actually *paying* a performer). The endless stream of tacky shops are perfect for buying gifts for (a) someone with a sense of humor, or (b) someone you don't really like. For a more relaxing time, rent in-line skates or a bike and roll up the path to Santa Monica. *Ocean Front Walk (btwn Venice Blvd. & Rose Ave.).*

4 Jody Maroni's Sausage Kingdom. Although Jody Maroni, self-proclaimed Sausage King, assures his customers that he's not making health food, these "haut dogs" are all natural, preservative free, and boast fancy flavorings such as cilantro, orange, fig, and apple. Only vegetarians will leave disappointed. *2011 Ocean Front Walk (north of Venice Blvd.).* ☎ *310/822-5639. www.jody maroni.com. Hot dogs $3–$8.*

5 ★ Muscle Beach. The famous outdoor gym originally resided just south of the Santa Monica Pier from the 1930s through the 1950s. Fitness gurus like Jack LaLanne and Joe Gold worked out here, as well as celebrities like Clark Gable, Kirk Douglas, and Jayne Mansfield. Later the gym migrated to facilities in Venice, where a young Arnold Schwarzenegger would stop in to pump up. Today the gym is still going strong. *Ocean Front Walk (2 blocks north of Venice Blvd.).*

6 ★ Venice Art Walls. These walls are the only remnants of "The Pit," an area popular with graffiti

Don't miss out on the delicious dogs at Jody Maroni's.

Look out for exploding biceps and more at Muscle Beach.

artists from 1961 to 1999. Today a permit is required to paint on the walls (weekends only). The goal is to nurture high-quality street art while minimizing the vandalism sometimes associated with it. *Ocean Front Walk (btwn Windward & Market sts.). www.veniceartwalls.com.*

7 ★★ Venice Beach Skate Park. Venice surfers-turned-boarders, the Z-boys, popularized skateboarding in the '70s largely by perfecting their techniques on the smooth concrete banks and dips of drained swimming pools. Therefore it's fitting that the park's design would mimic these pools, as well as a streetscape with steps, ramps, and rails. *Ocean Front Walk (at Market St.).*

8 ★★ Venice Murals by Rip Cronk. Venice loves its street murals. Some of the most memorable ones were created in the late '80s and early '90s by an artist named Rip Cronk. Look for the following: *Morning Shot* (at Speedway and 18th Court), which features a towering Jim Morrison; *Venice Reconstituted* (25 Windward at Speedway), a loose interpretation

Graffiti artists are welcome to display their best at the Venice Art Walls.

of Botticelli's *The Birth of Venus*; and *Homage to a Starry Night*, Cronk's nod to van Gogh (Wavecrest Ave. and Ocean Front Walk).

Head north on Ocean Front Walk, then east on Westminster Ave. for a couple of short blocks.

⑨ ★★ Abbot Kinney Boulevard. Compared to the sea of humanity on the boardwalk, this stretch of funky-chic shops and small cafes is refreshingly laid-back. But if you see something you gotta have, you better grab it—these stores specialize in the hard to find and one of a kind. Trawl for home furnishings and decor at Tortoise General Store, French 50s-60s, and Surfing Cowboys (1208, 1103, and 1624 Abbot Kinney Blvd.); or roll into Linus Bikes (1413½ Abbot Kinney Blvd.), which sells the coolest (and fairly affordable) bikes that look like they've been plucked out of a French new wave film. There's also a slew of great eats: Joe's Restaurant (1023 Abbot Kinney Blvd.) has been considered the best on the block for nearly 20 years; sophisticated and unpretentious Gjelina (1429 Abbot Kinney Blvd.) draws raves for its small plates; and Axe's cute courtyard is perfect for alfresco dining (1009 Abbot Kinney Blvd.). *Btwn Brooks Ave. & Venice Blvd.*

⑩ ★ Jin Patisserie. Relax in the tranquil garden of this Asian-influenced cafe. An afternoon tea offers French teas, finger sandwiches, scones (yes, with clotted cream), cookies, and cakes—all made fresh in the store. A box of artful chocolate truffles or French macaroons makes an excellent gift. *1202 Abbot Kinney Blvd., Venice.* ☎ *310/399-8801. www.jinpatisserie. com. Tues–Sun 10:30am–7pm. Afternoon tea $10–$19.*

Treat yourself to macaroon cakes and other delights at Jin Patisserie.

Silver Lake

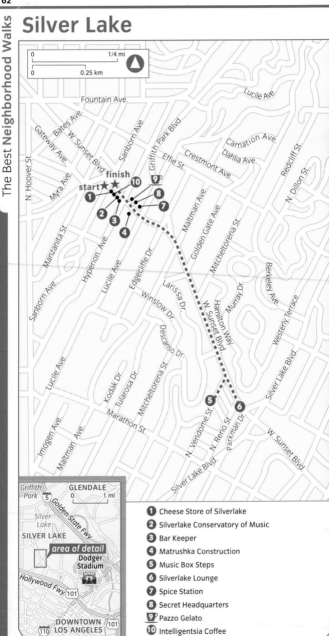

1 Cheese Store of Silverlake
2 Silverlake Conservatory of Music
3 Bar Keeper
4 Matrushka Construction
5 Music Box Steps
6 Silverlake Lounge
7 Spice Station
8 Secret Headquarters
9 Pazzo Gelato
10 Intelligentsia Coffee

Silver Lake is a bohemian enclave east of Hollywood. Once home to the first movie studios (Mack Sennett, Vitagraph, and Walt Disney) and later modernist architects (Neutra, Schindler), this hipster haven now offers one-of-a-kind shopping, eclectic eats, and a music scene that has arguably become a brand name (much like Brooklyn's Williamsburg). You can't see all of Silver Lake on foot, but the Sunset Junction makes for a happening hub. START: **Sunset and Santa Monica blvds.**

The Cheese Store of Silverlake is a gourmand's paradise.

① ★ Cheese Store of Silverlake. At this quaint shop, you can grab all the fixings for a gourmet picnic: artisanal cheeses, hard-to-find wines, cured meats, and chocolates. *3926 W. Sunset Blvd. ☎ 323/644-7511. www.cheesestoresl.com. Mon 10am–6pm; Tues–Sat 10am–6:45pm; Sun 11am–5pm.*

② ★ Silverlake Conservatory of Music. It's only fitting that Silver Lake, with its thriving indie music scene, would have its own school of rock. Flea, local music hero and bassist for the Red Hot Chili Peppers, founded the not-for-profit organization. *3920 W. Sunset Blvd. ☎ 323/665-3363. www.silverlake conservatory.com. Fri noon–9pm; Sat 10am–6pm.*

Head southeast on Sunset Blvd.

③ ★ Bar Keeper. If you've gotten caught up in the city's cocktail craze and are looking to set up your own

Mad Men–esque bar at home, get a load of this amazing array of bar paraphernalia—vintage glassware, seltzer bottles, martini shakers, old-school cocktail manuals, absinthe fountains, and bitters galore. *3910 W. Sunset Blvd. ☎ 323/669-1675. www.barkeepersilverlake.com. Mon–Thurs noon–6pm; Fri–Sat 11am–7pm; Sun 11am–6pm.*

④ ★ Matrushka Construction. If you want a taste of the local fashion flavor, you won't do better than the dresses made by Silver Laker Laura Howe. She'll even tailor them for you right there in her store, which *Los Angeles Magazine* recently named the "Best Boutique for a Sunset Junction Outfit." *3822 W. Sunset Blvd. ☎ 323/665-4513. www.matrushka.com. Mon–Fri noon–7pm; Sat–Sun 11am–6pm.*

Continue several blocks southeast on Sunset Blvd., and then go right at Vendome St.

⑤ ★ Music Box Steps. This small detour combines two of the

Laurel and Hardy struggle with a piano in The Music Box *(1932).*

neighborhood's hallmarks: steps (seriously, there are websites devoted to cataloging them all) and moviemaking history (Mack Sennett's Keystone Studios was just around the corner). It was here that the comedic duo Laurel and Hardy shot their 1932 Oscar-winning short, *The Music Box*, in which Stan and Ollie deliver a piano up this ludicrously long stairway. *Btwn 923 & 925 Vendome St.*

Return to Sunset Blvd. and head right.

6 ★★ **Silverlake Lounge.** A funky hole-in-the-wall with a cash-only bar, this neighborhood favorite segues from indie bands (Elbow, Vampire Weekend) on weekday nights to drag queens on weekends without ever skipping a beat. Don't be afraid to roll the dice on shows, especially on Monday, when it won't cost a thing to get in. For more on the Silver Lake music scene, see p 37. *2906 Sunset Blvd.* ☎ *323/663-9636. www.foldsilverlake.com. Cover $8 Tues–Thurs. Mon–Fri 5pm–2am; Sat–Sun 3pm–2am.*

Cross over to the other side of Sunset and head back northeast.

7 ★ **Spice Station.** Follow your nose into this aromatic sanctum for exotic spices—Szechuan peppercorns, Indian fenugreek, ghost pepper salt (the hottest in the world), sassafras bark—which would be overwhelming if it weren't for the friendly owners who encourage you to explore and sample. *3819 W. Sunset Blvd.* ☎ *323/660-3565. www. spicestationsilverlake.com. Mon, Wed 11am–6pm; Thurs–Fri 11am–8pm; Sat 10am–8pm; Sun noon–5pm.*

8 ★★ **Secret Headquarters.** Comic book collecting gets a sophisticated spin at this quiet and orderly store, whose leather armchairs and rich wood racks create a leisurely, library-like atmosphere. *3817 W. Sunset Blvd.* ☎ *323/666-2228. www. thesecretheadquarters.com. Mon–Sat 11am–9pm; Sun noon–7pm.*

9 ★ **Pazzo Gelato.** Cold treats face fierce competition in sunny Los Angeles, but this gelato and espresso bar recently earned "Best of L.A." from *L.A. Weekly*. *3827 W. Sunset Blvd.* ☎ *323/662-1410. www.pazzogelato.net. Sun–Thurs 11am–11pm; Fri–Sat 11am–midnight. Double scoop $4.*

10 ★★ **Intelligentsia Coffee.** Okay, now that you're fully acclimated to the Silver Lake scene, take a seat at this cafe and order one of the finest cups of java in town. Every cup is made fresh to order using the mighty Clover, the single-blast coffee machine with a cultlike following. Cup in hand, take a seat on the bustling patio and blend in among the locals: Grow your beard, ruminate, work on turning your screenplay into a concept album, or vice versa. Take a moment to observe the creative creatures in their own habitat. *3922 W. Sunset Blvd.* ☎ *323/663-6173. www.intelligentsiacoffee. com. Mon–Wed 6am–8pm; Thurs–Sat 6am–11pm; Sun 6am–8pm.* ●

Grab a cup of joe at Intelligentsia Coffee.

4 | The Best **Shopping**

Shopping Best Bets

Hippest Store for Guys & Gals
★★ American Rag Cie *150 S. La Brea Ave.* (p 73)

Best **Music Store**
★★★ Amoeba Music *6400 Sunset Blvd.* (p 77)

Best **Wine Store**
★★ Silver Lake Wine *2395 Glendale Blvd.* (p 78)

Best **Bookstore**
★★ Book Soup *8818 Sunset Blvd.* (p 71)

Best **Rock Star Fashions**
★ Logan Riese *517 N. Robertson Blvd.* (p 73)

Best **Funky Gift Shop**
★★ Wacko *4633 Hollywood Blvd.* (p 75)

Biggest **Scene**
★★★ Fred Segal *8100 Melrose Ave.* (p 73)

Best **Bargain Hunting**
★★ Rose Bowl Flea Market *1001 Rose Bowl Dr.* (p 74)

Most **Puzzling**
★ Puzzle Zoo *1413 Third St. Promenade* (p 76)

Sexiest Shop
★ Agent Provocateur *7961 Melrose Ave.* (p 77)

Best Place to **Find a Party Dress in a Jiffy**
★ Betsey Johnson *8050 Melrose Ave.* (p 73)

Best **Sneakers**
★ Undefeated *112½ S. La Brea Ave.* (p 78)

Best **Old-World Charm**
★ Santa Maria Novella *8411 Melrose Place* (p 75)

Best **Shopping for Tiny Dogs**
★ Fifi & Romeo Boutique *7282 Beverly Blvd.* (p 74)

Coolest **Kids' Clothing**
★★ La La Ling *1810 N. Vermont Ave.* (p 76)

Best **Art Gallery for Kids**
★★ Every Picture Tells a Story *1311-C Montana Ave.* (p 71)

Best **Comic Books**
★ Meltdown Comics & Collectibles *7522 W. Sunset Blvd.* (p 71)

Best **Vintage Couture**
★★ Decades *8214½ Melrose Ave.* (p 72)

Shop like a Pretty Woman on Rodeo Drive.

Santa Monica & the Beaches

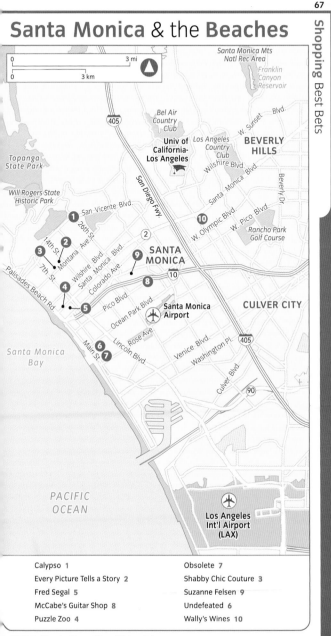

Calypso **1**

Every Picture Tells a Story **2**

Fred Segal **5**

McCabe's Guitar Shop **8**

Puzzle Zoo **4**

Obsolete **7**

Shabby Chic Couture **3**

Suzanne Felsen **9**

Undefeated **6**

Wally's Wines **10**

P 65: Fashion is girly and fun at Betsey Johnson.

Beverly Hills & the Westside

Shoreham Dr.

Horn Ave.

Nellas St.

N. Clark St.

Larrabee St.

Palm Ave.

Santa Monica Blvd.

West Hollywood Park

San Vicente Blvd.

Carmelita Ave.

N. Foothill Rd.

N. Elm Dr.

N. Maple Dr.

N. Palm Dr.

N. Hillcrest Rd.

N. Alpine Dr.

Carmelita Ave.

N. Rexford Dr.

N. Crescent Dr.

N. Canon Dr.

Santa Monica Blvd.

Beverly Gardens Park

Civic Center Dr.

N. Foothill Rd.

N. Maple Dr.

N. Palm Dr.

N. Oakhurst Dr.

S. Doheny Dr.

S. Wetherly Dr.

S. Almont Dr.

S. La Peer Dr.

S. Swall Dr.

S. Clark Dr.

Melrose Ave.

Rangely Ave.

Dorrington Ave.

Ashcroft Ave.

Rosewood Ave.

Beverly Blvd.

Robertson Blvd.

Alden Dr.

W. 3rd St.

Park Way

Burton Way

Dayton Way

Clifton Way

Clifton Way

N. Rodeo Dr.

Brighton Way

N. Crescent Dr.

N. Canon Dr.

N. Rexford Dr.

N. Elm Dr.

N. Maple Dr.

N. Doheny Dr.

N. Wetherly Dr.

N. Almont Dr.

N. La Peer Dr.

S. Swall Dr.

S. Clark Dr.

S. Robertson Blvd.

N. Arnaz Dr.

N. Hamel Dr.

N. Camden Dr.

Dayton Way

Wilshire Blvd.

BEVERLY HILLS

← (one block west)

Charleville Blvd.

S. Bedford Dr.

S. Peck Dr.

S. Camden Dr.

S. Rodeo Dr.

S. El Camino Dr.

S. Beverly Dr.

S. Reeves Dr.

S. Canon Dr.

S. Crescent Dr.

S. Elm Dr.

S. Rexford Dr.

S. Maple Dr.

S. Palm Dr.

S. Oakhurst Dr.

S. Doheny Dr.

S. Wetherly Dr.

S. Almont Dr.

S. La Peer Dr.

S. Swall Dr.

S. Clark Dr.

S. Robertson Blvd.

S. Arnaz Dr.

S. Hamel Rd.

Gregory Way

(2.5 miles south)

W. Olympic Blvd.

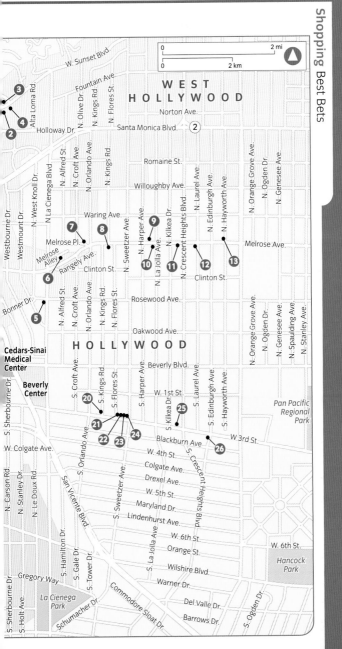

Hollywood, Los Feliz & Silver Lake

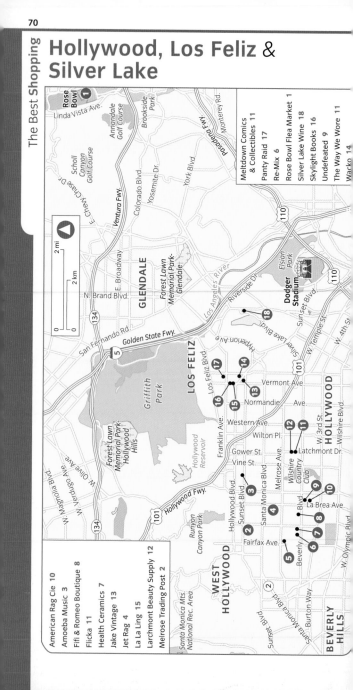

Meltdown Comics
& Collectibles 11
Panty Raid 17
Re-Mix 6
Rose Bowl Flea Market 1
Silver Lake Wine 18
Skylight Books 16
Undefeated 9
The Way We Wore 11
Wacko 14

American Rag Cie 10
Amoeba Music 3
Fifi & Romeo Boutique 8
Flicka 11
Health Ceramics 7
Jake Vintage 13
Jet Rag 4
La La Ling 15
Larchmont Beauty Supply 12
Melrose Trading Post 2

Shopping A to Z

Beauty

★ Larchmont Beauty Center
LARCHMONT   This mom-and-pop shop is one of the city's best collections of premium shampoos, soaps, candles, makeup, and hair products. *208 N. Larchmont Blvd. (btwn Third St. & Beverly Blvd.).* ☎ *323/461-0162. www.larchmontbeauty.com. AE, MC, V. Map p 70.*

★★ Ole Henriksen WEST HOLLYWOOD   Luxurious facials and a superb line of skincare products make this spa a hit among celebrities like Charlize Theron, Prince, and Leonardo DiCaprio. *8622 W. Sunset Blvd., west of Alta Loma Rd.* ☎ *310/854-7700. www.olehenriksen.com. AE, MC, V. Map p 68.*

Books

★★ Book Soup WEST HOLLYWOOD   The city's favorite independent bookstore has an amazing stock of books crammed into its nooks and crannies, a monstrous magazine rack, interesting clientele, and in-store author events that have included appearances by James Ellroy, Sarah Vowell, and Werner Herzog. *8818 Sunset Blvd., at Larabee St.* ☎ *310/659-3110. www.booksoup.com. AE, MC, V. Map p 68.*

★★ Every Picture Tells a Story
SANTA MONICA   Part children's bookstore, part art gallery celebrating the illustrations found in children's books. Check out limited-edition lithographs from *Charlotte's Web* and *Where the Wild Things Are,* and an original Dr. Seuss ink-and-crayon sketch from *The Cat in the Hat. 1311-C Montana Ave.* ☎ *310/451-2700. www.everypicture.com. AE, MC, V. Map p 67.*

★ Meltdown Comics & Collectibles HOLLYWOOD   The city's biggest comic store carries an incredible selection of comics and graphic novels including foreign, small press, and independently produced works. They also offer special events like book signings, art shows, and classes on creating comics. *7522 W. Sunset Blvd., at Sierra Bonita Ave.* ☎ *323/851-7223. www.meltcomics.com. AE, MC, V. Map p 70.*

★ Skylight Books LOS FELIZ   This warm and cozy shop specializes in literary fiction, film, and Los

Whatever your beauty product needs, you're sure to find them at Larchmont Beauty Center.

Angeles history. Staff recommendations are always spot on. *1816½ N. Vermont Ave., at Melbourne Ave.* ☎ *323/666-2202. www.skylight books.com. AE, MC, V. Map p 70.*

Department Stores

★★ Barneys New York BEVERLY HILLS   Fashion mavens navigate five luxurious floors of ready-to-wear from every designer on the planet. The women's shoes, bags, and beauty departments are especially alluring. Try the hoity-toity deli on the rooftop. *9570 Wilshire Blvd., at N. Camden Dr.* ☎ *310/276-4400. www.barneys.com. AE, MC, V. Map p 68.*

★★ Neiman Marcus BEVERLY HILLS   At this monument to retail escapism, a woman can rampage through the Manolo Blahniks in the highly regarded shoe department while her man waits patiently at the bar on the fourth floor. *9700 Wilshire Blvd. (btwn Santa Monica Blvd. & Brighton Way).* ☎ *310/550-5900. www.neimanmarcus.com. AE, MC, V. Map p 68.*

Discount Vintage & Vintage Couture

★★ Decades HOLLYWOOD   Stylists to the stars patrol the racks

here for vintage couture from Hermès, Gucci, and YSL. *8214½ Melrose Ave., at Harper Ave.* ☎ *323/655-1960. www.decadesinc.com. AE, MC, V. Map p 68.*

Jet Rag HOLLYWOOD   Here you'll find retro-style threads on the cheap. The $1 sale every Sunday is mayhem. *825 N. La Brea Ave.* ☎ *323/939-0528. AE, MC, V. Map p 70.*

Lily et Cie BEVERLY HILLS   For Oscar®-night fashion, stars like Penelope Cruz and Renee Zellweger peruse Rita Watnick's museum-quality selection of vintage gowns from Givenchy, Chanel, and Balmain. *9044 Burton Way, at Doheny Dr.* ☎ *310/724-5757. AE, MC, V. Map p 68.*

Polkadots and Moonbeams Vintage WEST HOLLYWOOD   This girly-girl shop is the perfect place to find vintage cocktail dresses. A few doors down is a sister store specializing in contemporary party wear. *8367 W. Third St., at S. Kings Rd.* ☎ *323/651-1746. www.polkadots andmoonbeams.com. AE, MC, V. Map p 68.*

★ The Way We Wore HOLLYWOOD   This friendly, two-level shop stocks dresses, shoes, and

Fun vintage dresses adorn the windows at Polkadots and Moonbeams.

purses from the 1890s to the 1970s. You'll find everything from Victorian gowns to beaded flapper dresses to groovy blouses by Pucci. *334 S. La Brea Ave.* ☎ *323/937-0878. www. thewaywewore.com. AE, MC, V. Map p 70.*

Fashion

★★ American Rag Cie HOLLY-WOOD This popular store features up-and-coming designers, well-selected vintage wear, retro sneakers, hip accessories, and a massive denim selection at their World Denim Bar—all guaranteed to make you cooler. *150 S. La Brea Ave. (btwn W. First & W. Second sts.).* ☎ *323/935-3154. www.amrag.com. AE, MC, V. Map p 70.*

★ Betsey Johnson WEST HOLLY-WOOD If you're looking for a sexy little number to wear to a party, check out the famous designer's colorful bouquet of playful, vintage-inspired dresses. *8050 Melrose Ave., at N. Laurel Ave.* ☎ *323/852-1534. www.betseyjohnson.com. AE, MC, V. Map p 68.*

★ Calypso WEST HOLLYWOOD Christiane Celle's elegant, French-inspired designs are comfortable and flowing, perfect for warm SoCal weather. *8635 W. Sunset Blvd., at Sunset Plaza Dr.* ☎ *310/652-4454. Also in Santa Monica at 225 26th St., at San Vicente Blvd.* ☎ *310/434-9601. www.calypso-celle.com. AE, MC, V. Map p 67.*

★★★ Fred Segal WEST HOLLY-WOOD No clothing store draws more celebrity shoppers than this ivy-covered landmark. The only thing reasonably priced is the parking, which is free. *8100 Melrose Ave.* ☎ *323/651-4129. Also in Santa Monica at 500 Broadway, at Fifth St.* ☎ *310/394-9814. www.fredsegal. com. AE, MC, V. Maps p 67 & 68.*

The landmark Fred Segal clothing store.

★ Jake Vintage LOS FELIZ If the retro-cool cads from *Swingers* were still styling their way through Hollywood nightclubs, this hip haberdasher would be their go-to source for natty, narrow-lapel suits from the 1940s through the 1960s. *4644 Hollywood Blvd., E. of Vermont Ave.* ☎ *323/662-5253. www.jakevintage. com. AE, MC, V. Map p 70.*

★★ Lisa Kline WEST HOLLYWOOD This trendy boutique is really two stores in one: young women (including celebrities) flock here for the bright, form-fitting fashions, while men going for the L.A. look can choose from the "right" kind of shirts, jeans, and jackets. *143 S. Robertson Blvd., at Alden Dr.* ☎ *310/385-7113. www.lisakline. com. AE, MC, V. Map p 68.*

★ Logan Riese WEST HOLLY-WOOD Rock your wardrobe with handcrafted inlaid leather jackets or skull-and-dagger silver jewelry from this Laguna Beach native whose bold, macho designs have been donned by Lenny Kravitz, Dave Navarro, and Jon Bon Jovi. *517 N. Robertson Blvd., at Melrose Ave.* ☎ *323/281-0007. www.loganriese. com. AE, MC, V. Map p 68.*

★ Madison WEST HOLLYWOOD This popular shop—the first of seven Madison boutiques in the city—keeps their loyal customers happy with creations from Vince, Marni, Helmut Lang, and Stella McCartney. *8115 Melrose Ave.* ☎ *323/651-3662. See website for more locations. www.madisonlos-angeles.com. AE, MC, V. Map p 68.*

★★★ **Maxfield** WEST HOLLYWOOD This concrete cathedral to avant-garde fashion showcases names like Yamamoto, Alexander McQueen, and Dolce & Gabbana in a casually bizarre setting that includes stuffed chickens, sex whips, and shrunken human heads (about $40 grand a pop). *8825 Melrose Ave.* ☎ *310/274-8800. AE, MC, V. Map p 68.*

★ **Noodle Stories** WEST HOLLYWOOD This collection of women's clothing emphasizes subtlety, simplicity, and sophistication. Designers include Comme des Garçons, Martin Margiela, and Yohji Yamamoto. *8323 W. Third St., at N. Flores St.* ☎ *323/651-1782. www.noodle stories.com. AE, MC, V. Map p 68.*

Oliver Peoples WEST HOLLYWOOD This fashionable optical shop sells top-quality shades and frames for stars (Jack Nicholson, Gwen Stefani) or folks that just want to look (and see) like them. *8642 W. Sunset Blvd., at Sunset Plaza Dr.* ☎ *310/657-2553. www.oliver peoples.com. AE, MC, V. Map p 68.*

★★ **Opening Ceremony** WEST HOLLYWOOD Once the home of Charlie Chaplin's dance studio, this sprawling space offers a series of rooms featuring high-fashion labels like Comme des Garçons, Band of Outsiders, and Rodarte. Browsers love the inviting layout and attitude-free staff. *451 N. La Cienega Blvd., at Rosewood Ave.* ☎ *310/652-1120. www.openingceremony.us. AE, MC, V. Map p 68.*

★★ **Paul Smith** WEST HOLLYWOOD Designer Paul Smith is celebrated for his snappy, British style, and his slightly mod shirts and suits will make

any man look like a million bucks. *8221 Melrose Ave., at N. La Jolla Ave.* ☎ *323/951-4800. www.paulsmith.co.uk. AE, MC, V. Map p 68.*

★ **Satine** WEST HOLLYWOOD This recently expanded store offers cutting-edge fashion from an eclectic mix of designers including Alexander Wang, Tsumori Chisato, and Balenciaga. *8134 W. Third St. (W. of Crescent Heights Blvd.).* ☎ *323/655-2142. www.satineboutique.com. AE, MC, V. Map p 68.*

★ **Trina Turk** WEST HOLLYWOOD This California designer is known for her retro-glam style that marries brightly colored patterns with classic silhouettes. *8008 W. Third St. (at S. Edinburgh Ave.).* ☎ *323/651-1382. www.trinaturk.com. AE, MC, V. Map p 68.*

Flea Markets

★ **Melrose Trading Post** HOLLYWOOD Every Sunday swarms of hipsters hunt for treasure buried in the over 200 stalls stuffed with clothes, shoes, jewelry, and funky housewares. *7850 Melrose Ave.* ☎ *323/655-7679. www.melrose tradingpost.org. Admission $2. Cash only. Every Sun. Map p 70.*

★★ **Rose Bowl Flea Market** PASADENA On the second Sunday of every month, locals flock to this massive outdoor marketplace with over 2,500 vendors to hunt for antique furniture, hard-to-find collectibles, and vintage clothing. *1001 Rose Bowl Dr.* ☎ *323/651-1382. www.rgcshows.com. Admission $8 adults, kids 11 & under free with an adult. Cash only. Second Sun of the month 9am–5pm. Map p 70.*

Gifts

★ **Fifi & Romeo Boutique** WEST HOLLYWOOD This luxury boutique for little pooches offers cashmere and angora sweaters, faux

Worn but regal treasures at the Rose Bowl Flea Market.

fur-trimmed coats, jewel-encrusted collars, and that sense of validation that tiny canines sometimes need. *7282 Beverly Blvd., at N. Poinsettia Place.* ☎ *323/857-7214. www.fifiand romeo.com. AE, MC, V. Map p 70.*

★ **OK** WEST HOLLYWOOD   Blown-glass vases, Japanese ceramics, vintage phones, modernist clocks, and a well-curated array of art and design books—unusual gift ideas abound at this gallery-like store. *8303 W. Third St., at S. Sweetzer Ave.* ☎ *323/653-3501. www. okstore.la. AE, MC, V. Map p 68.*

★ **Santa Maria Novella** WEST HOLLYWOOD   On Melrose Place, take a side-trip to Florence, Italy. This boutique carries soaps, lotions, and scents based on the same recipes used 400 years ago by the Dominican friars of Santa Maria Novella. *8411 Melrose Place, at N. Orlando Ave.* ☎ *323/651-3754. www.smnovella.it. AE, MC, V. Map p 68.*

★★ **Wacko** LOS FELIZ   Load up on kitschy stuff that you definitely don't need, but for some reason, you just have to have: bobble heads, wind-up robots, Mexican wrestling masks, Tiki mugs, *Yellow Submarine* lunchboxes. Rumor has it that Michael Jackson ran up quite a tab here shortly before he died. *4633 Hollywood Blvd., at Rodney Dr.* ☎ *323/663-0122. www.soapplant. com. AE, MC, V. Map p 70.*

Home Decor

H.D. Buttercup CULVER CITY   Fifty or so vendors present a wide array of high-end furniture and arty home decor in a 150,000-square-foot Art Deco building that was once home to the historic Helms Bakery. *3225 Helms Ave., at Washington Ave.* ☎ *310/558-8900. www.hdbuttercup. com. AE, DISC, MC, V. Map p 68.*

★★ **Heath Ceramics** HOLLYWOOD   This studio and store features exquisite tableware and tile with classic, mid-century designs. Each piece has been handcrafted in California by experienced artisans. *7525 Beverly Blvd., at Sierra Bonita Ave.* ☎ *323/ 965-0800. www.heathceramics.com. AE, MC, V. Map p 70.*

★ **Obsolete** SANTA MONICA   This art store/gallery carries visually arresting, creepy-cool pieces such as antique models of the human brain and sculptures made of found

This wooden girl model is one of the obscure and somewhat unsettling objects that can be found at Obsolete.

objects like baby-doll heads. Pottery Barn this ain't. *222 Main St. (btwn Rose Ave. & Marine St.).* ☎ *310/399-0024. www.obsoleteinc.com. AE, MC, V. Map p 67.*

Shabby Chic Couture SANTA MONICA   Now that Rachel Ashwell's brand of cozy and relaxed linens and furniture has become ubiquitous, she's upgraded the entire line to include what she calls "future heirlooms and magic." *1013 Montana Ave., at 10th St.* ☎ *310/394-1975. www.shabbychic.com. AE, MC, V. Map p 67.*

Jewelry
arp WEST HOLLYWOOD   This handsome jewelry store carries the organic, almost minimalist designs of Ted Muehling. *8311½ W. Third St., at Sweetzer Ave.* ☎ *323/653-7764. AE, MC, V. Map p 68.*

Suzanne Felsen WEST HOLLY-WOOD   Giving unusual gemstones a modern twist, this native Ange-leno is one of the city's most popular jewelry designers. *8332 Melrose Ave., at N. Kings Rd.* ☎ *323/653-5400. Also in Santa Monica at 2525 Michigan Ave.* ☎ *310/315-1972. www.suzannefelsen.com. AE, MC, V. Maps p 67 & 68.*

Wanna Buy a Watch WEST HOL-LYWOOD   Take the time to check out this shop's selection of high-end vintage watches like Rolex, Patek Philippe, and Cartier. *8465 Melrose Ave., at La Cienega Blvd.* ☎ *323/653-0467. www.wannabuyawatch.com. AE, DISC, MC, V. Map p 68.*

Kids
★ **Flicka** LARCHMONT   The clothes for infants and toddlers are sweet, trendy, and well-made. Finding the perfect baby-shower or birthday gift is a snap, and the free wrapping helps. *204 N. Larchmont Blvd. (btwn Beverly Blvd. & First St.).* ☎ *323/466-5822. AE, MC, V. Map p 70.*

★★ **La La Ling** LOS FELIZ   If your kid simply has to have what the Jolie-Pitt kids are wearing this sea-son, hit this funky shop stuffed with such designer duds as Paul Frank galoshes and rocker tees. *1810 N. Vermont Ave., at Melbourne Ave.* ☎ *323/664-4400. www.lalaling.com. MC, V. Map p 70.*

★ **Puzzle Zoo** SANTA MONICA   Conveniently located on the Third Street Promenade, this lively toy store specializes in puzzles (naturally)

Find the perfect gift for the baby or tod-dler in your life at Flicka.

For fun and filly lingerie, head to Panty Raid in Silver Lake.

as well as collectibles, such as action figures from *Star Wars, Lord of the Rings,* and *Austin Powers. 1413 Third St. Promenade, at Arizona Ave.* ☎ *310/393-9201. www.puzzlezoo. com. AE, MC, V. Map p 67.*

Lingerie

★ **Agent Provocateur** WEST HOLLYWOOD   The grande dame of Los Angeles lingerie, this sexy boutique sells high-end lingerie with matching price tags. You'll love the service you get from the ladies dressed in matching frocks. *7961 Melrose Ave., at N. Hayworth Ave.* ☎ *323/653-0229. www.agent provocateur.com. AE, MC, V. Map p 68.*

★ **Panty Raid** LOS FELIZ   Eastside hipsters shop here for its fun variety of frilly underthings from designers like Hanky Panky, Mary Green, and Cosabella. *1953 Hillhurst Ave., at Franklin Ave.* ☎ *323/668-1888. www.pantyraidshop.com. AE, MC, V. Map p 70.*

Music & Musical Instruments
★★★ **Amoeba Music** HOLLY-WOOD   In the war of music retailers, score one for the little guy—and by "little," I mean *huuuge* but

independently owned. The extra-large music store's staff—walking encyclopedias of music—don't mind you asking, "What's the name of that band . . . with that song; it kinda goes like . . . ?" *6400 Sunset Blvd., at Ivar Ave.* ☎ *323/245-6400. www.amoeba. com. DISC, MC, V. Map p 70.*

★★ **McCabe's Guitar Shop** SANTA MONICA   Faithfully serving local and itinerant musicians in Los Angeles for over 50 years, this homey shop sports the largest selection of stringed instruments in the state and is known for its intimate, backroom concerts featuring rootsy performers such as M. Ward, Steve Earle, and Lucinda Williams. *3101 Pico Blvd., at 31st St.* ☎ *310/828-4497. www.mccabes. com. AE, DISC, MC, V. Map p 67.*

Shoes
Diavolina WEST HOLLYWOOD For footwear and accessories that'll get you noticed, check out the huge selection from designers like Chloe and Marc Jacobs. *8741 W. Third St.* ☎ *310/550-1341. www.shopdiavolina. com. AE, MC, V. Map p 68.*

★ **Re-Mix** WEST HOLLYWOOD Most of these shoes—old-schoolers like wingtips, babydolls, and saddle

Treat yourself to a pair of stylish, sexy shoes from Diavolina.

The Beverly Hills Cheese Shop offers cheese, cheese, and more delicious cheese.

shoes—come from dead stock, or have been reproduced to match the vintage style. *7605½ Beverly Blvd., at N. Curson Ave.* ☎ *323/936-6210. www.remixvintageshoes.com. AE, DISC, MC, V. Map p 70.*

★ **Sigerson Morrison** WEST HOLLYWOOD This NYC export showcases sleek bags, shoes, and boots, and its sexy flat sandals have inspired a passionate legion of fans. *8307 W. Third St., at S. Sweetzer Ave.* ☎ *323/655-6133. www.sigersonmorrison.com. AE, DISC, MC, V. Map 68.*

★ **Undefeated** HOLLYWOOD Sneakerheads shuffle over to this shop for its incredible array of funky footwear. Don't be surprised if you see long lines of cool kids waiting for the release of exclusive limited-edition kicks from Nike, Vans, or Converse. *112½ S. La Brea Ave.* ☎ *323/937-6077. In Silver Lake: 3827 W. Sunset Blvd.* ☎ *323/668-1315. In Santa Monica: 2654-B Main St.* ☎ *310/399-4195. www.undftd.com. AE, MC, V. Maps p 67 & p 70.*

Specialty Foods & Wines

★★ **Beverly Hills Cheese Shop** BEVERLY HILLS Since 1967, cheese-lovers have flocked here for a staggering selection of heavenly cheeses, more than 500 varieties from around the globe. *419 N. Beverly Dr., at Brighton Way.* ☎ *310/278-2855. www.cheesestorebh.com. AE, DC, DISC, MC, V. Map p 68.*

Edelweiss Chocolates BEVERLY HILLS The old-fashioned chocolate shop, a Beverly Hills landmark since 1942, stays fresh by creating all their delectables on the premises. Happy customers have included Katherine Hepburn, Lauren Bacall, and Steven Spielberg. The fudge rocks. *444 N. Canon Dr., at Burton Way.* ☎ *310/275-0341. www.edelweisschocolates.com. AE, MC, V. Map p 68.*

★★ **Silver Lake Wine** SILVER LAKE This neighborhood shop focuses on top-notch, small-batch wines for all budgets. On Friday evenings in summer, they host popular wine-tasting events on the lovely grounds of the historic Hollyhock House at the Barnsdall Art Park ($20)—highly recommended. They also offer in-store tastings on Monday, Thursday, and Sunday. *2395 Glendale Blvd., at Brier Ave.* ☎ *323/662-9024. www.silverlakewine.com. AE, MC, V. Map p 70.*

★ **Wally's Wines** WESTWOOD Lovers of the grape know to hit this Westside warehouse for its vast selection and friendly, knowledgeable staff. Great gift baskets are also available. *2107 Westwood Blvd., at Mississippi Ave.* ☎ *310/475-0606. www.wallywine.com. AE, DISC, MC, V. Map p 67.* ●

Silver Lake Wine has something for you, no matter what your budget.

5 The Best of the **Outdoors**

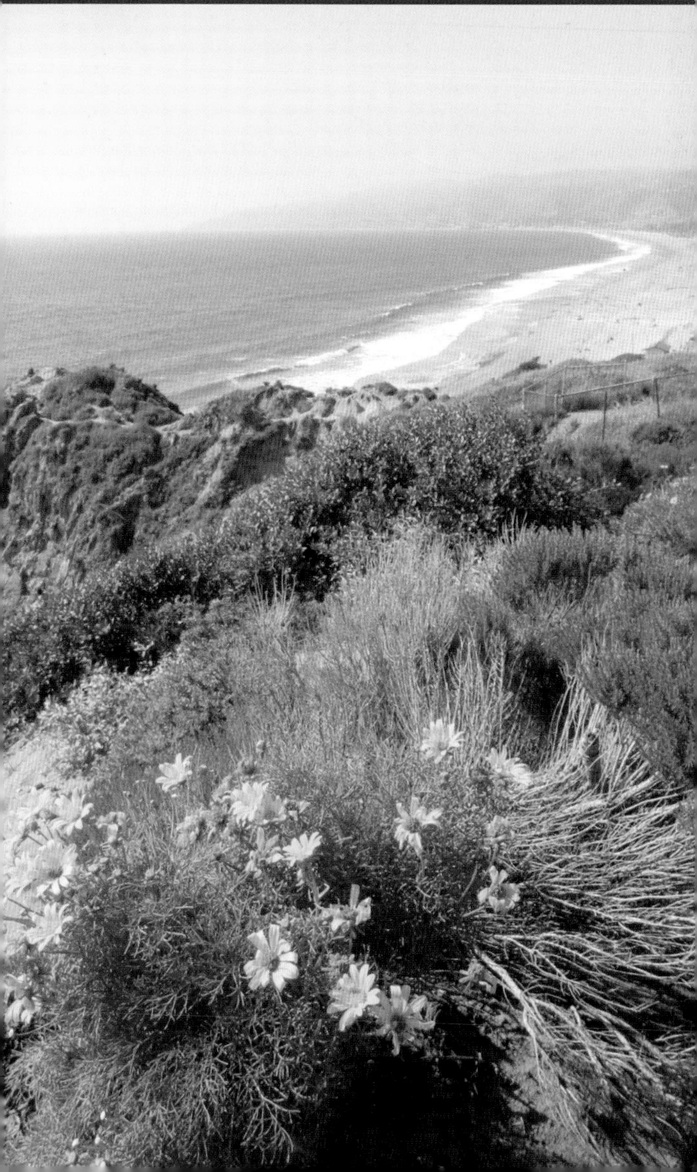

L.A.'s **Best Beaches**

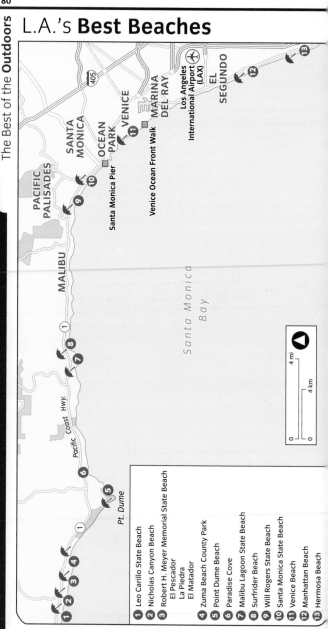

405

PACIFIC
PALISADES

SANTA
MONICA

OCEAN
PARK

VENICE

MARINA
DEL RAY

EL
SEGUNDO

Los Angeles
International Airport
(LAX)

Santa Monica Pier

Venice Ocean Front Walk

MALIBU

Santa Monica Bay

Pacific Coast Hwy.

Pt. Dume

1 Leo Carillo State Beach
2 Nicholas Canyon Beach
3 Robert H. Meyer Memorial State Beach
    El Pescador
    La Piedra
    El Matador
4 Zuma Beach County Park
5 Point Dume Beach
6 Paradise Cove
7 Malibu Lagoon State Beach
8 Surfrider Beach
9 Will Rogers State Beach
10 Santa Monica State Beach
11 Venice Beach
12 Manhattan Beach
13 Hermosa Beach

0   4 mi
0   4 km

Previous page: Picturesque Point Dume.

It's not if you're going to the beach, it's when. So when you do go, here's how you find the ones that are right for you. One glaringly obvious tip: Weekends are going to be much more crowded than other times, particularly if it's warm. And for God's sake, wear sunscreen.

① ★ Leo Carrillo State Beach.
Named after the actor who played Pancho, sidekick to the Cisco Kid in the 1950s television show, Leo Carrillo is a 1½-mile-wide sandy beach where Hollywood used to shoot beach-blanket flicks, earning the nickname Movie Beach. Kids love searching for hermit crabs in the tide pools and coastal caves. Family-friendly campgrounds are available; Wi-Fi is free for campers, and a Starbucks is a short drive away. Ahh, roughing it. *35000 W. Pacific Coast Hwy., Malibu.*

② Nicholas Canyon Beach.
Called Zeroes by locals, this sandy spot is usually far less crowded than nearby beaches such as Leo Carrillo or Zuma; perhaps the lack of a sign on Pacific Coast Highway has something to do with it. It's certainly no secret to local surfers, who dig the left point break on south swells. Families enjoy the easy access and picnic tables. *33850 W. Pacific Coast Hwy., Malibu.*

Windsurfers take advantage of a beautiful day at Leo Carrillo State Beach.

El Matador Beach.

③ ★★★ Robert H. Meyer Memorial State Beach (El Pescador, La Piedra, and El Matador). These three hidden coves are gems tucked against the Malibu cliffs. If you can manage your way down a short trail and/or rickety staircases, clean pockets of sand and alluring sea caves await you. Crowded summer weekends can kill the magical vibe, but if you make it midweek or, better yet, off season, you might be able stake out a patch of paradise. No lifeguard on duty. *32900, 32700 & 32350 W. Pacific Coast Hwy. (btwn Broad Beach & Decker Canyon rds.), Malibu.*

④ ★ Zuma Beach County Park. This huge and hugely popular stretch of white, sandy beach has the proverbial "something for everybody": swimming, surfing, bodyboarding, fishing, volleyball, snack bars, playground swings, restrooms, and plenty of parking. Weekends are a zoo, but weekdays are surprisingly tame. *30000 W. Pacific Coast Hwy. (btwn Kanan Dume & Encinal Canyon rds.), Malibu.*

General Beach Information

Most beaches are operated by the Los Angeles County Department of Beaches & Harbors (☎ 310/305-9503; www.labeaches.info).

For the surf report on Malibu beaches, call ☎ 310/457-9701. For the surf report on South Bay beaches, call ☎ 310/379-8471.

Beaches are generally open daily sunrise to sunset. Parking lots for county-run beaches typically charge $5 to $12.

Water pollution can be a factor, especially after heavy rains, when storm drains empty into the ocean. Before you head out, check www.watchthewater.org to make sure a specific beach has a current clean bill of health.

5 ★★ **Point Dume Beach.** Don't tell anybody, but this is my favorite beach in Los Angeles. The Point lies just south of Zuma, but it lacks Zuma's crowds (and, frankly, its amenities and activities, as well). Frolic in the surf, or hike up into the Point Dume State Preserve and take in the views (perfect for whale-watching during the Dec–Mar migration season). From the summit, you can descend to a smaller, isolated beach called Pirate's Cove. *7103 Westward Rd. (at the PCH), Malibu.*

6 **Paradise Cove.** This is technically a private beach, so it'll cost you $25 to drive in ($5 if validated with a $20 purchase at the Paradise Cove Cafe), or $5 to walk in. Families love—and on weekends, can overrun—this small, scenic cove where television's *Gidget* was filmed, while others enjoy drinking and dining with their toes in the sand. *28128 Pacific Coast Hwy., Malibu.* ☎ *310/457-9791. www.paradise covemalibu.com. Daily 8am–10pm.*

7 ★ **Malibu Lagoon State Beach.** Malibu Creek meets the Pacific Ocean at this lagoon, and the wetlands create a unique bird sanctuary, a pit stop for more than 200 species during their annual migrations. Watch the birds, watch the

surfers, go fishing on the Malibu Pier, or lounge on the beach. When you're ready to reengage your mind, pop into the **Adamson House** (☎ 310/456-8432; www. adamsonhouse.org; Wed–Sat 11am–3pm; guided tours $5 adults, $2 kids), renowned for its display of Malibu tiles; or try the **Malibu Lagoon Museum** (free admission), which traces the history of the area from the days of the Chumash Indians. *23200 Pacific Coast Hwy. (at Cross Creek Rd.), Malibu.*

8 **Surfrider Beach.** Next to the Malibu Pier is this surfing hot spot, probably the most-surfed break in the county. Arguably the birthplace of surfing in California, Surfrider still enjoys a fine reputation for the consistency of its summer waves, although local surfers aren't fond of sharing them with out-of-towners. *Part of Malibu Lagoon State Beach, 23200 Pacific Coast Hwy. (at Cross Creek Rd.), Malibu.*

9 **Will Rogers State Beach.** This 3-mile-long beach, with its gentle surf, playground and gymnastic equipment, and plenty of restrooms, is a favorite among families. A small pocket of the beach, affectionately called Ginger Rogers Beach, is known as a hot spot for

gay men. Active types head for the volleyball courts or hop on the South Bay Bicycle Path, which runs along the shoreline and ends 22 miles south in Torrance County Beach. *16000 Pacific Coast Hwy., Pacific Palisades.*

⑩ **Santa Monica State Beach.** White sands, restrooms, easy access with ample parking, hot dogs, and in full view of the Santa Monica Pier—sheesh, how much more can you ask of a beach so close to all the action? While it may not be a "get there early and camp out all day" type beach, it's a great way to combine beach time with other activities such as eating or shopping in Santa Monica or taking a scenic stroll along bluff-top Palisades Park. *400–2900 blocks of Ocean Ave., Santa Monica.*

⑪ ★★ **Venice Beach.** Consider the beach to be a sandy extension of wild Venice Boardwalk. It's about entertainment, not relaxation—the sound of waves crashing isn't quite as soothing when accompanied by an impromptu drum circle. You may as well rent some skates or a bike (try Venice Bike & Skates at 21 Washington Blvd.) and join the streams heading up and down the boardwalk. *3100 Ocean Front Walk, Venice.*

Volleyball is a major draw at Manhattan Beach.

⑫ **Manhattan Beach.** Surfing and volleyball are the two big draws on this big beach with small-town friendliness. More than 150 volleyball courts (for both pros and amateurs) dot the 2 miles of wide, flat beach. Surfers catch killer waves at El Porto at the north end of the beach. *Manhattan Beach Blvd. (at Highland Ave.), Manhattan Beach.*

⑬ ★ **Hermosa Beach.** Like its neighbor, Manhattan Beach, this beach community is proud of its surfing and volleyball. Pro volleyball tournaments are a regular feature and draw huge crowds. When the sun goes down, the bar scene on Pier Avenue heats up. *Hermosa Ave. (at 33rd St.), Hermosa Beach.*

Pelicans enjoy the sunshine at Malibu Lagoon State Beach.

Hikes

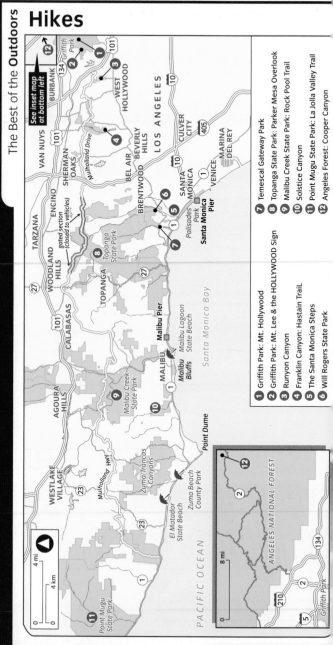

See inset map at bottom left

1 Griffith Park: Mt. Hollywood
2 Griffith Park: Mt. Lee & the HOLLYWOOD Sign
3 Runyon Canyon
4 Franklin Canyon: Hastain Trail
5 The Santa Monica Steps
6 Will Rogers State Park
7 Temescal Gateway Park
8 Topanga State Park: Parker Mesa Overlook
9 Malibu Creek State Park: Rock Pool Trail
10 Solstice Canyon
11 Point Mugu State Park: La Jolla Valley Trail
12 Angeles Forest: Cooper Canyon

Funny thing about folks in Los Angeles—they wrinkle their noses at the idea of walking a block to dinner, but call something a "hike," and it's a stampede of iPods and Nikes. Here are a few places to get out of the gritty city, or at least above it.

1 ★ Griffith Park: Mount Hollywood. A wide, sandy trail takes you to the top of Mount Hollywood, undoubtedly the best view in all of Griffith Park. Being the most popular hike in the city's most popular park, it can get crowded. Take the Charlie Turner Trailhead, which begins across from the Griffith Observatory, for a 2.5-mile loop. For a 5-mile version, start at the Ferndell Trail near the Ferndell Nature Museum. *Griffith Observatory, 2800 E. Observatory Rd.* ☎ *213/473-0800. www. griffithobservatory.org. Ferndell Nature Museum: Ferndell Dr. (north of Los Feliz Blvd.).* ☎ *323/666-5046. Trails open daily 6am–dusk.*

2 ★★ Griffith Park: Mount Lee and the Hollywood Sign. This is my favorite way to experience the sign, looking over the tops of the 45-foot-high letters at the city sprawled out below. Think about all the people who could be looking up at the Hollywood Sign right now for inspiration, and wave at them. *Take*

Beachwood Dr. north to Hollyridge Dr. Follow the Hollyridge Trail northeast. After ½ mile, take Mulholland Trail west. At Mount Lee Dr., head north & follow the trail to the back of the sign.

3 Runyon Canyon. An off-leash dog park just a bone's throw from Hollywood and Highland, the canyon's trails are always packed with people and their pooches. Make it to the highest point in the park, Indian Rock, and you'll earn a lovely panorama of Hollywood and beyond. Plus, there's something refreshing about spotting a celeb, baseball cap pulled low, dutifully picking up after his or her dog. *2000 N. Fuller Ave (at Hillside Ave.), Hollywood.* ☎ *323/666-5046. Daily dawn–dusk.*

4 Franklin Canyon: Hastain Trail. Tucked away between the San Fernando Valley and Beverly Hills, these 605 chaparral-covered acres offer a lake (originally a reservoir built in 1914 by William

C'mon—a little exercise won't kill ya. Go for a hike in Runyon Canyon. Enjoy the views while you're at it.

An intimate view at the Parker Mesa Overlook.

Mulholland), a small duck pond, and 5 miles of hiking trails, the most popular being the pretty Hastain Trail, a hearty 2.3-mile workout. Grab a map near the park's entrance at the Sooky Goldman Nature Center. *2600 Franklin Canyon Dr. (at Mullholland Dr.), Beverly Hills.* ☎ *310/858-7272. Head north on Beverly Dr., turn left on Coldwater/Beverly Dr. & turn left again on Beverly Dr. Go right at Franklin Canyon Dr.*

⑤ **Santa Monica Steps.** Enjoy hiking except for that pesky back-to-nature business? Here's a popular urban hike—actually more of a nightmarishly long set of stairs that will burn your legs and lungs. Locals come for an intense workout, with lovely views of the ocean—and of each other. Try the loop: Go up the concrete steps, jog a few hundred feet east on Adelaide Street, and come down the wooden steps. Repeat ad nauseam. *Fourth St. (btwn Adelaide St. & San Vicente Blvd.).*

⑥ ★ **Will Rogers State Park.** Good ol' Will Rogers left us his ranch, 186 acres at the western edge of the Santa Monica Mountains, to enjoy. A relatively easy hike lifts you into the countryside along the ranch's perimeter, where highlights include **Inspiration Point;** from here you can take in the gorgeous ocean and mountain views. *1501 Will Rogers Park Rd. (off Sunset*

Blvd.), Pacific Palisades. ☎ *310/454-8212. Daily 8am–sunset.*

⑦ ★ **Temescal Gateway Park.** The popular Canyon Loop follows a scenic ridgeline and then dips into a woodsy canyon, at the bottom of which is a small waterfall (don't get too excited—it barely trickles during the dry summer season). A steep climb out of the canyon yields expansive ocean views, and the adventurous can climb another half-mile up to Skull Rock, where the views are even better; both offer gentle ocean breezes to cool your brow. *15601 Sunset Blvd. (at Temescal Canyon Rd.), Pacific Palisades.* ☎ *310/454-1395. Daily sunrise–sunset.*

Feel the burn on the Santa Monica steps.

8 ★★★ **Topanga State Park: Parker Mesa Overlook.** The largest state park within the boundaries of a major city, Topanga is a whopper: 11,000 acres of grassland, live oak groves, and sandstone cliffs overlooking the Pacific Ocean. With 36 miles of trails (including some backbreakers that extend into the neighboring parks of Will Rogers and Point Mugu), you've got plenty of options. I recommend the hike from Trippet Ranch to the Parker Mesa Overlook, where you can absorb the stunning 360-degree views. *20825 Entrada Dr.* ☎ *310/455-2465. Daily 8am–sunset. From Pacific Coast Hwy., travel north on Topanga Canyon Blvd. & then turn right on Entrada Dr.*

9 ★ **Malibu Creek State Park: Rock Pool Trail.** Former owner Twentieth Century Fox fully exploited the park's "so close, yet so far away" quality, using it as a backdrop for movies *(Planet of the Apes, Tarzan)* and television shows *(M.A.S.H.).* An easy walk brings you to a refreshing Rock Pool, although it can get overcrowded on summer weekends. Try rock climbing along its volcanic rock walls. For a more serene water setting, head along the trail to Century Lake, set in a grove of redwoods. *M.A.S.H.* fans might want to trek farther down Crags Road to visit "Korea," where a couple of rusty jeeps appear to be the only casualties of the war. *1925 Las Virgenes Rd. (at Mulholland Dr.), Malibu.* ☎ *818/880-0367. Daily sunrise–sunset.*

10 ★ **Solstice Canyon.** For centuries, Chumash Indians used this beautiful coastal canyon for food and shelter, but a hike along the Solstice Canyon Trail will yield evidence of not-so-ancient ruins—an architecturally significant residence designed by the renowned Paul Williams that burned down in 1982.

The serene Rock Pool at Malibu Creek State Park.

The area, called Tropical Terrace, also features a lovely 30-foot waterfall and lush foliage. Play archaeologist, or simply sun on the large boulders in the creek. *Corral Canyon Rd. (at PCH), Malibu.* ☎ *805/370-2301. Daily 8am–sunset.*

11 ★★ **Point Mugu State Park: La Jolla Valley Trail.** A longer drive from Los Angeles than the other options, Point Mugu throws in plenty of incentives: 70 miles of hiking trails, 13,300 acres of state park, and miles of jagged coastline. The La Jolla Valley Trail cuts through rolling grasslands, lush canyons, and, in spring, blooming wildflowers and burbling waterfalls. The most dramatic vistas are along the oceanside hills on the way to Mugu Peak. *9000 W. Pacific Coast Hwy., Malibu.* ☎ *818/880-0350. Daily 7am–10pm.*

12 ★★ **Angeles National Forest: Cooper Canyon.** North of the Los Angeles basin loom the rugged San Gabriel Mountains, which make for great hiking in the late spring after the winter snow melts, creating lovely waterfalls like the 40-foot Cooper Canyon Falls. Take the Burkhart Trail for a relatively easy 3-mile loop to the falls and back; or if you're really adventurous (and fit), continue on Burkhardt Trail toward the Devil's Punchbowl and the edge of the "High" Mojave Desert. *Hwy. 2, or Angeles Crest Hgwy., at Burkhart Campground entrance rd.* ☎ *818/880-0350. Daily 7am–10pm.*

Griffith Park

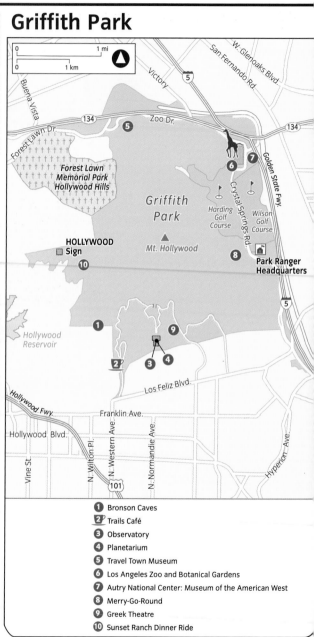

1. Bronson Caves
2. Trails Café
3. Observatory
4. Planetarium
5. Travel Town Museum
6. Los Angeles Zoo and Botanical Gardens
7. Autry National Center: Museum of the American West
8. Merry-Go-Round
9. Greek Theatre
10. Sunset Ranch Dinner Ride

Welsh mining millionaire Griffith J. Griffith (1850–1919) believed every great city needs a great park, and for Christmas in 1896, he gave 3,015 acres to the people of Los Angeles to create "a place of rest and relaxation for the masses, a resort for the rank and file." Today it is one of the largest urban parks in the United States and beloved by Angelenos. Daily 6am to 10pm. START: **Take the Canyon Dr. entrance to Griffith Park, then hike .25 mile past the Bronson Canyon parking lot.**

❶ ★ Bronson Caves. To the Batcave! These manmade caves, actually short tunnels, are the result of quarry operations to gather crushed rock for paving Sunset Boulevard and other major roads. Most folks will recognize the caves from the 1960s' *Batman* television series. The "exotic" location has appeared in countless films, as well—from sci-fi B-movies *(Teenagers from Outer Space)*, to Westerns *(The Searchers)*, to historical epics *(Julius Caesar)*. ⏱ *20 min. Canyon Dr. & Brush Canyon Trail.*

A monument to James Dean, who helped make the Griffith Observatory world famous in Rebel Without a Cause.

❷ ★ The Trails Café. Fuel up with organic coffee and homemade vegan snacks like avocado sandwiches with soy bacon and lavender shortbread cookies. Plus, free Wi-Fi. *2333 Fern Dell Dr. ☎ 323/871-2102. 8am–7pm.*

❸ ★★★ kids Griffith Observatory. After trying out a powerful telescope at nearby Mount Wilson, Griffith experienced an epiphany: "If all mankind could look through that telescope, it would change the world!" With that noble goal, he left the city money to create this observatory, which debuted in 1935. The original 12-inch Zeiss refracting telescope, which more people have looked through than any other on Earth, remains in prime condition and serves up to 600 visitors nightly. In the other copper-topped dome is the triple-beam solar telescope, which is used to observe the sun safely. ⏱ *1 hr. 2800 E. Observatory Rd. ☎ 213/473-0800. www.griffithobservatory.org. Free admission.*

❹ ★ kids Samuel Oschin Planetarium. This planetarium offers a state-of-the-art, star-studded experience called Centered in the Universe, which lets you experience the Big Bang, travel distant galaxies, and observe the overall structure of the universe—all without leaving your cushy seat. Tickets can be purchased only at the observatory, and they often sell out; try to buy tickets immediately upon your arrival. ⏱ *45 min. Tickets $7 ages 13 & over, $5 seniors, $3 kids 5–12. Kids 4 & under are not admitted. Tues–Fri noon–10pm; Sat–Sun 10am–10pm. Check www.griffithobservatory.org for showtimes.*

⑤ ★ kids Travel Town Museum.
In the late 1940s, park employee Charley Atkins and a few of his train-loving pals decided to create a "railroad petting zoo" to encourage kids to become engineers. Young kids, especially Thomas the Tank Engine fans, love exploring the steam-powered engines, vintage railcars, and cabooses. A miniature-train ride costs $2.50. For more train fun, head over to the Griffith Park & Southern Railroad (4400 Crystal Springs Dr.) on the other side of the park. ⏲ 30 min. 5200 Zoo Dr. ☎ 323/662-9678. www.traveltown. org. Free admission. Mon–Fri 10am–4pm; Sat–Sun 10am–5pm.

⑥ kids Los Angeles Zoo and Botanical Gardens. Current highlights include the junglelike Campo Gorilla Reserve, with western lowland gorillas; the Sea Life Cliffs, where you can watch the underwater antics of the sea lions through a glass tank; and Chimpanzees of Mahale Mountains, home to one of the largest groups of chimpanzees in the United States. As of this writing the Elephants of Asia, which will expand the elephant space into one of the largest in the country, is scheduled to open in 2011, and Rainforest of the Americas, scheduled to open in 2012, will present mixed species (mammals, reptiles, birds, and insects) in a tropical setting intended to immerse the visitor in a sensory experience, with a central theme of water, the

Visiting with kids? Be sure to stop at the Los Angeles Zoo.

Ornate revolvers on display at Gene Autry's Museum of the American West.

rainforest's key ingredient. ⏲ 1 hr. 5333 Zoo Dr., Griffith Park. ☎ 323/644-4200. www.lazoo.org. Admission $13 adults, $10 seniors, $8 kids 2–12, free for kids 1 & under. Labor Day through June daily 10am–5pm; July to Labor Day daily 10am–6pm.

⑦ ★ Autry National Center: Museum of the American West. This well-kept museum explores the "real" Old West as well as the mythology perpetuated by movies and television. Past exhibits include Dazzling Firearms, decorative pistols from the 19th and 20th centuries; and the Art of Native American Basketry, a dazzling selection from nearly 14,000 baskets, the largest collection in the world, at the Southwest Museum of the American Indian, also part of the Autry National Center. ⏲ 40 min. 4700 Western Heritage Way. ☎ 323/667-2000. www.the autry.org. Admission $9 adults, $5 seniors & students, $3 kids 3–12, free for kids 2 & under. Tues–Fri 10am–4pm; Sat–Sun 11am–5pm.

⑧ kids Merry-Go-Round. This carousel has delighted families since 1937. Jumping horses, bejeweled and brightly colored, spin around to the sounds of marches and waltzes from a Stinson band organ. A quick and easy way to make a kid happy. ⏲ 20 min. ☎ 323/665-3051. Rides $1.50 per person. Summer daily 11am–5pm; rest

The Hollywood Sign

Nine letters, 45 feet high—the Hollywood sign stands on Griffith Park's Mount Lee as an enduring symbol of the glitz and glamour of the entertainment industry and is one of the most recognizable signs on the planet. It began in 1923 as a billboard for a housing development called "Hollywoodland," and since this is Hollywood, a town booming with an energetic film industry, the developers had a sense of showmanship—4,000 blinking 20-watt bulbs lit the letters at night.

In 1932 Peg Entwistle, a struggling actress, exposed the dark reality of the Hollywood dream when she climbed to the top of the letter H and jumped to her death. The sign languished over the years, and in 1949 city boosters repaired and rebuilt the sign as "Hollywood" without the "land" and the light bulbs. By the 1970s the wood and sheet-metal structure was falling apart, and an unlikely alliance of private donors—Hugh Hefner, Alice Cooper, and Gene Autry—came to its rescue.

One of the best places to view the sign is from the lawn in front of the Griffith Observatory; other choice spots are the Hollywood & Highland Center, up Beachwood Canyon Drive, and Lake Hollywood. Or simply check out the webcams—and much more information—at www.hollywoodsign.org.

---

of year Sat–Sun 11am–5pm. Park Center (off Crystal Springs Dr. btwn the zoo & the Los Feliz entrance).

9 ★★ **Greek Theatre.** Tree lined and nestled in the hills, this 5,700-seat venue feels like an intimate version of the Hollywood Bowl. If you find one of your favorites playing there, jump on the opportunity. Recent acts include the Flaming Lips, the Dave Matthews Band, and a Super '70s Soul Jam Spectacular. The only downside is the stacked parking ($15) that can make exiting a show a long slog. ⏱ 2–2½ hr. 2700 Vermont Canyon Rd. ☎ 323/665-1927. www.greektheatrela.com. Tickets $30–$155.

10 **Sunset Ranch Dinner Ride.** Mount up and mosey through the twilight over the hills to a Mexican restaurant in Burbank. Take it easy on the margaritas, cowboy—you still have to ride the horse back. Day rides ($25–$40 per person) are also available and provide great photo ops for the Hollywood sign. ⏱ 4 hr. 3400 Beachwood Dr. ☎ 323/469-5450. www.sunsetranchhollywood.com. Reservations required. Dinner ride begins 4–5pm daily. Dinner ride $105 per person. Head north up Beachwood Dr.

End your day with a sunset horseback ride at Sunset Ranch.

Huntington Library & Gardens

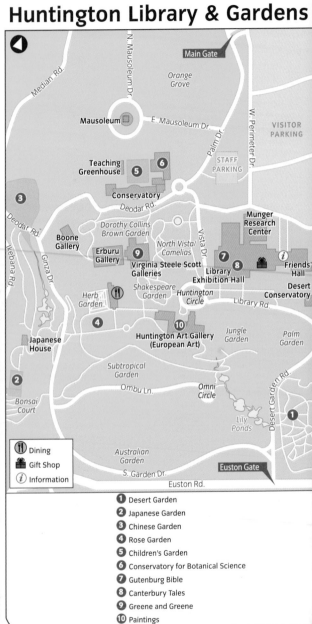

- Main Gate
- Median Rd.
- N. Mausoleum Dr.
- Orange Grove
- VISITOR PARKING
- Mausoleum
- E. Mausoleum Dr.
- W. Perimeter Dr.
- Palm Dr.
- Teaching Greenhouse ❺ ❻
- STAFF PARKING
- Conservatory
- Deodar Rd.
- Munger Research Center
- Deodar Rd.
- Dorothy Collins Brown Garden
- Boone Gallery
- Erburu Gallery ❾
- North Vista/ Camelias
- Vista Dr.
- Ikebana Rd.
- Ginza Dr.
- Virginia Steele Scott Galleries
- ❼ ❽ 🎁 ⓘ Friends' Hall
- Library Exhibition Hall
- Desert Conservatory
- Shakespeare Garden
- Herb Garden 🍴
- Huntington Circle
- Library Rd.
- ❹
- ❿
- Huntington Art Gallery (European Art)
- Jungle Garden
- Palm Garden
- Japanese House
- Subtropical Garden
- Ombu Ln.
- Omni Circle
- Desert Garden Rd.
- ❷
- Bonsai Court
- Lily Ponds
- ❶
- 🍴 Dining
- 🎁 Gift Shop
- ⓘ Information
- Australian Garden
- Euston Gate
- S. Garden Dr.
- Euston Rd.

❶ Desert Garden
❷ Japanese Garden
❸ Chinese Garden
❹ Rose Garden
❺ Children's Garden
❻ Conservatory for Botanical Science
❼ Gutenburg Bible
❽ Canterbury Tales
❾ Greene and Greene
❿ Paintings

Upon his death in 1927, railroad and real-estate tycoon Henry E. Huntington willed that his private 207-acre estate, near Pasadena, be opened to the public as a library, museum, and botanical gardens—now a triple shot of world-class attractions. With 14,000 species of plants landscaped across 120 acres, the magnificent gardens are best enjoyed at a leisurely pace (closing time is 4:30pm, and you'll need 2 hr. at the very least). *1151 Oxford Rd., San Marino.* ☎ *626/405-2100. www.huntington.org. Tues–Fri noon–4:30pm; Sat–Sun 10:30am–4:30pm; Tues closed. Admission $15 adults, $12 seniors 65 & up, $10 students and kids 12 & up, $6 kids 5–11, free for kids under 5 Mon–Fri. Admission $20 adults, $12 seniors 65 & up, $15 students and kids 12 & up, $6 kids 5–11, free for kids under 5 Sat–Sun. Free for everyone the 1st Thurs of the month.*

1 ★★ **Desert Garden.** Two dozen families (amounting to 5,000 species) of succulents, many imported from the Southwest and Mexican deserts, occupy 10 acres, making it one of the largest collections of its kind in the world. *Warning:* The gorgeous display can be a black hole for photography enthusiasts, who insist on "just one more" extreme close-up of a blooming ocotillo.

2 ★★★ **Japanese Garden.** True to Japanese tradition, this garden is a harmonious and multifaceted retreat, created through the disciplined interplay among the elements of water, rocks, and plants. Highlights include a stroll garden, picturesque moon bridge, Shoin-style house, and Bonsai court.

3 **Chinese Garden.** These 12 acres compose the largest classical garden of its kind outside mainland China. Highlights include a lake, teahouse, pavilions, and bridges, all linked by winding pathways designed to draw the visitor through a series of "poetic views." Key architectural elements—sculpted rocks, hand-crafted lattice windows, and roof tiles—were imported from China.

Succulents in the Desert Garden.

④ ★ Rose Garden. If you're like me and thought that roses only came in two varieties, red or not red, you're in for a shock: Here are 1,200 cultivars in a kaleidoscope of colors. To catch them in full bloom—between late April and early June—is breathtaking.

⑤ Children's Garden. The area is specifically designed to tickle the curiosity of children ages 2 to 7. Kinetic sculptures, water bells, a tunnel of prisms, misty rainbows, magnetic sand, a fog grotto—each of the hands-on experiences explores one or more of the four ancient elements: fire, water, earth, and air.

⑥ Conservatory for Botanical Science. Older children and adults enjoy the 16,000-square-foot, award-winning conservatory. It features interactive botanical exhibits, none more popular than the *Amorphophallus titanum,* known as the "Corpse Flower" because of its foul odor.

⑦ ★★★ Gutenberg Bible. With more than six million rare books and manuscripts, the Huntington is one of the largest research libraries in the world. Perhaps the most famous item on public display is a 1455 Gutenberg Bible, one of only 12 vellum (fine parchment, as opposed to paper) copies in the world. *Library Exhibition Hall.*

Make time for a pass through the impressive Rose Garden.

Chaucer's Canterbury Tales *is one of the highlights of Huntington Library & Gardens.*

⑧ ★★ Canterbury Tales. Created around 1410, the Ellesmere manuscript of Chaucer's *Canterbury Tales* features 464 pages of cursive text with floral borders and other meticulous decorations, such as 23 portraits of the pilgrim-storytellers, including Chaucer himself. Scholars consider it to be one of the most significant English-language manuscripts in existence. *Library Exhibition Hall.*

⑨ Greene and Greene. An excellent companion to a tour of the Greenes' Gamble House in Pasadena (their Arts and Crafts masterpiece; p 33), this permanent installation displays Greene-designed tables, chairs, lamps, and rugs. *Virginia Steele Scott Gallery of American Art.*

⑩ ★ Paintings. Henry's wife Arabella was the driving force behind the comprehensive collection of British and French art of the 18th and 19th centuries. Two highlights are the portraits that seem to be checking each other out: Thomas Gainsborough's *The Blue Boy* and Thomas Lawrence's *Pinkie.* *Huntington Art Gallery.* ●

Dining Best Bets

Best **Date Night**
★★★ Lucques $$$ 8474 Melrose Ave. (p 105)

Most **Like a Movie Set**
★★ Cicada $$$$ 617 S. Olive St. (p 102)

Best **Italian**
★★ Angelini Osteria $$$ 7313 Beverly Blvd. (p 101)

Best **Lunch at the Farmer's Market**
★ Loteria! Grill $ 6333 W. Third St. (p 105)

Best **Brunch**
★★★ Campanile $$$ 624 S. La Brea Ave. (p 102)

Best **Wine Selection**
★★★ A.O.C. $$$ 8022 W. Third St. (p 101)

Best **Korean BBQ**
★★ Soot Bull Jeep $$ 3136 Eighth St. (p 107)

Best **Steak**
★★★ Mastro's $$$$ 246 N. Canon Dr. (p 106)

Most **Creative Cuisine**
★★★ The Bazaar $$$$ 465 S. La Cienega Blvd. (p 101)

Best **Thai with Elvis**
★ Palms Thai $ 5900 Hollywood Blvd. (p 106)

Best **Sushi**
★★ Sushi Katsu-Ya $$ 11680 Ventura Blvd. (p 108)

Best **Cupcakes**
★ Sprinkles Cupcakes $ 9635 Little Santa Monica Blvd. (p 108)

Best **Seafood**
★★★ Providence $$$$ 5955 Melrose Ave. (p 107)

Most **Worth the Wait**
★★★ Pizzeria Mozza $$$ 641 N. Highland Ave. (p 107)

Best **Tacos**
★★ Kogi $ Various locations (p 105)

Best **Fine Dining**
★★★ Patina $$$$ 141 S. Grand Ave. (p 106)

Best **Cocktails**
★★★ Rivera $$$ 246 N. Canon Dr. (p 107)

Best **Cheap Vietnamese**
★ Pho Café $ 2841 W. Sunset Blvd. (p 106)

Best **Celebrity Sightings**
★★★ CUT $$$ 9500 Wilshire Blvd. (p 103)

The French dip sandwich and the sawdust floor are the trademarks of Philippe The Original.

Santa Monica & the Beaches

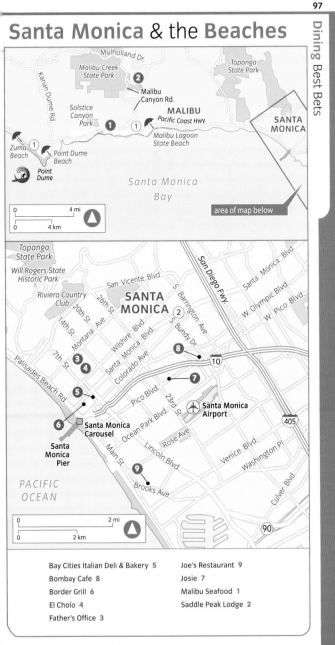

Bay Cities Italian Deli & Bakery 5

Bombay Cafe 8

Border Grill 6

El Cholo 4

Father's Office 3

Joe's Restaurant 9

Josie 7

Malibu Seafood 1

Saddle Peak Lodge 2

P 95: At the Border Grill in Santa Monica.

Beverly Hills & the Westside

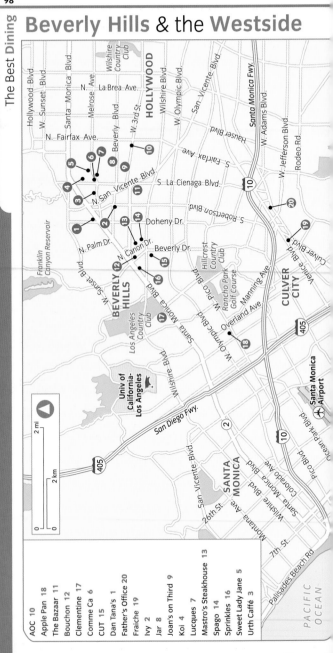

AOC 10
Apple Pan 18
The Bazaar 11
Bouchon 12
Clementine 17
Comme Ca 6
CUT 15
Dan Tana's 1
Father's Office 20
Fraiche 19
Ivy 2
Jar 8
Joan's on Third 9
Koi 4
Lucques 7
Mastro's Steakhouse 13
Spago 14
Sprinkles 16
Sweet Lady Jane 5
Urth Caffé 3

Hollywood, Los Feliz & Silver Lake

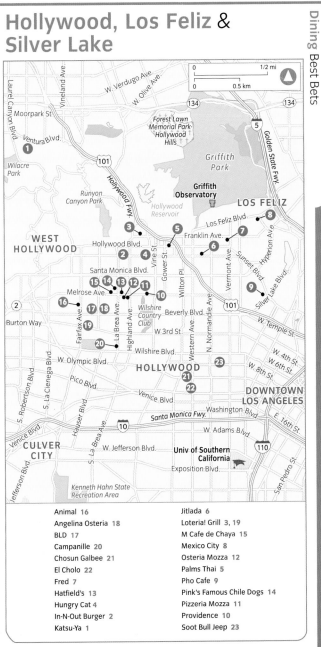

Animal **16**
Angelina Osteria **18**
BLD **17**
Campanile **20**
Chosun Galbee **21**
El Cholo **22**
Fred **7**
Hatfield's **13**
Hungry Cat **4**
In-N-Out Burger **2**
Katsu-Ya **1**

Jitlada **6**
Loteria! Grill **3, 19**
M Cafe de Chaya **15**
Mexico City **8**
Osteria Mozza **12**
Palms Thai **5**
Pho Cafe **9**
Pink's Famous Chile Dogs **14**
Pizzeria Mozza **11**
Providence **10**
Soot Bull Jeep **23**

Downtown

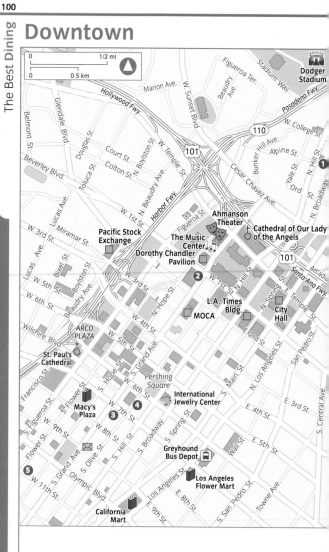

Bottega Louie 3
Cicada 4
Patina 2
Rivera 5
Yang Chow 1

Dining A to Z

★★ Angelini Osteria WEST HOL-
LYWOOD *ITALIAN* Chef/owner
Gino Angelini brings Roma right to
your plate with fresh ingredients
and his *mamma*'s authentic recipes.
The small, unpretentious room gets
loud, but that's what amazing food
does to people. Another good sign:
The crowd often includes Italians
and off-duty chefs. *7313 Beverly
Blvd., at Poinsettia Place.* ☎ *323/
297-0070. www.angeliniosteria.com.
Reservations recommended. Entrees
$20–$40. AE, MC, V. Lunch & dinner
Tues–Sun. Map p 99.*

★★ Animal FAIRFAX *NEW AMERI-
CAN* Meat lovers, rejoice. Hot
young chefs Jon Shook and Vinny
Dotolo prepare beef and pork in all
manners of deliciousness. They
even add bacon to their chocolate
crunch-bar dessert. *435 N. Fairfax
Ave., at Oakwood Ave.* ☎ *323/782-
9225. www.animalrestaurant.com.
Entrees $23–$37. AE, MC, V. Dinner
daily. Map p 99.*

★★★ A.O.C. WEST HOLLYWOOD
CALIFORNIAN/FRENCH Foodies
huddle over small plates—charcute-
rie, cheese (French, Italian, and
Spanish), skirt steak, fried oysters—
and sip on sublime wines in a
casual, chic setting. *8022 W. Third
St., at Crescent Heights Blvd.* ☎ *323/
653-6359. www.aocwinebar.com.
Reservations recommended. Small*

A shrimp dish at A.O.C.

plates $9–$18. AE, MC, V. Dinner
daily. Map p 98.*

★ Apple Pan WESTWOOD *BURG-
ERS* Gourmet burger craze be
damned—this old-school burger
joint hasn't changed a thing since it
opened in 1947. Plop down at the
counter and order a hickory burger,
then chase it with a slab of apple
pie. *10801 W. Pico Blvd., at Glendon
Ave.* ☎ *310/475-3585. www.apple
pan.com. Burgers $7. Cash only.
Lunch & dinner Tues–Sun. Map p 98.*

**★ Bay Cities Italian Deli &
Bakery** SANTA MONICA *DELI*
You'll swear off assembly-line, chain
restaurant sandwiches once you
sink your teeth into the legendary
Godmother—fresh baked Italian
bread stuffed with Genoa salami,
mortadella, capicola, ham, prosciutto, and provolone—at this local
favorite since 1925. *1517 Lincoln
Blvd., at Broadway.* ☎ *310/395-
8279. www.baycitiesitaliandeli.com.
Sandwiches $6–$12. MC, V. Lunch &
dinner Tues–Sun. Map p 97.*

★★★ The Bazaar BEVERLY HILLS
SPANISH In what must be the
city's splashiest dining room, Jose
Andres presents bold Spanish tapas
that showcase his mastery of molecular gastronomy. Marvel at the
"liquid olive" that dissolves in your
mouth or the *foie gras* wrapped in
cotton candy. *465 S. La Cienega
Blvd., in SLS Hotel.* ☎ *310/246-5555.
http://thebazaar.com. Tapas $5–$36.
AE, DC, DISC, MC, V. Dinner daily;
brunch Sat–Sun. Map p 98.*

★ BLD WEST HOLLYWOOD *NEW
AMERICAN* This popular cafe from
Grace's Neal Fraser pushes typical
diner fare into something far tastier
for breakfast, lunch, and dinner (get
it?). *7450 Beverly Blvd., at N. Vista*

A Japanese taco at The Bazaar.

St. ☎ 323/930-9744. http://bld restaurant.com. *Entrees $8–$27. AE, MC, V. Breakfast, lunch & dinner daily. Map p 99.*

★ **Bombay Cafe** WESTSIDE *INDIAN* Consistently rated among the best Indian restaurants in town, this popular but low-key Westside mainstay serves mouth-watering curries and kormas. *12021 W. Pico Blvd., at Bundy Dr.* ☎ 310/473-3388. www.bombaycafe-la.com. *Entrees $10–$21. MC, V. Lunch & dinner daily. Map p 97.*

★ **kids Border Grill** SANTA MON-ICA *MEXICAN* The Food Network's *Too Hot Tamales,* Mary Sue Milliken and Susan Feniger, present gourmet Mexican cuisine in a fiesta-like atmo-sphere (read: It can get *loud*). *Tres leches* cake is a must for dessert. Also, look for the Border Grill food truck (check website to track cur-rent location). *1445 Fourth St., at Santa Monica Blvd.* ☎ 310/451-1655. www.bordergrill.com. *Entrees $14–$30. AE, DC, DISC, MC, V. Lunch & dinner daily. Map p 97.*

★★ **Bottega Louie** DOWNTOWN *ITALIAN* You can't help but love a place that does so much and so well: modern Italian dishes, pizzas, small plates, desserts like gelato and macaroons, a bustling weekend brunch, a stylish bar, and a gourmet market and takeaway. *700 S. Grand Ave., at W. 7th St.* ☎ 213/802-1470 or 310/395-3200. www.bottega louie.com. *Entrees $9–$40. AE, MC,*

V. Lunch Mon–Fri; dinner daily; brunch Sat–Sun. Map p 100.

★★ **Bouchon** BEVERLY HILLS *FRENCH* The long-awaited brasse-rie from the world-renowned Thomas Keller delivers perfectly pre-pared French bistro fare with flaw-less service in a charming setting. The profiteroles are a must for des-sert. *235 N. Canon Dr., at Bundy Dr.* ☎ 310/271-9910. www.bouchon bistro.com. *Reservations recom-mended. Entrees $18–$36. AE, MC, V. Lunch & dinner daily. Map p 98.*

★★★ **kids Campanile** HOLLY-WOOD *CALIFORNIAN/MEDITERRA-NEAN* In a 1928 Tuscan-style building that once belonged to Charlie Chaplin, Mark Peel's restau-rant has made history on its own for nearly 20 years as one of the city's best restaurants. Grilled Cheese Night is a popular draw on Thurs-days, but nothing beats the deli-cious weekend brunch in the sunny courtyard. *624 La Brea Ave., at Wilshire Blvd.* ☎ 323/938-1447. www.campanilerestaurant.com. *Res-ervations recommended. Entrees $21–$38. AE, DC, DISC, MC, V. Lunch & dinner Mon–Sat; brunch Sun. Map p 99.*

★ **Chosun Galbee** KOREATOWN *KOREAN BBQ* The fresh, savory meats will delight any Korean BBQ connoisseur, while the spotless, sleek interior (polished steel, smoked glass, and slate floors) will ease newbies who are unfamiliar with tabletop cooking. *3330 W. Olympic Blvd., at Western Ave.* ☎ 323/734-3330. www.chosun galbee.com. *Entrees $12–$30. AE, MC, V. Lunch Mon–Fri; dinner daily. Map p 99.*

★★ **Cicada** DOWNTOWN *NORTH-ERN ITALIAN* Enjoy fine Italian dining in one of the city's most stun-ning Art Deco environments with Lalique glass doors, rich wood columns and paneling, a gold-leaf ceiling, and a grand stairway. No wonder most weekends are booked for weddings. *617 S. Olive St., btwn Sixth & Seventh sts.* ☎ *213/488-9488. www.cicadarestaurant.com. Reservations recommended. Entrees $21–$42. AE, DC, DISC, MC, V. Dinner Tues–Sun. Map p 100.*

★★ **Clementine** CENTURY CITY *BAKERY/SANDWICHES* This casual cafe and bakery wins you over by doing all the simple things righter than right. Scones, salads, sandwiches, and soups are all delish. Only downside: parking. *1751 Ensley Ave., at Santa Monica Blvd.* ☎ *310/552-1080. www.clementineonline. com. Entrees $8–$12. AE, MC, V. Breakfast, lunch & dinner Mon–Sat. Map p 98.*

★★ **Comme Ca** WEST HOLLY-WOOD *BRASSERIE* Pop into this hip brasserie for French favorites like coq au vin and braised short ribs, or, incongruously, one of the best burgers in town (available only at lunch or late-night—don't ask me why). Hand-crafted, market-fresh cocktails keep the bar bustling and loud. *8479 Melrose Ave., at La Cienega Blvd.* ☎ *323/782-1104. www.commecarestaurant.com. Entrees $22–$31. AE, DISC, MC, V. Lunch & dinner daily. Map p 98.*

★★★ **CUT** BEVERLY HILLS *STEAK-HOUSE* It's this simple: When Wolfgang Puck opens his first steak-house in a Richard Meier–designed room at one of the city's finest hotels, you go (as do celebrities— Tom Cruise is a huge fan) and sink your teeth into a perfectly seared Nebraskan corn-fed, 35-day aged USDA prime. *9500 Wilshire Blvd., at the Beverly Wilshire Hotel.* ☎ *310/276-8500. www.fourseasons.com/ beverlywilshire. Steaks $40–$120. AE, DISC, MC, V. Dinner Mon–Sat. Map p 98.*

★ **Dan Tana's** WEST HOLLYWOOD *ITALIAN* This dark and cozy hole-in-the-wall, a West Hollywood fixture since 1964, cooks up classic steaks and hearty Italian dishes for a multi-generational mix of industry heavy-weights, actors, rockers, hangers-on, and wannabes. *9071 Santa Monica Blvd., at Doheny Dr.* ☎ *310/275-9444. www.dantanasrestaurant.com. Reservations recommended. Entrees $22–$58. AE, MC, V. Dinner daily. Map p 98.*

★ **El Cholo** KOREATOWN *MEXICAN* L.A.'s oldest Mexican restaurant has drawn its share of celebs since it debuted in 1927 and claims to have been the first in the states to serve nachos. Try the green corn tamales and sample their famous margarita recipe. *1121 S. Western Ave., btwn 11th & 12th sts.* ☎ *323/734-2773. www.elcholo.com. Also in Santa Monica at 1025 Wilshire Blvd., at 11th St.* ☎ *310/899-1106. Entrees $10–$14. AE, DC, DISC, MC, V. Lunch & dinner daily. Map p 97.*

★★ **Father's Office** CULVER CITY *BURGERS* Finding a seat is competitive, and the menu inflexible— absolutely no substitutions and no ketchup. All is forgiven, however, when you sink your teeth into Sang Yoon's famous burger: dry-aged beef, Gruyere and Maytag blue cheese, caramelized onions, and smoked-bacon compote on a French roll. Incredible selection of craft beers. *3229 Helms Ave., at Venice Blvd.* ☎ *310/736-2224. www. fathersoffice.com. Reservations not accepted; minors not admitted. Entrees $5–$16. Lunch Fri–Sun; dinner daily. AE, MC, V. Map p 98.*

★★ **Fraiche** CULVER CITY *MEDI-TERRANEAN* Culver City is fast becoming a foodie destination with acclaimed restaurants like this. The decor is country casual, and the menu offers French and Italian–inspired dishes like lamb stew, duck-leg confit, and beef short-rib angolotti. *9411 Culver Blvd.* ☎ *310/839-6800. www.fraicherestaurantla.com. Reservations recommended. Entrees $10–$26. Lunch Mon–Fri; dinner daily. AE, DC, DISC, MC, V. Map p 98.*

★ kids **Fred 62** LOS FELIZ *DINER* A favorite among eastside hipsters, this retro-styled diner always hits its mark—Bearded Mr. Frenchy (corn-flake-encrusted French toast), Thai Cobb salad, or a mean tuna melt for late-night munchies. *1850 N. Vermont Ave., at Russell Ave.* ☎ *323/667-0062. www.fred62.com. Entrees $8–$14. MC, V. Breakfast, lunch & dinner daily 24 hr. Map p 99.*

★★★ **Hatfield's** WEST HOLLYWOOD *NEW AMERICAN* This classy place is all about the sophisticated, seasonal menu from husband-and-wife chef team Quinn and Karen Hatfield. Raves go to the *croque madame* served on brioche with yellowtail and prosciutto, and topped with a quail egg. *6703 Melrose Ave., at Citrus Ave.* ☎ *323/935-2977. www.hatfieldsrestaurant.com. Reservations recommended. Entrees $15–$36. AE, MC, V. Lunch Mon–Fri; dinner daily. Map p 99.*

★★ **Hungry Cat** HOLLYWOOD *SEAFOOD* Enjoy fantastic cocktails and fresh, well-executed seafood, such as Maine lobster rolls, in the heart of Hollywood. *1535 N. Vine St., at Sunset Blvd.* ☎ *323/462-2155. www.thehungrycat.com. Entrees $14–$50. AE, MC, V. Lunch & dinner daily. Map p 99.*

★ kids **In-N-Out Burger** HOLLYWOOD *BURGERS* With the freshest ingredients and no microwaves or freezers, this is the best fast-food burger in California. *7009 Sunset Blvd., at Orange Dr.* ☎ *800/786-1000. Multiple other locations.* *Burgers $4. AE, MC, V. Lunch & dinner daily. Map p 99.*

★ **Ivy** BEVERLY HILLS *NEW AMERICAN* With the paparazzi camped outside the white picket-fenced patio, this spot serves upscale comfort food to stars, power brokers, and tourists. *113 N. Robertson Blvd., btwn Beverly Blvd. & Third St.* ☎ *310/274-8303. Reservations recommended. Entrees $10–$38. AE, MC, V. Lunch & dinner daily. Map p 98.*

★★★ **Jar** WEST HOLLYWOOD *NEW AMERICAN* Stylish and elegant, Suzanne Tracht's steakhouse offers superb service and a refined take on pork chops, pot roast, and filet of beef. The Sunday brunch, featuring *chilaquiles* with *crème fraîche*, corn pancakes, and pecan sweet bread is a knockout. *8225 Beverly Blvd., at Harper Ave.* ☎ *323/655-6566. www.thejar.com. Reservations recommended. Entrees $21–$48. AE, DC, DISC, MC, V. Dinner daily; brunch Sun. Map p 98.*

★★ **Jitlada** HOLLYWOOD *THAI* This humble, strip-mall restaurant with authentic Southern Thai cuisine is celebrated for its flavorful curries, which will make your taste buds pop and your eyes water. The fearless opt for the fish kidneys. *5233½ W. Sunset Blvd., at N. Harvard Blvd.* ☎ *323/667-9809. www.jitlada.com. Entrees $6.95–$17. AE, MC, V. Lunch Tues–Sun; dinner daily. Map p 99.*

★★ **Joan's on Third** WEST HOLLYWOOD *BAKERY/SANDWICHES* This bakery and deluxe deli stocks a variety of gourmet salads and sandwiches, and to-die-for cupcakes. A perfect pit stop while shopping on Third Street. *8350 W. Third St., at Kings Rd.* ☎ *323/655-2285. www.joansonthird.com. Sandwiches & salads $10–$13. AE, MC, V. Lunch & dinner daily. Map p 98.*

★★ Joe's Restaurant VENICE *CALIFORNIAN* Sophisticated food in an unpretentious setting, Joe's has been the most bankable meal in Venice for 20 years. The three-course lunch menu ($18) offers a great bang for your buck, perfect on days spent shopping along Abbott Kinney. *1023 Abbot Kinney Blvd., btwn Westminster Ave. & Broadway.* ☎ *310/399-5811. www.joesrestaurant.com. Reservations recommended. Entrees $14–$28. Lunch & dinner Tues–Sun. AE, MC, V. Map p 97.*

★★★ Josie SANTA MONICA *NEW AMERICAN* Gourmands seek out Josie Le Balch's nuanced American cuisine with French and Italian flair. *2424 Pico Blvd., at 25th St.* ☎ *310/581-9888. www.josierestaurant.com. Reservations recommended. Entrees $25–$38. AE, MC, V. Dinner daily. Map p 97.*

★★ Kogi *KOREAN* Roy Choi's four food trucks roam the sprawling metropolis, tweeting their locations to followers hungry for Kogi tacos, which combine Korean barbecue with traditional Mexican tortillas and veggies. Savor their signature taco, Korean short ribs, or the popular spicy pork taco, or something a little

Cupcakes at Joan's on Third.

Follow the Kogi truck at Twitter.com/ KOGIBBQ to track down their Korean BBQ tacos.

more offbeat, like kimchi quesadillas. *Various locations; check www.kogi bbq.com or twitter.com/kogibbq. Tacos & burritos $2–$7. Cash only. Lunch & dinner daily.*

★ Koi WEST HOLLYWOOD *SUSHI* The sushi is very good, but just as many people come for the "scene"—the young and the beautiful trying to be in the right place at the right time. *730 N. La Cienega Blvd., btwn Melrose & Willoughby aves.* ☎ *310/659-9449. www.koi restaurant.com. Reservations recommended. Entrees $13–$27. AE, DC, DISC, MC, V. Dinner daily. Map p 98.*

★ Loteria! Grill FARMERS MARKET *MEXICAN* For years this unassuming stand has drawn lines of locals for its authentic Mexican fare. A new outpost in Hollywood (6627 Hollywood Blvd.; ☎ 323/465-2500), a "real" restaurant you might say, is spacious and modern with a *grande* selection of tequilas. *Farmers Market at Third St. & Fairfax Ave.* ☎ *323/930-2211. www.loteriagrill.com. Entrees $8–$21. MC, V. Breakfast, lunch & dinner daily. Map p 99.*

★★★ Lucques WEST HOLLYWOOD *MEDITERRANEAN* James Beard Award–winning chef and titan of the Los Angeles culinary scene, Suzanne Goin dazzles with her simple but sophisticated Cal-Med menu in a warm, intimate atmosphere—the small brick building was once the carriage house of silent-comedian

Harold Lloyd. Sunday Supper offers a three-course *prix fixe* dinner, a bargain at $45. *8474 Melrose Ave., at La Cienega Blvd.* ☎ *323/655-6277. www.lucques.com. Reservations recommended. Entrees $16–$44. AE, DC, MC, V. Lunch Tues–Sat; dinner daily. Map p 98.*

★ **M Café de Chaya** WEST HOLLYWOOD *VEGETARIAN* If "flavorful macrobiotic" sounds oxymoronic to you, prepare to be surprisingly satisfied by the panini and rice bowls at this hot spot for starlets and the health-obsessed. *7119 Melrose Ave., at La Brea Ave. Also at 9343 Culver Blvd., Culver City & 9433 Brighton Way, Beverly Hills.* ☎ *323/525-0588. www.mcafedechaya.com. Entrees $5–$14. AE, MC, V. Breakfast, lunch & dinner daily. Map p 99.*

★★ kids **Malibu Seafood Fresh Fish Market & Cafe** MALIBU *SEAFOOD* This walk-up-and-order shack serves some of the freshest seafood on the coast. You can't miss with fish and chips or lobster. BYOB and no corkage fee. *25653 Pacific Coast Hwy. (1½ miles north of Malibu Canyon Rd.).* ☎ *310/456-3430. www.malibuseafood.com. Entrees $5–$20. MC, V. Lunch & dinner daily. Map p 97.*

★★★ **Mastro's Steakhouse** BEVERLY HILLS *STEAK* Score a martini and a perfectly grilled double porterhouse at this swank, low-lit steakhouse in the heart of Beverly Hills. Somewhere, the Rat Pack is smiling. *246 N. Canon Dr., btwn Clifton & Dayton ways.* ☎ *310/888-8782. www.mastrosrestaurants.com. Reservations recommended. Entrees $26–$63. AE, MC, V. Dinner daily. Map p 98.*

★ kids **Mexico City** LOS FELIZ *MEXICAN* Friendly and fun, this is my absolute favorite place in L.A. for margaritas and enchiladas. *2121 Hillhurst Ave., at Avocado St.* ☎ *323/661-7227. www.mexicocityla.com. Entrees $10–$20. AE, MC, V. Lunch Wed–Sun; dinner daily. Map p 99.*

★★ **Osteria Mozza** HOLLYWOOD *ITALIAN* After opening the casual Pizzeria Mozza next door, the formidable team of Nancy Silverton and Mario Batali went upscale with this sleek Italian restaurant, one of the hottest tickets in town. *6602 Melrose Ave., at Highland Ave.* ☎ *323/297-0100. www.mozza-la.com. Reservations recommended. Entrees $25–$36. AE, MC, V. Dinner daily. Map p 99.*

★ **Palms Thai** THAI TOWN *THAI* Gobble up authentic Thai specialties while the Thai Elvis croons the classics. *5900 Hollywood Blvd., at Bronson St.* ☎ *323/462-5073. www.palmsthai.com. Entrees $5–$20. AE, MC, V. Lunch & dinner daily. Map p 99.*

★★★ **Patina** DOWNTOWN *FRENCH/NEW AMERICAN* For a world-class dining experience, sample Joachim Splichal's ambitious cuisine in this stunning space tucked inside the Walt Disney Concert Hall. *141 S. Grand Ave., at Second St. (in Walt Disney Concert Hall).* ☎ *213/972-3331. www.patinagroup.com/patina. Reservations recommended. Entrees $36–$46. AE, MC, V. Dinner Tues–Sun. Map p 100.*

★ **Pho Café** SILVER LAKE *VIETNAMESE* The Vietnamese noodle soups and crepes are fresh, cheap,

A plate is perfected at Lucques.

and unbelievably tasty. The lack of a sign lets you know it's too cool for its random strip-mall location. *2841 W. Sunset Blvd., at Silver Lake Blvd.* ☎ *213/413-0888. Entrees $5–$10. Cash only. Lunch & dinner daily. Map p 99.*

★ **Pink's Hot Dogs** HOLLYWOOD *HOT DOGS* Slinging hot dogs since 1939, Pink's is a Hollywood legend that has folks lining up for a fix at all hours of the day. Michelle Obama and the First Daughters stopped by on their last visit to town. *709 N. La Brea Ave., at Melrose Ave.* ☎ *323/ 931-4223. www.pinkshollywood. com. Chili dog $3. Cash only. Breakfast, lunch & dinner daily. Map p 99.*

★★★ **Pizzeria Mozza** HOLLY-WOOD *PIZZA* Since opening with a bang in 2006, this highbrow pizzeria has had foodies fighting for tables. The pizza's distinctive crust—puffy, crispy, yet chewy—sets the stage for artisanal toppings such as squash blossoms with Burrata, little-neck clams, or (my favorite) fennel sausage. *641 N. Highland Ave. (at Melrose Ave.).* ☎ *323/297-0101. www.mozza-la.com. Reservations recommended. Entrees $10–$28. AE, MC, V. Lunch & dinner daily. Map p 99.*

★★★ **Providence** HOLLYWOOD *SEAFOOD* Known for its exquisitely prepared seafood, Michael Cimarusti's restaurant is considered one of the best in the country. *5955 Melrose Ave., at Cole Ave.* ☎ *323/460-4170. www.providencela.com. Entrees $21–$49. AE, MC, V. Lunch Fri; dinner daily. Map p 99.*

★★★ **Rivera** DOWNTOWN *LATIN* Close to all the action near L.A. Live and the Staples Center, this elegant restaurant also contains a sense of exuberance in its big, bold, and authentic Latin flavors; plates decorated with stencils and spices; and

At Pho Café, in Silver Lake.

an amazing selection of fresh cocktails, including flights of tequilas infused with seasonal ingredients like Cara Cara oranges. *1050 S. Flower St., at Eleventh St.* ☎ *213/ 749-1460. www.riverarestaurant. com. Entrees $12–$29. AE, DC, DISC, MC, V. Lunch Mon–Fri; dinner daily. Map p 100.*

★★ **Saddle Peak Lodge** CALA-BASAS *NEW AMERICAN/GAME* This former hunting lodge is worth the drive to the Malibu hills for its rustic beauty and fabulous game dishes. *419 Cold Canyon Rd., at Piuma Rd.* ☎ *818/222-3888. www. saddlepeaklodge.com. Reservations recommended. Entrees $29–$54. AE, MC, V. Dinner Wed–Sun; brunch Sat–Sun. Map p 97.*

★★ **Soot Bull Jeep** KOREATOWN *KOREAN BBQ* Indifferent service, thick air, and a no-frills interior—none of this matters; the charcoal grill at your table gives the marinated meat a sensational, smoky flavor. *3136 Eighth St., at Catalina St.* ☎ *213/387-3865. Entrees $12–$25. AE, MC, V. Lunch & dinner daily. Map p 99.*

★★★ **Spago** BEVERLY HILLS *CALIFORNIA* Wolfgang Puck's groundbreaking restaurant continues to live up to the dazzle. Make it easy on yourself and order the tasting menu. *176 N. Canon Dr., at Wilshire Blvd.* ☎ *310/385-0880. www. wolfgangpuck.com. Reservations*

Pink's is popular with the late-night crowd.

recommended. Entrees $17–$66; tasting menu $125. AE, MC, V. Lunch & dinner daily. Map p 98.

★ **Sprinkles Cupcakes** BEVERLY HILLS *DESSERT* This cute cupcakery with a cult following has lines spilling out onto the sidewalk and some of the most delectable cupcakes you'll ever stuff in your mouth. Careful, the red velvet might melt your brain. *9635 Little Santa Monica Blvd. (2 blocks west of Rodeo Dr.).* ☎ 310/274-8765. www.sprinkles.com. Cupcakes $3.25. Mon–Sat 9am–7pm; Sun 10am–6pm. Map p 98.

★★ **Sushi Katsu-Ya** STUDIO CITY *SUSHI* Before teaming up with SBE Entertainment to launch a string of glammed-up sushi joints on prime L.A. real estate (like Hollywood and Vine), Katsuya Uechi, one of four master sushi chefs in Los Angeles, made waves in the valley with his flawless sushi, amazing baked crab rolls, and signature spicy tuna on

crispy rice. *11680 Ventura Blvd., at Colfax Ave.* ☎ 818/985-6976. www.katsu-yagroup.com. Reservations recommended. Sushi & rolls $4–$12. AE, MC, V. Dinner daily. Map p 99.

★ **Sweet Lady Jane** WEST HOLLYWOOD *BAKERY/DESSERT* These scrumptious cakes and cupcakes are big hits for parties and gifts. Try the Tripleberry. *8360 Melrose Ave., at N. Kings Rd.* ☎ 323/653-7145. www.sweetladyjane.com. Sandwiches & desserts $6.50–$10. Mon–Sat 8:30am–11:30pm; Sun 10am–6pm. Map p 98.

★ **Urth Caffé** WEST HOLLYWOOD *BAKERY/SANDWICHES* Enjoy the sunny patio of this health-conscious cafe—a favorite of the boys in *Entourage*—which prepares gourmet salads, quiches, panini, and guilt-free pastries with all-natural ingredients. *8565 Melrose Ave., at Westmount Dr.* ☎ 310/659-0628. www.urthcaffe.com. Entrees $5.95–$13. AE, MC, V. Breakfast, lunch & dinner daily. Map p 98.

★ **Yang Chow** CHINATOWN *CHINESE* Try their signature slippery shrimp at this top-rated Mandarin and Szechuan spot in Chinatown. *819 N. Broadway, at Alpine St.* ☎ 213/625-0811. www.yangchow.com. Entrees $10–$15. AE, MC, V. Lunch & dinner daily. Map p 100. ●

Game, such as the ostrich meat pictured here, is the draw at Saddle Peak Lodge.

Nightlife Best Bets

Best **Happy Hour**
★ Copa d'Oro 217 Broadway
(p 114)

Best **Dive Bar**
★ Frolic Room 6245 Hollywood
Blvd. (p 116)

Best **Lounge Act**
★ Marty and Elaine at The Dresden 1760 N. Vermont Ave. (p 114)

Best **Gay Bar**
★★ The Abbey 692 N. Robertson
Blvd. (p 116)

Most **Historic Bar**
★★★ Formosa Cafe 7156 Santa
Monica Blvd. (p 114)

Best **Burlesque**
★ Bordello 901 E. First St. (p 115)

Best **Jukebox**
★ 4100 Bar 4100 Sunset Blvd.
(p 115)

Best **One-Man Band**
★★★ Jon Brion at Largo at the
Coronet 366 N. La Cienega Blvd.
(p 119)

Best **Biergarten**
★ Red Lion Tavern, 2366 Glendale
Blvd. (p 115)

Best **Cutting-Edge Music
Scene**
★★ The Echo/Echoplex, 1822 Sunset Blvd and 1154 Glendale Blvd.
(p 119)

Best **Vodka Selection**
★ Bar Lubitsch, 7702 Santa Monica
Blvd. (p 114)

Best **Poolside Waterbeds**
★★ Roof Bar at the Standard
Downtown, 550 S. Flower St. (p 118)

Best **Fruity Cocktails with
Funny Names**
★ Tiki-Ti, 4427 W. Sunset Blvd.
(p 115)

Most **Muy Caliente!**
★ Conga Room, 800 W. Olympic
Blvd. (p 116)

Most **Prohibition-Era Cocktails**
★★★ The Varnish, 118 E. Sixth St.
(p 115)

Best **Place to Catch the Big
Game**
★ Capitol City, 1615 N Cahuenga
Blvd. (p 120)

The poolside Roof Bar of the Standard Hotel.

Beverly Hills & the Westside

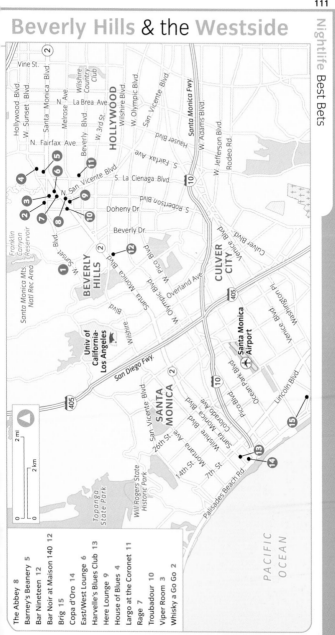

The Abbey 8
Barney's Beanery 5
Bar Nineteen 12
Bar Noir at Maison 140 12
Brig 15
Copa d'Oro 14
East/West Lounge 6
Harvelle's Blues Club 13
Here Lounge 9
House of Blues 4
Largo at the Coronet 11
Rage 7
Troubadour 10
Viper Room 3
Whisky a Go Go 2

P 109: The world-famous Grauman's Chinese Theatre.

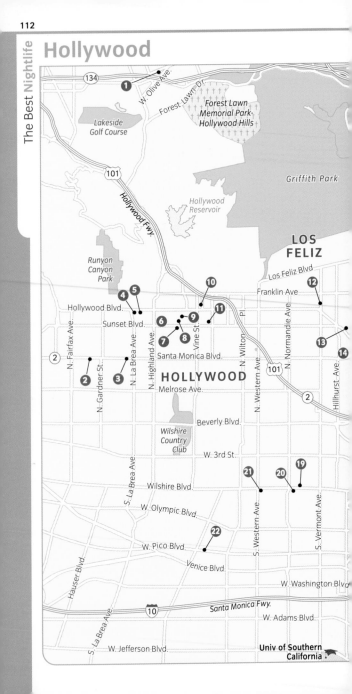

Hollywood

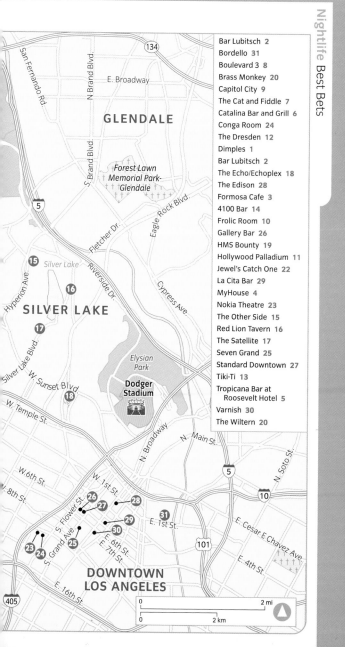

Bar Lubitsch 2
Bordello 31
Boulevard 3 8
Brass Monkey 20
Capitol City 9
The Cat and Fiddle 7
Catalina Bar and Grill 6
Conga Room 24
The Dresden 12
Dimples 1
Bar Lubitsch 2
The Echo/Echoplex 18
The Edison 28
Formosa Cafe 3
4100 Bar 14
Frolic Room 10
Gallery Bar 26
HMS Bounty 19
Hollywood Palladium 11
Jewel's Catch One 22
La Cita Bar 29
MyHouse 4
Nokia Theatre 23
The Other Side 15
Red Lion Tavern 16
The Satellite 17
Seven Grand 25
Standard Downtown 27
Tiki-Ti 13
Tropicana Bar at
  Roosevelt Hotel 5
Varnish 30
The Wiltern 20

Nightlife A to Z

Bars & Pubs

★ Bar Lubitsch WEST HOLLY-WOOD   This Russian-themed vodka parlor offers 200 kinds of vodka for you and your comrades and the Red Room in back to dance off its effects. *7702 Santa Monica Blvd., at Spaulding Ave.* ☎ *323/654-1234. Map p 112.*

The Brig VENICE   A friendly, mixed crowd downs drinks in a hip and modern space with a DJ spinning on most nights. *1515 Abbot Kinney Blvd., at California Ave.* ☎ *310/399-7537. www.thebrig.com. Map p 111.*

★ Cat and Fiddle HOLLYWOOD   This classic and always reliable pub offers cheap pints of English ale during happy hour (Mon–Thurs 4–7pm), darts, and a garden courtyard overflowing with ambience. *6530 W. Sunset Blvd. (btwn N. Highland Ave. & Vine St.).* ☎ *323/468-3800. www. thecatandfiddle.com. Map p 112.*

★ Copa d'Oro SANTA MONICA   You've probably never tasted anything like these creative cocktails, made with the freshest ingredients—fruits and herbs straight from the Santa Monica Farmers Market. The "Happy Depression" menu is a

bargain: $5 cocktails from 6 to 8pm. *217 Broadway (at Second St.).* ☎ *310/576-3030. www.copadoro. com. Map p 111.*

★ The Dresden LOS FELIZ   As you imbibe, enjoy the musical stylings of Marty and Elaine, the legendary lounge act you might remember from the movie *Swingers*. Don't leave before they bust out their version of *Stayin' Alive*. *1760 N. Vermont Ave. (at Kingswell Ave.).* ☎ *323/665-4294. www.thedresden. com. Map p 112.*

★ The Edison DOWNTOWN   This nostalgic nightclub, which occupies the sub-basement of a 100-year-old building, takes its design cues from a previous tenant—a power plant. Cocktails are serious business here, especially the monthly Radio Room night, when visiting mixologists from around the country gather to create their most ambitious and delicious libations. *108 W. Second St., at Main St.* ☎ *213/613-2000. www.edisondowntown.com. Map p 112.*

★★★ Formosa Cafe WEST HOLLYWOOD   Opened in 1939 and declared a city landmark in 1991, this trolley-car bar is perfect if you

The Formosa Cafe is a Hollywood landmark.

The bartender sports a dirndl dress at the Red Lion Tavern.

like your drinks dripping with nostalgia—Marilyn, Sinatra, and Elvis have all tippled here. *7156 Santa Monica Blvd., at Formosa Ave.* ☎ *323/850-9050. Map p 112.*

★ **4100 Bar** SILVER LAKE   Snake through the velvet curtain, kick back in the red glow of the vaguely Asian decor, and take in the eclectic crowd and the sounds of the stellar jukebox. *4100 Sunset Blvd. (at Manzanita St.).* ☎ *323/666-4460. Map p 112.*

★ **Red Lion Tavern** SILVER LAKE Waitresses in dirndl dresses, an enviable collection of beer steins, sausage platters, and the largest assortment of German beers this side of München—*wunderbar!* *2366 Glendale Blvd., at Brier Ave.* ☎ *323/662-5337. www.redliontavern.net. Map p 112.*

★ **Seven Grand** DOWNTOWN This watering hole serves over 300 premium whiskeys including a 30-year-old Macallan Scotch that'll bump you back more than a C-note for a glass. The "gentleman of leisure" vibe is completed with dark woods, dim lighting, a couple pool tables, and a kitschy jackalope motif. *515 W. Seventh St., at Grand Ave.* ☎ *213/614-0737. www.seven grand.la. Map p 112.*

★ **Tiki-Ti** LOS FELIZ   Try the exotic cocktails—the Blood and Sand, the Great White Shark, Ray's

Mistake—at what may be the world's tiniest tiki hut, serving loyal locals since 1961. *4427 W. Sunset Blvd., at Virgil Place.* ☎ *323/669-9381. www.tiki-ti.com. Map p 112.*

★★★ **The Varnish** DOWNTOWN The mixologists at this speakeasy-style bar—the entrance is an unmarked door in the back of Cole's restaurant—craft meticulous cocktails like the Penicillin, a single-malt Scotch with honey, lemon, and crystallized ginger, on a single slab of ice. If you're lucky, a jazz pianist will slip behind the antique upright for a little ragtime. *118 E. Sixth St. (at Main St.).* ☎ *213/622-9999. www. thevarnishbar.com. Map p 112.*

Dance Clubs

★ **Bordello** DOWNTOWN   This intimate space awash in red velvet presents a wide variety of neo-burlesque shows—the best is the professionally choreographed Harlow Gold on Sunday nights. *901 E. First St., at Vignes St.* ☎ *213/687-3766. www.bordellobar.com. Cover $10–$25. Map p 112.*

★ **Boulevard 3** HOLLYWOOD   At the former Hollywood Athletic Club

Go for a fruity cocktail at Tiki-Ti.

(established in 1924 with charter members such as Chaplin and DeMille), this club offers a huge dance floor as well as a courtyard retreat with cozy cabanas. Call ahead for reservations, but you may still have to rely on the kindness of bouncers, if there is such a thing. *6523 W. Sunset Blvd., at N. Hudson Ave.* ☎ *323/466-2144. www.boulevard3.com. Cover $20. Map p 112.*

★ **Conga Room** DOWNTOWN
Co-owned by Jennifer Lopez, Jimmy Smits, Sheila E., and will.i.am., this may be the city's hottest—it's certainly the swankiest—spot for Latin music and dancing. And if your salsa is a little rusty, relax—lessons are available (free with cover charge, $10 without) from 8 to 9pm before the club opens on Thursday and Saturday nights. *800 W. Olympic Blvd. (at Figueroa St.), suites A160 & A260.* ☎ *213/749-0445. www.congaroom.com. Cover $15–$45. Map p 112.*

★★ **La Cita Bar** DOWNTOWN
Saturday and Sunday offer authentic salsa and ranchera-style dancing, while the rest of the week, especially Thursday nights, features DJs spinning for shimmying hipsters from Echo Park and Silver Lake. *336 S. Hill St. (at W. Third St.).* ☎ *213/687-7111. www.lacitabar.com. Cover Thurs–Fri $5–$10. Map p 112.*

My House HOLLYWOOD   This hot spot feels like a rock star's mansion and caters to young Hollywood and their entourages. Bottle-service reservations, which are costly, are the only guaranteed way through the door. *7080 Hollywood Blvd. (at N. La Brea Ave.).* ☎ *323/960-3300. www.myhousehollywood.com. Cover $20–$30. Map p 112.*

Dive Bars
★ **Frolic Room** HOLLYWOOD
Slumped next to the high-flying Pantages Theatre, this bar is refreshingly untouched by Hollywood's wave of regentrification. It's got an exuberant neon sign on the outside and a fading wallpaper mural of yesteryear celebrities on the inside. *6245 Hollywood Blvd., at Argyle Ave.* ☎ *323/462-5890. Map p 112.*

★ **HMS Bounty** KOREATOWN
Attached to the lobby of the historic Gaylord apartment building, this bar has cheap drinks, a half-baked nautical theme, and waitresses who have seen it all, buster. Slide into the booth once favored by Jack "Just the facts, ma'am" Webb. *3357 Wilshire Blvd., at S. Kenmore Ave.* ☎ *213/385-7275. Map p 112.*

Gay & Lesbian Bars & Clubs
★★ **The Abbey** WEST HOLLYWOOD   This indoor/outdoor cafe

A gay night out in West Hollywood includes a stop at The Abbey.

and bar has long been considered ground zero of West Hollywood's gay and lesbian nightlife. *692 N. Robertson Blvd. (at Santa Monica Blvd.).* ☎ *310/289-8410. www. abbeyfoodandbar.com. Map p 111.*

★ **East/West Lounge** WEST HOL-LYWOOD   Gay professionals chill at this upscale club, which serves specialty drinks (like pureed-fruit martinis) in a plush, conversation-friendly setting. *801 Larrabee St., at Santa Monica Blvd.* ☎ *310/360-6186. www.eastwestlounge.com. No cover. Map p 111.*

Here Lounge WEST HOLLYWOOD   This lounge and dance club successfully mixes gay and lesbian nights. On Thursday and Friday nights, ladies strut their stuff. *696 N. Robertson Blvd., at Santa Monica Blvd.* ☎ *310/360-8455. www.herelounge. com. Cover $10. Map p 111.*

Jewel's Catch One MID-CITY   This multiroom dance party started in 1972 as the nation's first black gay-and-lesbian disco, and most nights offers a mix of house, hip-hop, and salsa for ladies of all colors. *4067 W. Pico Blvd. (btwn Norton & 12th aves.).* ☎ *323/734-8849. www.jewelscatchone.com. Cover $10. Map p 112.*

The Other Side SILVER LAKE   If you're looking for something a little more low-key than go-go-go WeHo, head to the Eastside and this casual and friendly piano bar, a neighborhood favorite for decades. *2538 Hyperion Ave., 1 block south of Griffith Park Blvd.* ☎ *323/661-0618. www.flyingleapcafe.com. No cover. Map p 112.*

Rage WEST HOLLYWOOD   Each night has a different theme, but the basic formula is this: hot young men dancing. *8911 Santa Monica Blvd., at N. San Vicente Blvd.* ☎ *310/652-7055. www.ragewesthollywood. com. Cover $5–$15. Map p 111.*

Bar Noir at Maison 140.

Best Websites for Gay Nightlife

For more information on the gay and lesbian scene, check out www. gogaywesthollywood.com or www. frontiersweb.com.

Hotel Bars

★ **Bar Nineteen12 at the Beverly Hills Hotel** BEVERLY HILLS   A cocktail at this elegant bar is an excellent way to experience this Los Angeles landmark without doling out the dough for a stay. *9641 Sunset Blvd.* ☎ *310/276-2251. www.barnineteen12.com. Map p 111.*

★★ **Bar Noir at Maison 140** BEVERLY HILLS   This cozy hideaway dressed in black, white, and red is the perfect place for a romantic rendezvous. Try the Lady Godiva, their signature chocolatey-vodka drink. During Happy Hour, 5 to 7pm daily, bartenders use a vintage absinthe fountain to pour glasses of the Green Fairy. *140 S. Lasky Dr. (btwn Charleville & Wilshire blvds.).* ☎ *310/281-4000. www.maison140 beverlyhills.com. Map p 111.*

★★ **Gallery Bar at the Millennium Biltmore Hotel** DOWNTOWN At this opulent, old-school bar in one of downtown's most stunning buildings, specialties include six types of Manhattans and a delicious martini called the Black Dahlia (named after the infamous "Black Dahlia" murder victim, Elizabeth Short, who supposedly had her last drink here). Weekend nights feature live jazz music. *506 S. Grand Ave.* ☎ *213/624-1011. www. millenniumhotels.com. Map p 112.*

★★ **Roof Bar at the Standard Downtown** DOWNTOWN Plop onto the waterbed of a poolside red pod and drink in views of the twinkling skyscrapers. *550 S. Flower St. (btwn W. Fifth & W. Sixth sts.).* ☎ *213/892-8080. www.standard hotel.com. Cover $10–20 Fri & Sat nights & Sun afternoon. Map p 112.*

★ **Tropicana Bar at the Roosevelt Hotel** HOLLYWOOD This poolside bar with a midcentury, Palm Springs vibe is still a prime Hollywood see-and-be-seen locale. Looking for something a bit quieter at this historic hotel? Cozy up to the dark and glamorous Library Bar in the lobby. *7000 Hollywood Blvd., at N. Orange Dr.* ☎ *323/466-7000.*

www.hollywoodroosevelt.com. Map p 112.

Karaoke

Caffe Brass Monkey KOREATOWN The only trouble at this popular dive is choosing from 75,000 songs or, for first-timers, finding the door (on Mariposa, not Wilshire). The karaoke kicks off at 9pm on Monday and Tuesday, 4pm on Wednesday and Friday, 7pm on Thursday, and 8pm on weekends. *659 Mariposa Ave., at Wilshire Blvd.* ☎ *213/381-7047. www.cafebrass monkey.com. No cover. 2-drink minimum. Map p 112.*

★ **Dimples** BURBANK This valley mainstay, which debuted in 1982, claims to be the first karaoke club in the western hemisphere. Your performance is projected on multiple screens, a video wall, cable access, and the Internet—enjoy your newfound stardom. *3413 W. Olive Ave., at N. Lima St.* ☎ *818/842-2336. www.dimplesshowcase.com. Open 6pm–2am, Mon–Sat. Fri–Sat cover $5 after 10pm. Map p 112.*

Live Music & DJs

★ **Catalina Bar and Grill** HOLLYWOOD Cooking up classic jazz in

Tropicana Bar at the Roosevelt Hotel.

Hollywood for 20 years, this 250-seat dinner club has hosted legends like Dizzy Gillespie, Art Blakey, and Wynton Marsalis. *6725 W. Sunset Blvd., at Highland Ave.* ☎ *323/466-2210. www.catalinajazzclub.com. Cover $10–$35. 2-drink or dinner minimum. Map p 112.*

★ ★ **The Echo/Echoplex** SILVER LAKE These sister clubs to the now defunct Spaceland share a building (but not an address) and pack solid lineups of indie artists for in-the-know audiences. Thom Yorke of Radiohead played an unannounced show here recently. *The Echo: 1822 Sunset Blvd. Echoplex: 1154 Glendale Blvd.* ☎ *213/413-8200. www.attheecho.com. Cover $5–$14. Map p 112.*

Harvelle's Blues Club SANTA MONICA This dark, old-school nightclub presents authentic blues every night of the week. *1432 Fourth St., at Santa Monica Blvd.* ☎ *310/395-1676. www.harvelles.com. Daily 8pm–2am; shows begin at 9:30pm. Cover $5–$10. Map p 111.*

★ **Hollywood Palladium** HOLLYWOOD This large streamline-moderne venue has been a fixture on the Hollywood music scene since Frank Sinatra topped the bill at its opening in 1940. Recent acts include Jay-Z, Bob Dylan, and the Pixies. *6215 W. Sunset Blvd. (btwn Vine & Gower sts.).* ☎ *323/962-7600. www.livenation.com. Tickets $20–$150. Map p 112.*

★ **House of Blues** HOLLYWOOD This slick, well-run venue hosts major acts from all genres. Try the Sunday gospel brunch, which serves up live gospel music and a buffet of Southern cuisine. *8430 W. Sunset Blvd., at N. Olive Dr.* ☎ *323/848-5100. www.houseofblues.com. Tickets $20–$50. Map p 111.*

A line forms outside the popular night spot Largo.

★★ **Largo at the Coronet** WEST HOLLYWOOD This is a quiet, sit-down venue for intimate musical performances (Eels, Fiona Apple) and comedic acts (Sarah Silverman, Patton Oswalt). Friday nights with producer, performer, and musical mad scientist Jon Brion are extraordinary. *366 N. La Cienega Blvd. (at Oakwood Ave.).* ☎ *310/855-0350. www.largo-la.com. Cover $10–$30. Map p 111.*

★ **Nokia Theatre L.A. Live** DOWNTOWN Part of a massive entertainment complex, this 7,100-seater presents major acts like Pink Floyd, Neil Young, and Mary J. Blige, as well as special events like the Emmy Awards and the finals of American Idol. *777 Chick Hearns Court (at the Staples Center).* ☎ *213/763-6030. www.nokiatheatrelalive.com. Cover $10–$30. Map p 112.*

The Satellite SILVER LAKE Formerly 3-star Spaceland, darling indie-rock club of discriminating music bloggers, the Satellite is just

The legendary Whisky a Go Go on Sunset Boulevard.

opening as we go to print. Check their lineup to see if the likes of Beck and Arcade Fire return. ☎ 323/661-4380. www.clubspaceland.com. Cover $7–$12; free on Mon. Map p 112.

★★★ **Troubadour** WEST HOLLY-WOOD   Opened in 1957, this club has played a pivotal role in the careers of Elton John, Tom Waits, Guns N' Roses, and countless more. Today's lineup veers toward indie sensations like Clap Your Hands Say Yeah, the Fiery Furnaces, and Art Brut. *9081 Santa Monica Blvd., at N. Doheny Dr.* ☎ 310/276-6168. www.troubadour.com. Tickets $10–$15. Map p 111.

Viper Room HOLLYWOOD   The small club, probably best known as the site of River Phoenix's death, packs a calendar full of up-and-coming rockers. Big names (Tom Petty, Pearl Jam) sometimes drop in for surprise sets. *8852 W. Sunset Blvd., at Larrabee St.* ☎ 310/358-1880. www.viperroom.com. Tickets $10–$15. Map p 111.

★★ **Whisky a Go Go** HOLLY-WOOD   This legendary venue still presents a variety of musical acts—mostly hard rockin'—including tribute bands to the greats that once played here: Led Zeppelin, Van Halen, and the Doors. *8901 W.*

Sunset Blvd., at N. San Vicente Blvd. ☎ 310/652-4202. www.whiskyago go.com. Tickets $8–$40. Map p 111.

★ **The Wiltern** MID–LOS ANGELES This Art Deco landmark presents popular indie acts (Broken Social Scene, Ween, the National) that have outgrown the Troubadour or Spaceland. *3790 Wilshire Blvd., at Western Ave.* ☎ 213/380-5005. www.livenation.com. Tickets $20–$50. Map p 112.

Sports Bars

★★ **Barney's Beanery** WEST HOLLYWOOD   This historical roadhouse-style bar and restaurant is a colorful and unpretentious place to quaff beers (choose from 132 types) as you watch sports or shoot pool. *8447 Santa Monica Blvd., at N. Olive Dr.* ☎ 323/654-2287. www.barneys beanery.com. Map p 111.

★ **Capitol City** HOLLYWOOD Located along the nightlife-rich Cahuenga Corridor (Cahuenga Blvd. btwn Hollywood and Sunset), this upscale sports bar offers an airy 7,000-square-foot space, choice beers on tap (Chimay, Guinness), good grub, and plenty of gargantuan plasma screens. *1615 N. Cahuenga Blvd.* ☎ 323/465-1750. www.cap citysports.com. Map p 112. ●

8 The Best Arts & Entertainment

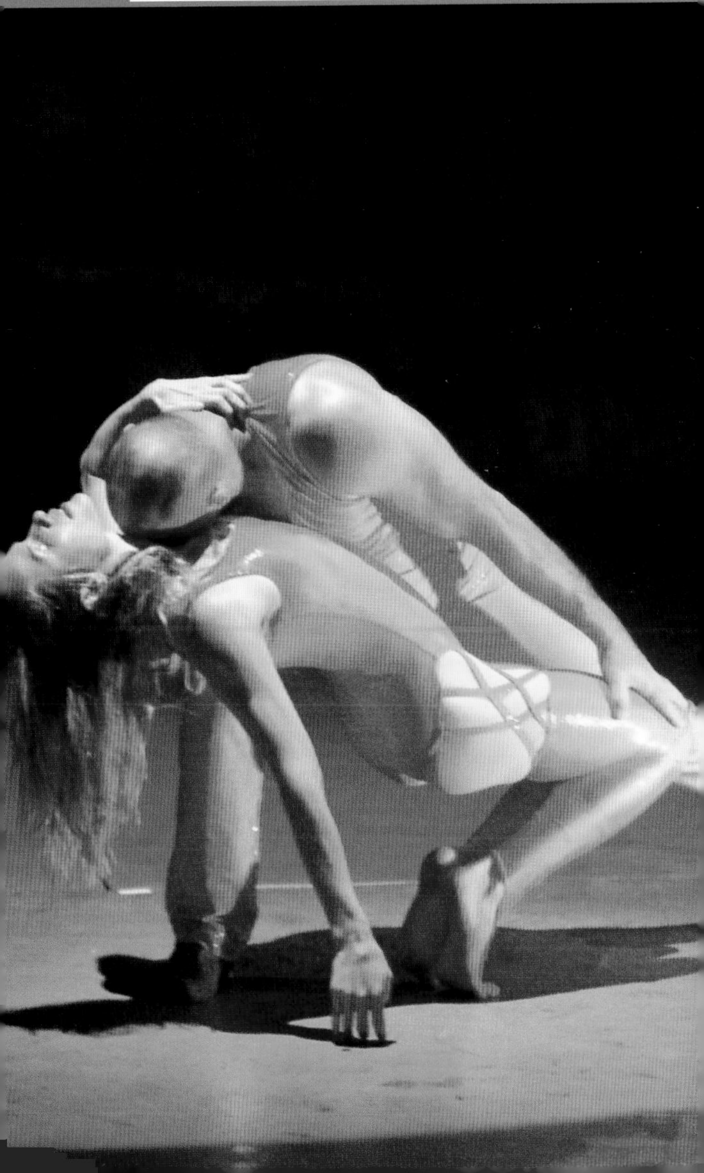

Arts & Entertainment Best Bets

Best **Movie Theater for Cinephiles**
★★ ArcLight Cinemas *6160 W. Sunset Blvd. (p 128)*

Best **Acoustics**
★★★ Walt Disney Concert Hall *111 S. Grand Ave. (p 126)*

Best **Chance to Do the Wave**
★★ Dodger Stadium *1000 Elysian Park Ave. (p 131)*

Best **Theater for a Broadway Musical**
★★ Pantages Theatre *6233 Hollywood Blvd. (p 132)*

Best **Place to See an Opera**
★ Dorothy Chandler Pavilion *135 N. Grand Ave. (p 126)*

Best **Chance to See Jack Nicholson**
★★ Staples Center *1111 S. Figueroa St. (p 131)*

Best **Old Hollywood Movie Experience**
★★★ Grauman's Chinese Theatre *6925 Hollywood Blvd. (p 128)*

Best **Concert Under the Stars**
★★★ Hollywood Bowl *2301 N. Highland Ave. (p 126)*

Best **Place to Get Your Kicks**
★ Home Depot Center *1000 E. Victoria St. (p 131)*

Most **Thought Provoking**
★ Museum of Tolerance *9786 W. Pico Blvd. (p 130)*

Best **Ongoing Auditions for Saturday Night Live**
★★ Groundlings *7307 Melrose Ave. (p 127)*

Best **Movie Theater for Kids**
★ El Capitan Theatre *6838 Hollywood Blvd. (p 128)*

Most **Baffling**
★★ Museum of Jurassic Technology *9341 Venice Blvd. (p 130)*

Best **Place to Admire Beyonce's Dress**
★★ Grammy Museum *1111 S. Figueroa St. (p 129)*

Most **Unpredictable Comedy**
★ Upright Citizens Brigade *1111 S. Figueroa St. (p 128)*

A scene from David Mamet's Speed the Plow *at Geffen Playhouse.*

Hollywood

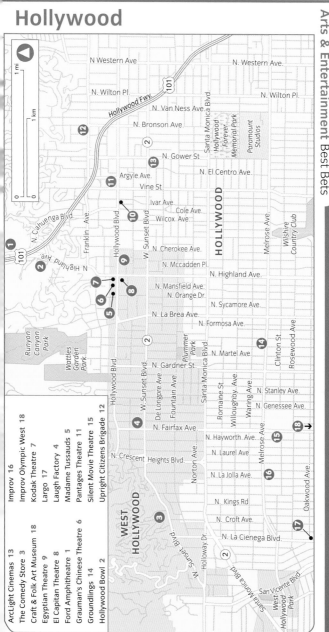

ArcLight Cinemas 13
The Comedy Store 3
Craft & Folk Art Museum 18
Egyptian Theatre 9
El Capitan Theatre 8
Ford Amphitheatre 1
Grauman's Chinese Theatre 6
Groundlings 14
Hollywood Bowl 2

Improv 16
Improv Olympic West 18
Kodak Theatre 7
Largo 17
Laugh Factory 4
Madame Tussauds 5
Pantages Theatre 11
Silent Movie Theatre 15
Upright Citizens Brigade 12

P 121: Performers at the Ford Amphitheatre.

Downtown

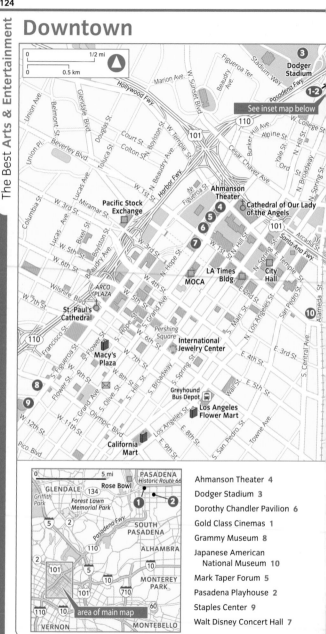

Ahmanson Theater 4

Dodger Stadium 3

Dorothy Chandler Pavilion 6

Gold Class Cinemas 1

Grammy Museum 8

Japanese American
  National Museum 10

Mark Taper Forum 5

Pasadena Playhouse 2

Staples Center 9

Walt Disney Concert Hall 7

Westwood

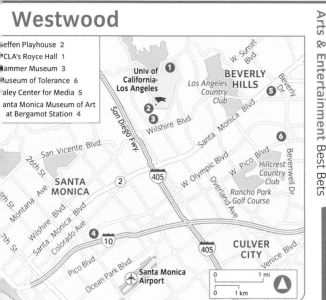

Geffen Playhouse **2**
UCLA's Royce Hall **1**
Hammer Museum **3**
Museum of Tolerance **6**
Paley Center for Media **5**
Santa Monica Museum of Art
  at Bergamot Station **4**

South Bay

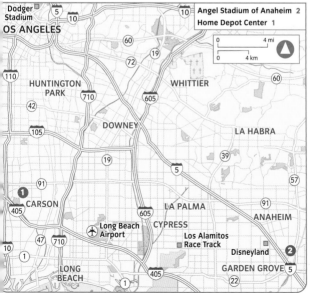

Angel Stadium of Anaheim **2**
Home Depot Center **1**

Arts & Entertainment A to Z

Classical Music, Opera & Dance

★ Dorothy Chandler Pavilion

DOWNTOWN The 3,200-seat auditorium is home to the nation's fourth-largest opera company, which continues to garner acclaim under the bold guidance of artistic director Plácido Domingo. Also, Dance at the Music Center hosts touring dance troupes such as the American Ballet Theatre. *135 N. Grand Ave. (btwn W. Temple & First sts.).* ☎ *213/972-8001 or 213/972-0711. www.musiccenter. org. Tickets $20–$220. Map p 124.*

Ford Amphitheatre HOLLY-

WOOD HILLS For an outdoor amphitheater, this is an intimate setting—no seat is more than 96 feet away from the stage—in which to enjoy a diverse schedule of music, theater, and unique dance performances, such as *Troupe Vertigo,* a retro circus-floor show set to swing jazz music. *2580 Cahuenga Blvd. E. (near Hwy. 101).* ☎ *323/461-3673. www.fordamphitheatre.org. Tickets $5–$75. Map p 123.*

★★★ Hollywood Bowl HOLLY-

WOOD In 1922 the city's finest musicians, the Los Angeles Philharmonic, played the city's finest outdoor venue, the Hollywood Bowl. Thankfully, the tradition continues.

Non-classical acts including jazz, world music, and rock fill out the rest of the schedule. *2301 N. Highland Ave.* ☎ *323/850-2000. www. hollywoodbowl.com. Tickets $1–$300. Map p 123.*

★ UCLA's Royce Hall WEST-

WOOD This 1929 beauty, one of the first buildings on the UCLA campus, has been likened to Carnegie Hall in terms of the quality of both its acoustics and its roster of performers over the years. George Gershwin, Ella Fitzgerald, Albert Einstein, Frank Zappa, and Mikhail Baryshnikov have all graced the stage. *On the UCLA campus, 405 Hilgard Ave. (at Sunset Blvd.).* ☎ *310/825-2101. www.uclalive.org. Tickets $22–$100. Map p 125.*

★★★ Walt Disney Concert

Hall DOWNTOWN Take any opportunity to attend a performance at this hall—a masterpiece for the eyes and ears. *111 S. Grand Ave., at First St.* ☎ *323/850-2000. www.laphil.com. Tickets $15–$142. Map p 124.*

Comedy

★ Comedy Store WEST HOLLY-

WOOD Started in 1972 by Pauly Shore's folks, this landmark club

The L.A. Opera performs Puccini's La Bohème *at Dorothy Chandler Pavilion.*

rollicking improv-based sketch shows. *8162 Melrose Ave., at N. Kilkea Dr.* ☎ *323/651-2583. http:// west.ioimprov.com. Tickets $13–$18. Map p 123.*

★ **Largo** WEST HOLLYWOOD Although known more for its excellent musical lineup, the venue also features comedy nights with names like Sarah Silverman, Paul F. Tompkins, and Patton Oswalt. *366 N. La Cienega Blvd. (at Oakwood Ave.).* ☎ *310/855-0350. www.largo-la. com. Cover $10–$30. Map p 123.*

★ **Laugh Factory** WEST HOLLY-WOOD Other than Michael "Kramer" Richards's infamous meltdown in 2006, Jamie Masada's club has been consistently bringing the funny since 1979, when Richard Pryor headlined the first show. Check out the All Star Comedy shows on weekends, when big names like Dane Cook have been known to sneak onstage for an unscheduled set. *8001 Sunset Blvd., at Laurel Ave.* ☎ *323/656-1336. www.laughfactory.com. Tickets $20–$45. Map p 123.*

U.C.L.A.'s Royce Hall.

features three separate rooms for funny business. Alumni include Richard Pryor, John Belushi, David Letterman, Andy Kaufman, Sam Kinison, and Gallagher. *W. Sunset Blvd., at Olive Dr.* ☎ *323/650-6268. www. thecomedystore.com. Tickets $10–$20, plus 2-drink minimum. Map p 123.*

★★ **Groundlings** HOLLYWOOD For improv and sketch comedy in L.A., nothing beats Groundlings, whose long list of funny alumni includes Will Ferrell, Lisa Kudrow, Phil Hartman, and Maya Rudolph. *7307 Melrose Ave., at Poinsettia Place.* ☎ *323/934-4747. www. groundlings.com. Tickets $11–$22. Map p 123.*

Improv WEST HOLLYWOOD At some point in their careers, all the big-time stand-up comedians have played Budd Friedman's club: Steve Martin, Robin Williams, Jay Leno, Billy Crystal, George Carlin, and Eddie Murphy. *8162 Melrose Ave., at N. Kilkea Dr.* ☎ *323/651-2583. www.improv.com. Tickets $13–$18. Map p 123.*

iO West HOLLYWOOD Founded by the Zen master of improvisational comedy, the late Del Close, this club jams its schedule with a variety of

Groundlings' impressive alumni include comedian/actress Jennifer Coolidge.

The El Capitan Theatre in Hollywood.

★ Upright Citizens Brigade

HOLLYWOOD The tiny theater rivals Groundlings for sketch-comedy supremacy, and the yuks per bucks ratio cannot be beat. *5919 Franklin Ave., at Bronson Ave.* ☎ *323/908-8702. www.ucbtheatre. com. Tickets $1–$8. Map p 123.*

Film

★★ ArcLight Cinemas

HOLLYWOOD Reserved seating, audio that exceeds THX standards, a "black box" distraction-free design, and extra-wide seats with ample legroom—this is simply the most luxurious movie theater in Hollywood. *6160 W. Sunset Blvd., at Vine St.* ☎ *323/464-1478. www.arclightcinemas.com. Tickets $7.75–$16.50. Map p 123.*

★★ Egyptian Theatre

HOLLYWOOD Home of the not-for-profit American Cinematheque, this historic showplace offers a program that dares to call film art: rare prints of 70mm classics, director retrospectives, film festivals, and in-person Q&A sessions with filmmakers and actors. *6712 Hollywood Blvd., at Las Palmas Ave.* ☎ *323/466-3456. www.egyptiantheatre.com. Tickets $9–$11. Map p 123.*

★ El Capitan Theatre

HOLLYWOOD Dancing Disney characters and a "Mighty Wurlitzer" pipe organ entertain the crowd before screenings of Disney/Pixar blockbusters at this historic theater, which hosted the world premiere of *Citizen Kane* in 1941. *6838 Hollywood Blvd., at Highland Ave.* ☎ *800/347-6396. Tickets $16–$30. Map p 123.*

★★ Gold Class Cinemas

PASADENA Battling the ArcLight for the town's supreme cinematic experience, this luxury movie theatre offers plush orange recliners, spaced generously apart in pairs—there no more than 40 seats in any auditorium. Need a little something? Push the small glowing button on your side table to summon a ninja-like server who'll bring you an extra pillow or some refreshments—say, Wagyu beef sliders and a Makers Mark Manhattan. *47 Miller Alley.* ☎ *626/639-2260. www.goldclass cinemas.com. Tickets $22–$29. Map p 124.*

★★★ Grauman's Chinese Theatre

HOLLYWOOD Catch a flick at the most famous movie theater on the planet, unless it's closed off for a star-studded, red-carpet, flashbulb-popping premiere. *6925 Hollywood Blvd., at Highland Ave.* ☎ *323/464-6266. www.manntheatres.com. Tickets $9–$12. Map p 123.*

Silent Movie Theatre HOLLY-WOOD For decades this theatre has kept alive the art of silent films. On Silent Wednesdays, enjoy the rare opportunity to see the antics of stars like Buster Keaton, Charlie Chaplin, and Harold Lloyd on the big screen. The rest of the week you can catch offbeat programming like a triple feature of groovy van films from the '70s. *611 N. Fairfax Ave., at Clinton St.* ☎ *323/655-2520. www.cinefamily.org. Tickets $10. Map p 123.*

Smaller Museums

Craft and Folk Art Museum MIRACLE MILE Running the gamut between traditional folk art and contemporary arts and crafts, this small and often-overlooked museum offers exhibits far off the beaten path: the history and art of tarot cards, dioramas of a multi-generational circus family, Palestinian embroidery, and Carnaval headdresses. Don't miss the museum shop, great for gift hunting. *5814 Wilshire Blvd. (btwn Fairfax & La Brea aves.).* ☎ *323/937-4230. www.cafam.org. Tues–Fri 11am–5pm; Sat–Sun noon–6pm. $5 adults, $3 seniors & students, free for children under 12; free for all 1st Wed of the month.*

★★ Grammy Museum DOWN-TOWN Part of the L.A. Live entertainment behemoth, this four-story, 30,000-square-foot museum celebrates all forms of music as well as the art and technology of recording that music. Check out one-of-a-kind memorabilia like Jim Morrison's poetry books and the first guitar Elvis Presley ever played; or dabble in the interactive studios and learn how to mix tracks. *800 W. Olympic Blvd.* ☎ *213/744-7432. www.grammymuseum.org. Sun–Fri 11:30am–7:30pm; Sat 10am–7:30pm. Admission $13 adults, $12 students & seniors, $11 kids 6–17, free for kids 5 & under.*

★ Hammer Museum WESTWOOD This museum has a smattering of paintings by European masters—Cezanne, Rembrandt, and van Gogh—and a lovely sculpture garden, but it's best known for its contemporary collection and edgy special exhibits such as Robert Crumb's take on the Book of Genesis. *10899 Wilshire Blvd., at Westwood Blvd.* ☎ *310/443-7000. www.hammer.ucla.edu. Tues–Wed & Fri–Sat 11am–7pm; Thurs 11am–9pm; Sun 11am–5pm. Admission $7 adults, $5 seniors, free for kids 17 & under; free for all on Thurs.*

★ Japanese American National Museum DOWNTOWN In a modern architectural marvel in Little Tokyo, this poignant museum

An interactive display at the Grammy Museum.

examines the Japanese experience in America, including the sad chapter during the early years of World War II when Japanese Americans were interned in camps in California. *369 E. 1st St.* ☎ *213/625-0414. www.janm. org. Wed–Sat 11am–5pm. Admission $9 adults, $5 seniors, $5 students & kids 6–17, free for kids 5 & under.*

Madame Tussauds HOLLY-WOOD   Although the management of this $55-million facility prefers the term "attraction" rather than "wax museum," this tourist draw located right off Grauman's courtyard is most definitely a wax museum, but by far the better (though more expensive) of the two on the block. Don't forget your camera since you'll probably want a shot of you flirting with Johnny Depp. *6933 Hollywood Blvd.* ☎ *323/798-1670. www.madametussauds.com. Mon–Thurs 10am–8pm; Fri–Sun 10am–10pm. Admission $25 adults, $20 seniors, $18 students & kids 4–12, free for kids 3 & under.*

★★ Museum of Jurassic Technology CULVER CITY   You start with the nonsequitur name, and become more baffled the deeper you delve into the museum's intricacies—which is precisely what creator/curator David Wilson wants. A 2001 recipient of a McArthur "genius grant," Wilson promotes confusion as "a vehicle to open people's minds." If this sounds like gobbledygook, wait until you see the "Eye of the Needle" exhibit, featuring a

sculpture of Pope John Paul II placed within the eye of a needle. *9341 Venice Blvd.* ☎ *310/836-6131. www.mjt. org. Thurs 2–8pm; Fri–Sun noon–6pm. Suggested donation: $5 adults, $3 seniors & visitors 12–21, free for children under 12.*

★ Museum of Tolerance CENTURY CITY   This internationally acclaimed museum is anchored by its dramatic Holocaust exhibit, where visitors take a 70-minute tour back in time to Nazi Germany. Interactive high-tech exhibits zero in on other issues of intolerance: genocide in Rwanda, White Supremacy, and the proliferation of hate speech on the Web. *9786 W. Pico Blvd.* ☎ *310/553-8403. www.museumof tolerance.com. Mon–Fri 10am–5pm; Sun 11am–5pm. Admission $15 adults, $12 seniors, $11 students & kids 5–18, free for kids 4 & under.*

Paley Center for Media BEVERLY HILLS   In a polished building designed by Richard Meier, this museum treats television, an often-derided form of mass entertainment, as a legitimate and significant art form, and offers 150,000 television programs and commercials for your viewing pleasure. *465 N. Beverly Dr.* ☎ *310/786-1000. www.paleycenter. org. Tues–Sun noon–5pm. Suggested donation: $10 adults, $8 students & seniors, $5 kids 14 & under.*

★ Santa Monica Museum of Art at Bergamot Station SANTA MONICA   This noncollecting

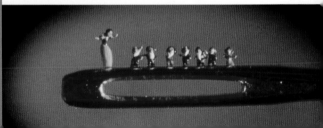

Willard Wigan's microminiature sculpture of Snow White and the Seven Dwarfs on the head of a needle at the Museum of Jurassic Technology.

museum is the focal point of the industrial-looking Bergamot Station, Southern California's largest complex of art galleries. After checking out a contemporary art exhibit on, say, the "Mama of Dada," California artist Beatrice Wood, take a stroll through the surrounding score of galleries. *2525 Michigan Ave. ☎ 310/586-6488. www.smmoa.org. Tues–Sat 11am–6pm. Free admission.*

Sports Venues

Angel Stadium of Anaheim
ANAHEIM In 2002 the Los Angeles Angels clinched the World Series here on their home turf, a user-friendly venue that is actually accessible by public transportation. *2000 Gene Autry Way, at S. State College Blvd. ☎ 888/796-HALO. www.angels.mlb.com. Tickets $5–$125. Map p 125.*

★★ kids Dodger Stadium
DOWNTOWN Built in 1962 to welcome the Dodgers from Brooklyn, this is one of Major League Baseball's classic stadiums, and currently the third oldest in use. *1000 Elysian Park Ave., at Stadium Way. ☎ 866/DODGERS. www.dodgers.com. Tickets $6–$225. Map p 124.*

★ Home Depot Center CARSON This 27,000-seat soccer-only stadium is the home field for both Chivas U.S.A. and the Los Angeles Galaxy. *1000 E. Victoria St., at Tamcliff Ave. ☎ 213/480-3232. www.homedepotcenter.com. Tickets $10–$250. Map p 125.*

Santa Anita Racetrack ARCADIA Play the ponies at the oldest (established in 1934) and finest racetrack in southern California. Be sure to look for the statue of Seabiscuit, winner of the 1940 Santa Anita Handicap. *285 W. Huntington Dr., Arcadia. ☎ 626/574-7223. www.santaanita.com. Admission $5–$20.*

David Beckham helps sell out the L.A. Galaxy soccer games played at the Home Depot Center.

★★ Staples Center DOWNTOWN This state-of-the-art sporting palace plays home to the NHL's Los Angeles Kings, as well as the NBA's Los Angeles Clippers and 2010 World Champion Los Angeles Lakers. Enjoy some of the best celeb-spotting in town. *1111 S. Figueroa St., at 11th St. ☎ 213/742-7300. www.staplescenter.com. Tickets $10–$275. Map p 124.*

Theaters

Actors' Gang CULVER CITY Co-founded in 1982 by Tim Robbins, this experimental theater ensemble specializes in skewering the classics (Shakespeare, Ibsen, and Chekhov), garnering over 100 awards for their risk-taking productions. *9070 Venice Blvd., at Culver Blvd. ☎ 310/838-4264. www.theactorsgang.com. Tickets $25.*

★★ Ahmanson Theater DOWNTOWN Enjoying the largest theatrical subscription base on the West Coast, the venue offers exclusive Los Angeles engagements of Tony Award–winning productions such as *Who's Afraid of Virginia Woolf?*, *Doubt*, *Jersey Boys*, and *Sweeney Todd*. *135 N. Grand Ave., at W. Temple St. ☎ 213/628-2772. www.centertheatregroup.org. Tickets $20–$100. Map p 124.*

Laurence Fishburne and Angela Bassett in a Pasadena Playhouse production of the August Wilson play Fences.

★ **Geffen Playhouse** WESTWOOD This striking venue near UCLA is known for showcasing film and television actors (Annette Bening, Matthew Modine) in an eclectic lineup of works that mixes satire, farce, musical, and biography. *10886 Le Conte Ave., at Westwood Blvd.* ☎ *310/208-5454. www.geffenplayhouse.com. Tickets $35–$110. Map p 125.*

Kirk Douglas Theatre CULVER CITY This intimate 300-seat theater is an oft-overlooked member of the Center Theatre Group (which includes Ahmanson Theater and Mark Taper Forum) and tends to present more adventurous works such as a musical fable by David Mamet. *9820 Washington Blvd., at Duquesne Ave.* ☎ *213/628-2772. Tickets $20–$40.*

★ **Kodak Theatre** HOLLYWOOD This sparkling new home of the Academy Awards lends the Hollywood and Highland megaplex some much-needed street cred. The venue also hosts a variety of special events such as magic revues, musicals (*Sesame Street Live,* Disney's *High School Musical*), and Cirque de Soleil extravaganzas. *6801 Hollywood Blvd., at Highland Ave.* ☎ *323/308-6300. www.kodaktheatre.com. Tickets $23–$150. Map p 123.*

★ **Mark Taper Forum** DOWNTOWN This intimate, 750-seat theater benefits from its thrust stage, which projects into the audience, allowing the action to be viewed from three sides. Sparkling from a $30-million overhaul, the internationally acclaimed venue presents innovative works by contemporary playwrights such as David Mamet, John Patrick Shanley, and John Guare. *135 N. Grand Ave., at W. Temple St.* ☎ *213/628-2772. www. centertheatregroup.org. Map p 124.*

★★ **Pantages Theatre** HOLLYWOOD Home to the Academy Awards ceremony from 1949 to 1959, this lavishly restored Art Deco landmark presents hit Broadway musicals such as *Wicked, Stomp, Cats,* and *Chicago. 6233 Hollywood Blvd., at Argyle Ave.* ☎ *323/468-1770. www.broadwayla.org. Tickets $81–$300. Map p 123.*

Pasadena Playhouse PASADENA This historic theater, founded in 1917 and granted the title "State Theater of California" in 1937, has launched many Hollywood actors such as Raymond Burr, Gene Hackman, and Dustin Hoffman. *39 S. El Molino Ave., at E. Green St.* ☎ *626/356-7529. www.pasadenaplayhouse.org. Tickets $31–$60. Map p 124.* ●

Lodging Best Bets

Best **Service**
★★★ Four Seasons Beverly Hills
$$$$ *300 S. Doheny Dr. (p 142)*

Most **Romantic**
★★★ Hotel Bel-Air $$$$ *701 Stone Canyon Rd. (p 143)*

Most **Iconic**
★★★ Beverly Hills Hotel & Bungalows $$$$$ *9641 Sunset Blvd. (p 140)*

Best **Value**
★ Elan Hotel $$ *8435 Beverly Blvd. (p 141)*

Best **Spot for Shopaholics**
★★★ Beverly Wilshire $$$$ *9500 Wilshire Blvd. (p 140)*

Best **Bed & Breakfast**
★★ Channel Road Inn $$$ *219 W. Channel Rd. (p 140)*

Most **Exclusive**
★★★ Chateau Marmont $$$$ *8221 Sunset Blvd. (p 140)*

Most **Kid-Friendly**
★★ Loews Santa Monica Beach $$$ *1700 Ocean Ave. (p 144)*

Best **Boutique Hotel**
★★ Maison 140 $$$ *140 S. Lasky Dr. (p 144)*

Most **"Hollywood"**
★★ Hollywood Roosevelt Hotel
$$$ *7000 Hollywood Blvd. (p 142)*

Best **Sunday Brunch**
★★★ The Langham Huntington
$$$$ *1401 S. Oak Knoll Ave. (p 143)*

Best **Views**
★★★ Shutters on the Beach $$$$ *1 Pico Blvd. (p 145)*

Best **Design**
★★ SLS Hotel $$$$ *465 S. La Cienega Blvd. (p 145)*

Most **Rock 'n' Roll**
★★ Sunset Marquis Hotel & Villas
$$$ *1200 Alta Loma Rd. (p 146)*

Best **Business Hotel**
★★★ L'Ermitage $$$$ *9291 Burton Way (p 144)*

Best **Hotel Bar**
★ Millennium Biltmore Hotel $$$ *506 S. Grand Ave. (p 144)*

Best **Hotel Spa**
★★★ The Peninsula Beverly Hills
$$$$ *9882 S. Santa Monica Blvd. (p 145)*

Best **Pool Scene**
★ W Los Angeles $$$ *930 Hilgard Ave. (p 146)*

A luxurious room at the Four Seasons Beverly Hills.

Santa Monica & the Beaches

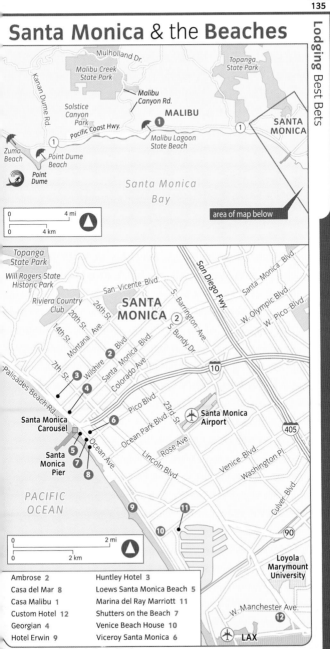

Mulholland Dr.

Malibu Creek State Park

Topanga State Park

Kanan Dume Rd.

Malibu Canyon Rd.

Solstice Canyon Park

MALIBU

Pacific Coast Hwy.

Malibu Lagoon State Beach

① 1

SANTA MONICA

Zuma Beach

① 1

Point Dume Beach

Point Dume

Santa Monica Bay

area of map below

0 ———— 4 mi
0 ———— 4 km

Topanga State Park

Will Rogers State Historic Park

San Vicente Blvd.

Riviera Country Club

20th St.

26th St.

SANTA MONICA

S. Barrington Ave.

San Diego Fwy.

Santa Monica Blvd.

② 2

S. Bundy Dr.

W. Olympic Blvd.

W. Pico Blvd.

14th St.

Montana Ave.

Wilshire Blvd.

② 2

Santa Monica Blvd.

Colorado Ave.

7th St.

③ 3

④ 4

Palisades Beach Rd.

Pico Blvd.

10

23rd St.

Santa Monica Airport

405

Santa Monica Carousel

⑥ 6

Ocean Park Blvd.

Rose Ave.

Santa Monica Pier

⑤ 5

⑦ 7

⑧ 8

Ocean Ave.

Lincoln Blvd.

Venice Blvd.

Washington Pl.

Culver Blvd.

PACIFIC OCEAN

⑨ 9

⑪ 11

⑩ 10

90

Loyola Marymount University

0 ———— 2 mi
0 ———— 2 km

W. Manchester Ave.

⑫ 12

✈ LAX

Ambrose **2**	Huntley Hotel **3**
Casa del Mar **8**	Loews Santa Monica Beach **5**
Casa Malibu **1**	Marina del Ray Marriott **11**
Custom Hotel **12**	Shutters on the Beach **7**
Georgian **4**	Venice Beach House **10**
Hotel Erwin **9**	Viceroy Santa Monica **6**

> 140: The Casa del Mar in Santa Monica.

Beverly Hills & the Westside

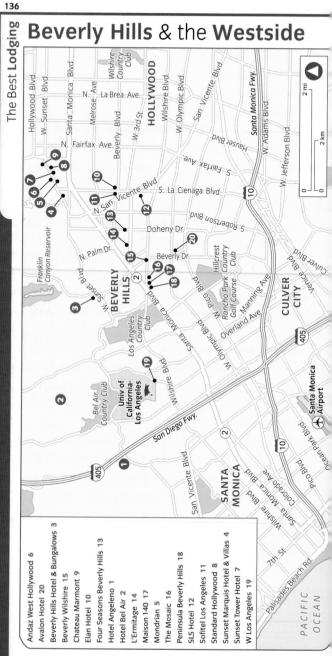

Hollywood

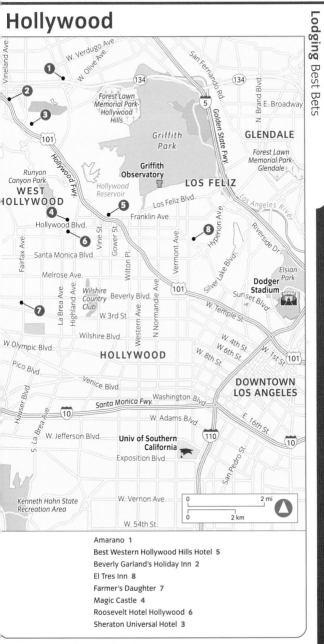

Amarano **1**
Best Western Hollywood Hills Hotel **5**
Beverly Garland's Holiday Inn **2**
El Tres Inn **8**
Farmer's Daughter **7**
Magic Castle **4**
Roosevelt Hotel Hollywood **6**
Sheraton Universal Hotel **3**

Downtown

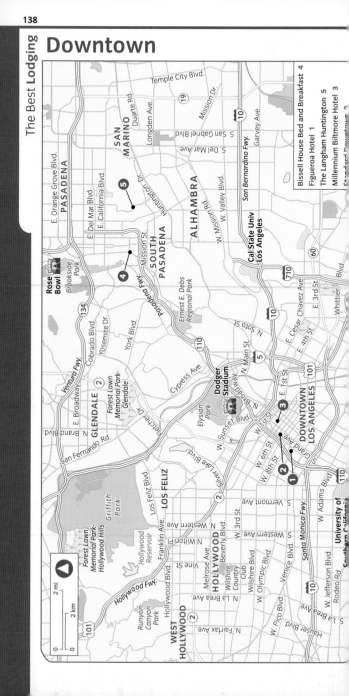

Lodging A to Z

★★ The Ambrose SANTA MONICA This Asian-meets-Craftsman–style hotel in a quiet, residential Santa Monica neighborhood is the "greenest" choice for lodging in the city. A free continental breakfast is provided by Urth Caffe and includes organic fresh fruit and pastries, and Starbucks fair-trade coffee. Other perks: free parking, unlimited Wi-Fi, and Aveda bath products. *1255 20th St. (btwn Wilshire Blvd. & Arizona Ave.).* ☎ *310/315-1555. www.ambrose hotel.com. 77 units. Doubles $225–$259. AE, DISC, MC, V. Map p 135.*

★ Andaz West Hollywood WEST HOLLYWOOD This is the infamous "Riot Hyatt" where rock 'n' roll will never die, although it will get older and more sophisticated, with sedate decor, and a refined restaurant featuring French-inspired cuisine and master mixologists behind the bar. Check out the views of the Strip and beyond from the rooftop pool. *8401 Sunset Blvd. (at Kings Rd.).* ☎ *323/656-1234. www.westhollywood. hyatt.com. 262 units. Doubles $245–$340. AE, DC, DISC, MC, V. Map p 136.*

★★ Avalon Hotel BEVERLY HILLS Formerly the apartments of starlets such as Marilyn Monroe, the building has been redone in a winking '50s style with designer accessories (Charles Eames, George Nelson). The pool courtyard is a groovy scene; if you seek peace and quiet, ask for a room in the Canon building across the street. *9400 W. Olympic Blvd. (at S. Canon Dr.).* ☎ *310/277-5221. www.avalonbeverlyhills.com. 84 units. Doubles $280–$320. AE, DC, MC, V. Map p 136.*

★ Best Western Hollywood Hills Hotel HOLLYWOOD All the contemporary-style rooms feature a fridge, a microwave, and Wi-Fi. Downstairs is the 101 Coffee Shop, typically packed with scruffy hipsters. Hollywood is a short walk, and a Metro Line stop is 3 blocks away. *6141 Franklin Ave. (btwn N. Gower St. & Argyle Ave.).* ☎ *323/464-5181. www.bestwesterncalifornia.com. 84 units. Doubles $116–$149. AE, DISC, MC, V. Map p 137.*

kids Beverly Garland's Holiday Inn UNIVERSAL CITY A pool, tennis courts, free Wi-Fi, friendly staff, easy freeway access, and a free shuttle to Universal Studios make this a great option for families. *4222 Vineland Ave. (at Hwy. 101).* ☎ *818/980-8000. www.beverlygarland.com.*

The pool at the Avalon Hotel.

255 units. Doubles $159–$209. AE, MC, V. Map p 137.

★★★ Beverly Hills Hotel & Bungalows BEVERLY HILLS The legendary "Pink Palace" opened in 1912 and still retains its golden-age glamour, ritziness, impeccable service, and that famous pink facade, which was immortalized on the cover of the Eagles' album *Hotel California*. *9641 Sunset Blvd. (at Beverly Dr.).* ☎ 310/276-2251. *www. thebeverlyhillshotel.com. 204 units. Doubles $480–$590. AE, DC, DISC, MC, V. Map p 136.*

★★★ Beverly Wilshire BEVERLY HILLS Directly across from Rodeo Drive stands this swanky, Four Seasons–managed hotel, originally built in 1928. The hotel's restaurant— Wolfgang Puck's hit steakhouse, CUT—is a major celebrity magnet. *9500 Wilshire Blvd. (at Beverly Dr.).* ☎ 310/275-5200. *www.fourseasons. com/beverlywilshire. 395 units. Doubles $395–$575. AE, DC, DISC, MC, V. Map p 136.*

★ Bissell House Bed and Breakfast PASADENA Set in a historic and architecturally rich neighborhood, this restored, antiques-filled Victorian built in 1887 is a comfy and cozy alternative to the typical L.A. hotel experience. *201 Orange*

The iconic sign of the Beverly Hills Hotel.

Grove Ave. (at Columbia St.). ☎ 626/441-3535. *www.bissellhouse.com. 5 units. Doubles $195–$350. AE, MC, V. Map p 138.*

★★★ Casa del Mar SANTA MONICA This resort hotel recaptures the glamour of its past as a 1920s beach club, with a rooftop pool and a sumptuous, velvet-draped lobby. Rooms offer ocean views, chaise longues, and large, white-marble bathrooms with whirlpool tubs and Murad products. *1910 Ocean Way (at Pico Blvd.).* ☎ 310/581-5533. *www.hotelcasadelmar.com. 129 units. Doubles $365–$630. AE, DC, DISC, MC, V. Map p 135.*

★ Casa Malibu Inn MALIBU Book well in advance to snag these simple and clean beachfront digs that won't blow your budget. *22752 Pacific Coast Hwy. (at Sweetwater Canyon Dr.).* ☎ 310/456-2219. *21 units. Doubles $129–$299. AE, MC, V. Map p 135.*

★★ Channel Road Inn SANTA MONICA This warm, well-run B&B in a 1910 colonial revival house boasts beautiful rooms—each with a private bath—a hillside hot tub, and an ideal location that's only a short walk to Will Rogers State Beach. *219 W. Channel Rd.* ☎ 310/459-1920. *www.channelroadinn. com. 15 units. Doubles $225–$365; includes full breakfast & afternoon tea. AE, MC, V.*

★★★ Chateau Marmont WEST HOLLYWOOD Built in 1927 in the mold of a Loire Valley castle, this landmark hotel prides itself on its exclusivity and privacy, which is probably why so many celebrities feel comfortable misbehaving here. The rooms, suites, cottages, and bungalows are individually decorated (Gothic, Arts and Crafts, midcentury, Spanish), but all bask in the glow of Hollywood's golden era. *8221 Sunset Blvd. (at Havenhurst Dr.).*

The eclectic and elegant lobby of the Chateau Marmont.

☎ 323/656-1010. www.chateau marmont.com. 63 units. Doubles $370–$480. AE, DC, MC, V. Map p 136.

★ **Custom Hotel** AIRPORT This budget option near LAX draws a young crowd (but not too young—no kids allowed) with its reasonable rates, quirky decor—dog portrait bedspreads, flock of sheep dolls in the lobby—and DJ-fueled pool parties in the summer. *8639 Lincoln Blvd. (at Manchester Ave.).* ☎ 310/645-0400. www.customhotel.com. 250 units. Doubles $100–$210. AE, DC, DISC, MC, V. Map p 135.

★★★ **kids** **Disney's Grand Californian Hotel & Spa** DISNEY-LAND The grand lobby will wow you with its massive stone hearth, soaring ceiling with skylights and exposed beams, and Arts and Crafts–style fixtures and furniture. Request a room (all are spacious and comfy) with a view of Disney's California Adventure park. *1600 S. Disneyland Dr.* ☎ 714/635-2300. www.disneyland.com. 745 units. Doubles $260–$390. AE, DC, DISC, MC, V.

★ **Elan Hotel** WEST HOLLYWOOD This small, clean, modern, and perfectly located boutique hotel does the little things to keep its campers happy; there's complimentary wine and cheese in the afternoons and free Wi-Fi throughout the hotel. *8435 Beverly Blvd. (at N. Croft Ave.).*

☎ 323/658-6663. www.elanhotel.com. 49 units. Doubles from $155–$269. AE, DC, MC, V. Map p 136.

★ **El Tres Inn** SILVER LAKE This recent (and sorely needed) addition to the Eastside offers funky-chic suites—basically small apartments—with handy kitchenettes, living rooms, Mexican folk art, 52-inch flatscreens, iPod speaker docks, and coolest of all, turntables stocked with groovy vinyl. *4439 Sunset Blvd. (above El Chavo Restaurant).* ☎ 323/666-6351. www.eltresinn.com. 3 units. Suites $175–$225. AE, MC, V. Map p 137.

For luxurious digs near Disneyland, book a room at Disney's Grand Californian Hotel & Spa. Photo © Disney Enterprises, Inc.

Dark woods and warm colors characterize the rooms at the Figueroa Hotel.

★ **Farmer's Daughter** WEST HOLLYWOOD   You can't help but smile at this budget motel's crazy-cowpoke style: plaid curtains, denim bedspreads, thrift-store art, a recurring rooster motif, and a better-than-average supply of rusty pitchforks. And boy howdy—it's right across from the Farmers Market and CBS Television Center, where many guests try out for *The Price Is Right*. *115 S. Fairfax Ave. (at W. First St.).* ☎ *323/937-3930. www.farmersdaughterhotel. com. 66 units. Doubles $175–$255. AE, DISC, MC, V. Map p 137.*

★ **Figueroa Hotel** DOWNTOWN Downtown adventurers might enjoy this moderately priced hotel with eclectic, exotic decor such as Moroccan chandeliers, Indian fabrics, Mexican tiles, and hand-woven Afghani kilims. A pool and patio bar complete the urban oasis. *939 S. Figueroa St. (at Olympic Blvd.).* ☎ *213/627-8971. www.figueroahotel.com. 285 units.*

Doubles $144–$205. AE, DC, MC, V. Map p 138.

★★★ **Four Seasons Beverly Hills** BEVERLY HILLS   Fabulousness and impeccable service in Beverly Hills—this is for those who are living the dream, baby. The hotel caters to the entertainment industry, and a stay here practically guarantees a celeb sighting. *300 S. Doheny Dr. (at Burton Way).* ☎ *800/332-3442. www.fourseasons.com/beverly wilshire. 285 units. Doubles $385–$450. AE, DC, DISC, MC, V. Map p 136.*

★★ **Georgian** SANTA MONICA This Art Deco masterpiece facing Santa Monica beach combines a lot of luxury and a bit of history—during Prohibition Bugsy Siegel opened a speakeasy in the hotel's basement. *1415 Ocean Ave. (btwn Santa Monica Blvd. & Broadway).* ☎ *800/538-8147 or 310/395-9945. www. georgianhotel.com. 84 units. Doubles $220–$265. AE, DC, DISC, MC, V. Map p 135.*

★★ **Hollywood Roosevelt Hotel** HOLLYWOOD   This hotel, site of the first Academy Awards in 1929, has been restored to its former glory—just ask the ghost of Montgomery Clift, who some say still haunts the building. Teddy's nightclub, the Library Lounge, and the Tropicana

Kick back and relax at the pool at the Four Seasons Beverly Hills.

The ultramodern lobby of the Huntley Hotel.

poolside bar draw throngs of young partiers. *7000 Hollywood Blvd. (at N. Orange Dr.).* ☎ *800/950-7667 or 323/ 466-7000. www.hollywoodroosevelt. com. 302 units. Doubles $230–$316. AE, DC, DISC, MC, V. Map p 137.*

★ **Hotel Amarano** BURBANK This sleek boutique hotel is an excellent choice for valley accommodations. With a business center, meeting spaces, and high-speed Wi-Fi, it's especially appealing for guests who may be mixing business with pleasure. *322 N. Pass Ave. (btwn W. Oak & 134 Fwy.).* ☎ *818/ 842-8887. www.hotelamarano.com. 100 units. Doubles $185–$299. AE, DISC, MC, V. Map p 137.*

★ **Hotel Angeleno** WESTSIDE In a can't-miss-it circular tower that looms over the 405 freeway, this friendly boutique hotel offers pie-shaped rooms with balconies and modern yet casual decor. A complimentary car service can zip you over to the Getty Center, UCLA, or other nearby attractions. *170 N. Church Lane (at I-405 & Sunset Blvd.).* ☎ *866/264-3536 or 310/476-6411. www.hotelangeleno.com. 209 units. Doubles $159–$239. AE, DC, DISC, MC, V. Map p 136.*

★★★ **Hotel Bel-Air** BEL-AIR Pink stucco buildings are nestled among 12 tranquil acres with manicured gardens, canopies of bougainvillea, old-as-dirt sycamores and live oaks,

fragrant flowers, and a swan lake. In late 2009 the one-of-a-kind hotel began a massive multiyear renovation to update rooms and add a 12,000-square-foot spa as well as additional villas. *701 Stone Canyon Rd. (north of Sunset Blvd.).* ☎ *800/648-4097 or 310/472-1211. www.hotel belair.com. 91 units. Doubles $485–$600. AE, DC, DISC, MC, V. Map p 136.*

★ **Hotel Erwin** VENICE For travelers determined to experience the human zoo that is Venice Beach, the best option may be this colorful boutique hotel located just off the boardwalk. Amenities may be light, but there's a relaxing rooftop lounge that overlooks the ocean. *1697 Pacific Ave. (at 17th Ave.).* ☎ *800/786-7789 or 310/452-1111. www.joiedevivre. com. 88 units. Doubles $229–$309. AE, DC, DISC, MC, V. Map p 135.*

★★ **Huntley Hotel** SANTA MONICA Bed down in postmodern coolness at this hotel close to the beach and prime Santa Monica shopping. It may be worth a stay just to score a white-leather seat at the white-hot bar, the Penthouse. *1111 Second St. (at California Ave.).* ☎ *310/394-5454. www.thehuntleyhotel.com. 209 units. Doubles $215–$399. AE, DISC, MC, V. Map p 135.*

★★★ **The Langham Huntington** PASADENA Set on 23 acres among lush gardens in the foothills of the San Gabriel Mountains, this

The Ritz-Carlton Huntington in Pasadena is now the Langham Huntington.

beautiful hotel, built in 1906, makes a great base for exploring downtown L.A., as well as the museums and architectural homes of Pasadena. The Terrace Restaurant offers a wonderful, relaxed Sunday brunch. *1401 S. Oak Knoll Ave. (at Hillcrest Ave.).* ☎ *626/568-3900. www.pasadena.langhamhotels.com. 380 units. Doubles $279–$399. AE, DC, MC, V. Map p 138.*

★★★ **L'Ermitage** BEVERLY HILLS The Asian-influenced rooms are huge, luxurious, and serene, with marble bathrooms and platform beds with bedside controls for lighting and climate. The work desks are actually for working—each is outfitted with a printer/copier/scanner— and the hotel will even provide you with free personalized business cards and stationery. *9291 Burton Way, at N. Foothill Rd.* ☎ *800/800-2113 or 310/278-3344. www.raffles. com. 119 units. Doubles $380–$575. AE, DC, DISC, MC, V. Map p 136.*

★★ **kids Loews Santa Monica Beach** SANTA MONICA   Kids and pets receive special attention, and adults love the palm tree–lined lobby, ocean views, heated pool, spa and fitness center, and easy access to Santa Monica Pier and Third Street Promenade. *1700 Ocean Ave., at Colorado Ave.* ☎ *800/235-6397 or 310/458-6700. www.santamonicaloewshotel.com.*

342 units. Doubles $349–$479. AE, DC, DISC, MC, V. Map p 135.

kids Magic Castle HOLLYWOOD Walkable to Hollywood Boulevard and a Red Line stop, this apartment complex turned motel offers large, sparsely designed rooms, most with fully equipped kitchens. *7025 Franklin Ave. (btwn Highland & La Brea aves.).* ☎ *800/741-4915 or 323/851-0800. www.magiccastlehotel.com. 40 units. Doubles $150–$236. AE, DC, DISC, MC, V. Map p 137.*

★★ **Maison 140** BEVERLY HILLS Originally a boarding house owned by Lillian Gish, this superchic boutique hotel blends elements that are French, Far East, and far out. Stroll nearby Rodeo Drive and then cozy up in the dark and velvety Bar Noir, the trystiest hotel bar around. *140 S. Lasky Dr. (btwn Wilshire & Charleville blvds.).* ☎ *800/670-6182 or 310/281-4000. www.maison140beverly hills.com. 43 units. Doubles $225–$275. AE, DC, MC, V. Map p 136.*

★ **Millennium Biltmore Hotel** DOWNTOWN   Architecture lovers should consider a stay at this 1923 historic landmark for its stunning lobby, halls, and ballrooms, which have been used for Oscar ceremonies, JFK's 1960 DNC

A guest room at Maison 140.

headquarters, and, of course, movie locations (Ghostbusters, Beverly Hills Cop). The rooms, while elegant, are rather small. *506 S. Grand Ave. (at W. Fifth St.).* ☎ *213/624-1011. www.millenniumhotels.com. 683 units. Doubles $159–$375. AE, DC, DISC, MC, V. Map p 138.*

★ **Mondrian** WEST HOLLYWOOD This stylish white-on-white high-rise is best known for its poolside bar, the exclusive Skybar, which maintains its status as one of Hollywood's hottest see-and-be-seen scenes. A $20-million renovation has spruced up the rooms. *8440 W. Sunset Blvd. (at Queens Rd.).* ☎ *800/606-6090 or 323/650-8999. www.mondrianhotel.com. 237 units. Doubles $305–$405. AE, DC, DISC, MC, V. Map p 136.*

★★ **Mosaic Hotel** BEVERLY HILLS This small but seriously swanky hotel charms with its soothing decor, high-end amenities, and no-attitude service, and rates are a mite more reasonable than other luxury digs in Beverly Hills. *125 S. Spalding Dr.* ☎ *800/463-4466 or 310/278-0303. www.mosaichotel. com. 49 units. Doubles $285–$520. AE, DC, MC, V. Map p 136.*

★★★ **The Peninsula Beverly Hills** BEVERLY HILLS You'll get an opulent, European-style room and flawless service if you can fork out the cash to luxuriate in this garden-like oasis, arguably the finest hotel in the city. Be pampered at the world-class Peninsula Spa or enjoy a private cabana at the rooftop pool. *9882 S. Santa Monica Blvd. (at Wilshire Blvd.).* ☎ *800/462-7899 or 310/551-2888. www.peninsula.com. 196 units. Doubles $395–$555. AE, DC, DISC, MC, V. Map p 136.*

★ **kids Sheraton Universal Hotel** UNIVERSAL STUDIOS Convenience and location make this a popular choice for families eager to hit Universal Studios, Warner Bros. Studios, or Hollywood. *333 Universal Hollywood Dr., at Lankershim Blvd.* ☎ *800/325-3535 or 818/980-1212. www.sheraton.com/universal. 451 units. Doubles $208–$289. AE, DC, DISC, MC, V. Map p 137.*

★★★ **Shutters on the Beach** SANTA MONICA This shingled building on the sand combines the luxury of a fine hotel with the breeziness of a beach cottage. Watch the sun set on the ocean from your own private balcony. *1 Pico Blvd. (at Neilson Way).* ☎ *800/334-9000 or 310/458-0030. www.shuttersonthe beach.com. 198 units. Doubles $395–$575. AE, DC, DISC, MC, V. Map p 135.*

★★ **SLS Hotel** BEVERLY HILLS The first luxury hotel from relentless nightlife impresario Sam Nazarian buzzes with energy. Philippe Starck spearheaded the design, both sophisticated and over-the-top, mixing clean lines and muted tones with larky elements like a mounted glass deer head. *465 S. La Cienega Blvd. (btwn Colgate Ave & Clifton Way).* ☎ *310/274-7777. www.sls hotels.com. 297 units. Doubles $169–$350. AE, DC, DISC, MC, V. Map p 136.*

★ **Sofitel Los Angeles** WEST HOLLYWOOD This hotel offers slick elegance and easy access to oodles of shopping—Beverly Center, Third Street, Robertson Boulevard. Slip into the hotel's trendy Stone Rose Lounge for a late-night cocktail. *8555 Beverly Blvd., at La Cienega Blvd.* ☎ *310/278-5444. www.sofitella.com. 295 units. Doubles $270–$345. AE, DC, DISC, MC, V. Map p 136.*

★ **Standard Downtown** DOWNTOWN Accommodations are cheeky and modern, but you come here to groove at the retro-style rooftop pool and bar, with its red pod beds and skyscraper views. *550 S. Flower St. (btwn W. Fifth & W. Sixth sts.).* ☎ *213/892-8080. www. standardhotel.com. 205 units. Doubles $245–$285. AE, DC, DISC, MC, V. Map p 138.*

★ **Standard Hollywood** HOLLYWOOD The vibe is "motel as pop art." In the lobby you'll find bubble chairs dangling over shag carpeting, beanbag pod chairs, and a hot chick lounging in a glass display behind the check-in desk. Rooms can get loud when a party's pumping poolside, which is nearly always. *8300 Sunset Blvd., at Sweetzer Ave.* ☎ *323/650-9090. www.standardhotel.com. 139 units. Doubles $165–$295. AE, DC, DISC, MC, V. Map p 136.*

★★ **Sunset Marquis Hotel & Villas** WEST HOLLYWOOD A Mediterranean oasis off the Sunset Strip, this all-suite hotel has long catered to the high-profile musician crowd (Stones, U2, Eminem); there's even a state-of-the-art recording studio in the basement. The Bar 1200 can be impossible to get into, unless you're a hotel guest or famous, or both. *1200 Alta Loma Rd. (btwn Sunset Blvd. & Halloway Dr.).* ☎ *310/657-1333. www.sunsetmarquis hotel.com. 114 units. Doubles $345–$530. AE, DC, DISC, MC, V. Map p 136.*

★★ **Sunset Tower Hotel** WEST HOLLYWOOD A 1929 Art Deco landmark that has seen tenants such as Frank Sinatra, Marilyn Monroe, and Howard Hughes, this hotel takes a straight-faced look back at Hollywood's heyday, and presents a grown-up's version of the Sunset Strip. Rooms have views, comfortable beds, and Kiehl's toiletries. *8358 W. Sunset Blvd. (btwn Crescent Heights & La Cienega blvds.).* ☎ *323/654-7100. www.sunsettowerhotel.com. 74*

units. *Doubles $225–$325. AE, DISC, MC, V. Map p 136.*

★ **Venice Beach House** VENICE No designer decor, no high-end amenities, but most importantly, no attitude—this charming B&B occupies a historic Craftsman bungalow just a block from Venice Beach. Half of the rooms have private bathrooms. *15 30th Ave. (at Speedway).* ☎ *310/823-1966. www.venicebeach house.com. 9 units, 5 with private bathroom. Doubles $145–$235. AE, MC, V. Map p 135.*

★★ **Viceroy Santa Monica** SANTA MONICA This glamorous retreat features what I'd call groovy-colonialism decor, two outdoor pools with swank cabanas, and the destination bar Cameo. *1819 Ocean Ave. (at Pico Blvd.).* ☎ *800/670-6185 or 310/260-7500. www.viceroysanta monica.com. 162 units. Doubles $340–$415. AE, DC, DISC, MC, V. Map p 135.*

★ **W Los Angeles** WESTWOOD This sleek, all-suite hotel near UCLA makes a good base for exploring the Westside. Enjoy WET, the heated outdoor pool ringed by chaise longues and cabanas. During the summer, movies screen poolside. *930 Hilgard Ave. (at Le Conte Ave.).* ☎ *800/W-HOTELS (946-8357) or 310/208-8765. www.starwood.com/ whotels. 258 units. Doubles from $299. AE, DC, DISC, MC, V. Map p 136.* ●

A guest room at the W Los Angeles.

10 The Best Day Trips & Excursions

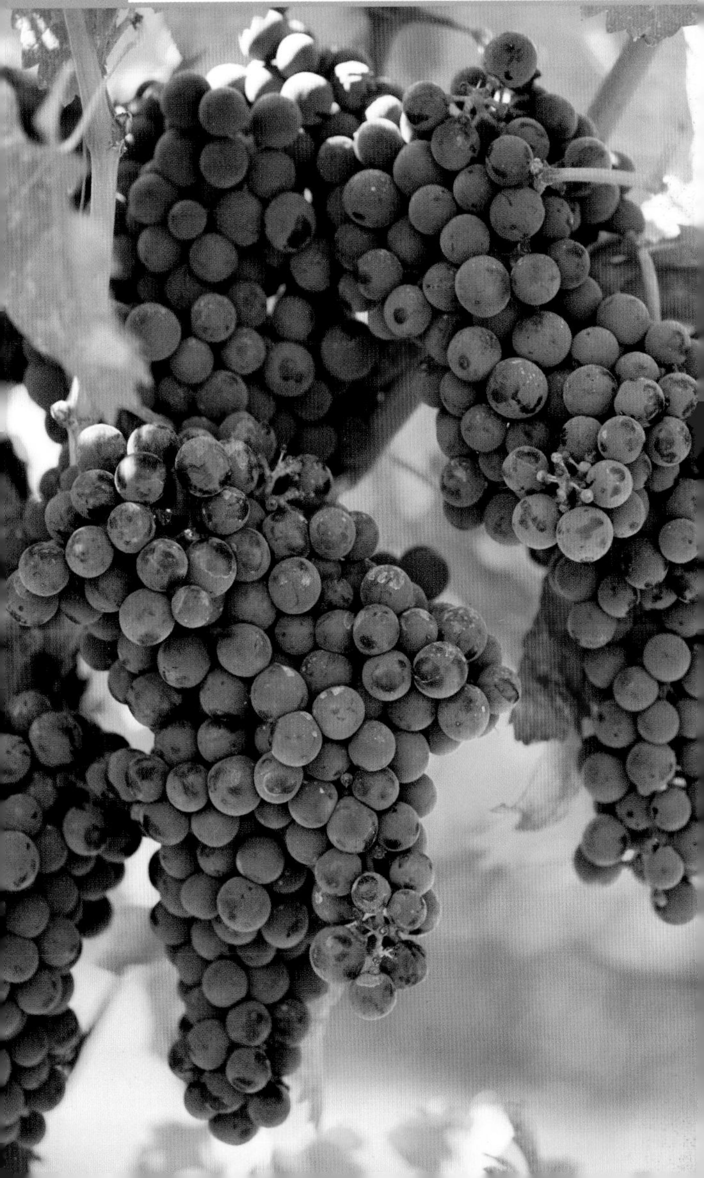

Disneyland Resort

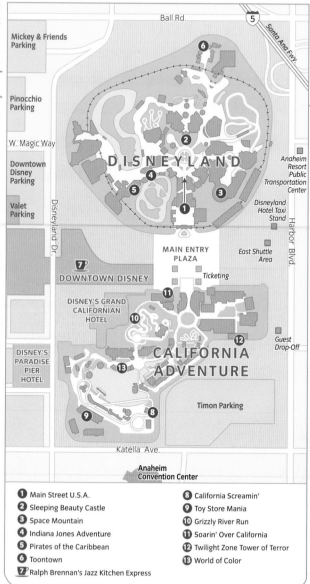

Ball Rd.

5

Santa Ana Fwy.

Mickey & Friends Parking

6

Pinocchio Parking

W. Magic Way

DISNEYLAND

2

Downtown Disney Parking

4

Valet Parking

5

3

1

Anaheim Resort Public Transportation Center

Disneyland Hotel Taxi Stand

Disneyland Dr.

MAIN ENTRY PLAZA

East Shuttle Area

7 DOWNTOWN DISNEY

Ticketing

11

DISNEY'S GRAND CALIFORNIAN HOTEL

10

12

Guest Drop-Off

DISNEY'S PARADISE PIER HOTEL

CALIFORNIA ADVENTURE

13

Harbor Blvd.

9

8

Timon Parking

Katella Ave.

Anaheim Convention Center

1 Main Street U.S.A.
2 Sleeping Beauty Castle
3 Space Mountain
4 Indiana Jones Adventure
5 Pirates of the Caribbean
6 Toontown
7 Ralph Brennan's Jazz Kitchen Express

8 California Screamin'
9 Toy Store Mania
10 Grizzly River Run
11 Soarin' Over California
12 Twilight Zone Tower of Terror
13 World of Color

Previous page: Grapes on the vine in the Santa Ynez Wine Country.

In 1955, Walt Disney unveiled his whimsical amusement park, ★★★ **Disneyland,** featuring 18 attractions spread across 160 acres surrounded by orange groves. Today it's a Californian icon and a mandatory stop for fun-seeking families. **Disneyland Resort** encompasses the original park, called the "Happiest Place on Earth"; ★★ **Disney's California Adventure,** a thrill-driven theme park added in 2001 as an homage to the Golden State; three Disney hotels; and **Downtown Disney,** a shopping, eating, and entertainment complex.

① ★ **Main Street U.S.A.** An idealization of small-town America at the turn of the 20th century, Main Street takes you back to an innocent time of ice-cream parlors, barber-shop quartets, horse-drawn trolleys, and shiny fire engines. Above the firehouse (but not available to the public) is the room where Walt often stayed during the park's construction; it remains fully furnished with a lamp in the front window that shines eternally as a tribute. *Entrance, Disneyland.*

② ★ **Sleeping Beauty Castle.** Modeled after Bavaria's romantic Schloss Neuschwanstein, the turreted, 77-foot-tall castle appears even grander due to the forced perspective of its architecture, which tricks the eye, especially from a distance. One of the spires is deliberately missing a small patch of

gold-leaf, per instructions from Walt, who never wanted to think of the park as complete. The castle is one of the park's original 17 attractions. *Entrance to Fantasyland, Disneyland.*

③ ★★ **Space Mountain.** The pitch-blackness of outer space denies the power of sight, but this roller coaster—the park's most adrenaline-pumping ride, around since 1977—is an assault on the rest of your senses. *Tomorrowland, Disneyland.*

④ ★★★ **Indiana Jones Adventure.** Showcasing some of the park's best special effects, this rumble-tumble ride dodges arrows, explosions, snakes, and collapsing bridges, illustrating that archaeology is not the safest choice of professions. The tumbling boulder gets me every time. *Adventureland, Disneyland.*

The grand turreted castle marks the entrance to Fantasyland at Disneyland.

⑤ ★★ Pirates of the Caribbean. With the success of the three *Pirates of the Caribbean* movies, this richly detailed ride has been upgraded with new special effects, story elements, voices, and an animated version of Johnny Depp's character, Captain Jack Sparrow. Thankfully, the off-putting display of lascivious pirates chasing "wenches" has been cut. *New Orleans Sq., Disneyland.*

⑥ ★ Toontown. This part of the park—inspired by *Who Framed Roger Rabbit*—is meant to look as though you tripped into a cartoon: Everything is bright and poofy, and you can't find a straight line (or a straight face) anywhere. Little kids love meeting Mickey or Goofy, and romping around the playground. *Toontown, Disneyland.*

⑦ Ralph Brennan's Jazz Kitchen Express. The tastiest snack option in Downtown Disney is this Big Easy–themed restaurant, where you can chow down on Cajun-style po' boys, crab cakes, fried catfish, jambalaya, and authentic New Orleans desserts like beignets and bread pudding. *1590 S. Disneyland Dr., Downtown Disney.* ☎ 714/776-5200. www.rbjazz kitchen.com. *Items $5–$10.*

⑧ ★★ California Screamin'. Paradise Pier evokes the great beachfront amusement parks of yesteryear such as Santa Monica or Venice. This classic roller coaster, one of the fastest rides in either park, does a vertical loop along the outline of Mickey's head. *Paradise Pier, Disney's California Adventure.*

⑨ ★★ Toy Story Mania! Don your 3-D glasses, and ride through a virtual midway of booths with interactive *Toy Story* characters. Use the toy cannon on your vehicle to toss rings, throw pies, and shoot darts at your targets. *Paradise Pier, Disney's California Adventure.*

⑩ ★ Grizzly River Run. Every amusement park needs a ride to cool you down on a hot day, right? This white-water-raft trip around Grizzly Peak—the bear-shaped mountain is the park's centerpiece—splashes through mine shafts and caves before dropping your raft down a geyser-filled gorge. *Grizzly Peak Recreation Area, Golden State, Disney's California Adventure.*

⑪ ★★★ Soarin' Over California. Rush over to this virtual ride, a state-of-the-art simulation of a hang-glider ride over the best parts of the state. Wheeee, there's Yosemite! And thanks to special olfactory effects, you'll smell those pines and oranges

Need to cool off? Head straight for Grizzly River Run. Photo © Disney Enterprises, Inc.

How to Conquer (& Enjoy) Disneyland

The parks get extremely crowded, especially on holidays and summer weekends, so a little preparation and strategy may stave off a lot of frustration. Here are a few tips for maximizing your visit:

1. Purchase tickets online prior to your visit (consider package deals, which can offer substantial discounts). If you have only 1 day and you're determined to see everything, opt for the Park Hopper pass; it costs a little more than the 1-Day 1-Park ticket, but it gets you into both parks.
2. Use the FASTPASS. At popular rides with long lines, you'll find automated FASTPASS machines where you can receive a voucher with a later boarding time (say, an hour or two later) and return at that designated time, then bypass the long line (suckers!) and enter the FASTPASS gate for a much shorter wait.
3. Arrive a half-hour before the gates open.
4. Have a plan; know which attractions you (or more importantly, your kids) most want to see.
5. Go against the grain—take advantage during mealtimes or parades, when lines may be shorter.
6. Stay at the resort (or nearby), and follow the schedule perfected by wily veterans of the park—hit as much as possible as early as possible, retreat in the afternoon to recharge, then return with renewed vigor for the evening festivities.

Oh, and remember: You're having fun!

1313 S. Harbor Blvd., Anaheim. ☎ *714/781-4565. www.disneyland.com. 1-Day 1-Park: $72 adults & kids 10 & up; $62 kids 3–9. 1-Day Park Hopper: $97 adults & kids 10 & up; $87 kids 3–9. Free for kids 2 & under.*

as you fly by. *Condor Flats, Golden State, Disney's California Adventure.*

⑫ ★★ The Twilight Zone Tower of Terror. So, does it sound like fun to plummet down an abandoned elevator shaft in the creepy Hollywood Tower Hotel, the tallest building in the entire resort? The *Twilight Zone* tidbits make the buildup to the heart-stopping climax excruciatingly tense. *Hollywood Pictures Backlot, California Adventure.*

⑬ ★★★ World of Color. This nighttime extravaganza is a dazzling display of music, light, color, fire, animation, and water. Some 1,200 individually controlled fountains are coordinated to create spectacular

flowing shapes, and sheets of mist form a multilayered movie screen for animated clips. *Paradise Park, Disney's California Adventure.*

Thrill-seekers will love The Twilight Zone Tower of Terror. Photo © Disney Enterprises, Inc.

Santa Catalina Island

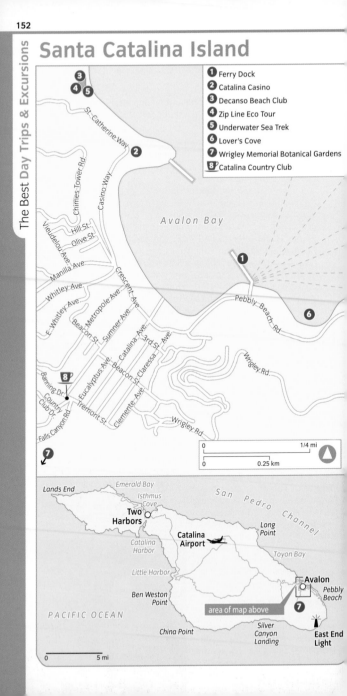

1 Ferry Dock
2 Catalina Casino
3 Decanso Beach Club
4 Zip Line Eco Tour
5 Underwater Sea Trek
6 Lover's Cove
7 Wrigley Memorial Botanical Gardens
8 Catalina Country Club

Only 22 miles off the California coast (and still in L.A. County), this rugged island feels like another world—unspoiled land, clean air, crystal-clear waters, and, except for the golf carts, no traffic. Chewing-gum magnate William Wrigley, Jr., purchased the island in 1919 as a remote playground for the exploding population of southern California; today a nonprofit foundation, the Catalina Island Conservancy, owns 88% of the island and is committed to protecting its natural resources.

1 Getting There. If you feel like splurging, take a 15-minute helicopter ride over the water and touch down at the helipad near Avalon, the island's only city. The thrilling jaunt provides amazing views of the coastline, and along the way you might spot some whales and dolphins. From 8am until sunset ★★★ **Island Express helicopters** fly out of San Pedro and Long Beach (near the *Queen Mary*). Not recommended for kids or the severely skittish. Most folks opt for the ★ **Catalina Express ferry,** an hour-long ride also departing from San Pedro and Long Beach. Because you'll be taking a round-trip, you can try both air and sea travel. *Island Express helicopters:* ☎ 310/510-2525. *www.island express.com. $86 1-way; round-trip $164. Reservations required. Catalina Express ferry: Long Beach, San Pedro & Dana Point.* ☎ 800/481-3470. *www.catalinaexpress.com. Approximately 30 daily departures. One-way: $33.25 adults, $30 seniors, $25.50 children; round-trip: $66.50 adults, $60 seniors, $51 children. Reservations required.*

2 ★ Catalina Casino. On landing, make for the distinct round building that dominates the bay. This Moorish-style palace was erected in 1929 as an entertainment destination (no, not gambling) where big-band legends such as Benny Goodman used to pack in crowds at the **Casino Ballroom** in the '30s and '40s. There's also a glamorous, Art Deco movie house, the **Avalon Theatre,** and the **Catalina Island Museum,** which illustrates 7,000 years of island history. The best way to experience the casino is a 50-minute tour

Boats anchored in the Santa Catalina harbor in Avalon.

Catalina's Wild Side: Two Harbors

If you want to get a better look at the rugged natural beauty of Catalina and escape the throngs of beachgoers, head over to **Two Harbors,** the quarter-mile "neck" at the island's northwest end that gets its name from the "twin harbors" on each side, known as the Isthmus and Catalina Harbor. An excellent starting point for campers and hikers, Two Harbors also offers just enough civilization for the less-intrepid traveler.

The **Banning House Lodge** (☎ 800/626-1496; www.visittwo harbors.com) is a 12-room bed-and-breakfast overlooking the isthmus. The clapboard house was built in 1910 for Catalina's pre-Wrigley owners and has seen duty as on-location lodging for movie stars like Errol Flynn and Dorothy Lamour. Peaceful and isolated, the simply furnished but comfortable lodge has spectacular views of both harbors.

Everyone chows at **The Harbor Reef Restaurant** (☎ 310/510-4215), on the beach. This nautical, tropical-themed saloon/restaurant serves breakfast, lunch, and dinner, the latter consisting of hearty steaks, ribs, freshly caught swordfish, and buffalo burgers in summer. Be sure to try the saloon's potent house drink, the "buffalo milk." One word of advice: It's not buffalo milk.

The waters in Lover's Cove are a snorkeler's paradise.

1 Casino Way, Avalon. (☎ 310/510-8687; 2pm daily; $17.50 adults, $15.75 seniors, $13.25 kids).

❸ ★ **Descanso Beach Club.** Located around the point from the casino, this cozy beach cove is a relaxing place to enjoy a cocktail in the sun, especially if you spring for a private cabana ($125 per day). Stop by the activity center to sign up for various adventures (kayaking, stand-up paddle-boarding, as well as ❹ and ❺) and island tours such as the Flying Fish Boat Trip or the Cape Canyon Tour. ☎ 310/510-7410. www.visitcatalinaisland.com. Beach admission $2. Open late spring through mid-Oct.

❹ ★★ **Zip Line Eco Tour.** Starting in the hills above Avalon, you'll make five adrenaline-filled "runs" (or "zips") through Descanso Canyon on a zip line 300 feet above the canyon floor. ⏱ *2 hr. including orientation.* ☎ *800/626-1496. $92.50.*

5 ★ Underwater Sea Trek. Explore Catalina's kelp forests and pristine marine environment by diving 20 feet underwater using a technique called "Snuba," an easy-to-master hybrid of snorkeling and scuba diving. You may even spot a stray bat ray or octopus. ⏱ *1½ hr.* ☎ *800/626-1496. $69. Ages 12 & up only.*

6 ★★ Lover's Cove. Enjoy snorkeling in these clear, shallow waters, an ideal spot for observing the rich marine life—spotted calico bass; opaleye; and the not-shy, neon-orange garibaldi. **Catalina Snorkeling Adventures** (☎ 877/766-7535; www.catalinasnorkelscuba.com) can rent you all the gear necessary to explore the cove; they also conduct 1½-hour marine eco-tours ($39 per person; reservations required). *Lover's Cove Marine Preserve, southeast of the harbor.*

7 ★ Wrigley Memorial & Botanical Gardens. Head up into Avalon Canyon to see the Romanesque Wrigley Memorial (the views from the tower are splendid) and a 37-acre garden of rare desert plants, many of which are endemic to Catalina. *1400 Avalon Canyon Rd.* ☎ *310/510-2288. Admission $5 adults; free for kids under 13. Daily 8am–5pm.*

8 ★★ Catalina Country Club. The spring-training clubhouse of the Chicago Cubs from 1921 to 1951, this elegant Mission-style building is now the island's best restaurant for fine dining. *1 Country Club Dr., Avalon.* ☎ *310/510-7404. Reservations recommended. Entrees $10–$34 dinner. Lunch & dinner daily. AE, DISC, MC, V.*

The elegant dining room at the Catalina Country Club.

Palm Springs

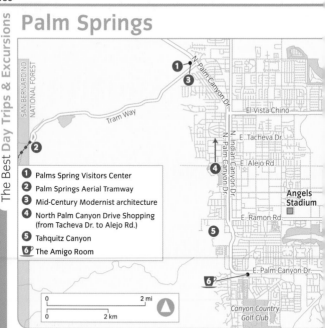

- **1** Palms Spring Visitors Center
- **2** Palm Springs Aerial Tramway
- **3** Mid-Century Modernist architecture
- **4** North Palm Canyon Drive Shopping (from Tacheva Dr. to Alejo Rd.)
- **5** Tahquitz Canyon
- **6** The Amigo Room

Map labels: San Bernardino National Forest, Tram Way, El Vista Chino, N. Palm Canyon Dr., N. Indian Canyon Dr., N. Palm Canyon Dr., E. Tacheva Dr., E. Alejo Rd., Angels Stadium, E. Ramon Rd., E. Palm Canyon Dr., Canyon Country Golf Club

0 — 2 mi / 0 — 2 km

Palm Springs first kicked up dust as a Hollywood getaway in the 1920s, and by the '50s and '60s, serious money—the kind that builds golf courses and architecturally significant second homes—began pouring in. Today this sunny resort town is popular with golf- and tennis-playing retirees, gays and lesbians, and hipsters craving a throwback to the Rat Pack era.

1 ★ **Palm Springs Visitor Center.** Originally designed as a gas station in 1965 by Albert Frey (1903–1998), this Palm Springs landmark is known for its soaring rooflines, which non-laymen call a "hyperbolic paraboloid." Various maps and brochures are available. *2901 N. Palm Canyon Dr., Palm Springs.* ☎ *800/347-7746 or 760/778-8418. www.visitpalmsprings. com. Daily 9am–5pm.*

2 ★★ **Palm Springs Aerial Tramway.** The world's largest tram cars take you on a steep vertical cable ride that climbs 2½ miles

from the dusty desert floor to the alpine forest of Mount San Jacinto. At the Mountain Station, you can take in views (all the way to the Salton Sea) at the observation deck, picnic, eat or grab a drink at either of two restaurants, visit the gift shop, or watch a short film about the tramway. *1 Tram Way, off Hwy. 111, Palm Springs.* ☎ *888/515-TRAM or 760/322-4800. www. pstramway.com. Admission $23 adults, $21 seniors, $16 kids 3–12, free for kids 2 & under. Mon–Fri 10am–8pm; Sat–Sun 8am–8pm.*

Tram runs every 30 min., last tram down at 9:45pm.

③ ★★★ Mid-Century Modernist architecture. For stunning examples of Mid-Century Modernism, specifically of the subgenre known as Desert Modernism, there is no place hotter than Palm Springs. Swing by the visitor center (**①**), buy a map created by the **Palm Springs Modern Committee** (www.ps modcom.com), and take the self-guided tour. Highlights include Richard Neutra's 1946 masterpiece, the **Kaufman Desert House;** John Lautner's imaginative **Elrod House,** which appeared in the James Bond flick *Diamonds Are Forever;* and Bill Krisel's **Elvis Honeymoon Hideaway,** once known as "the House of Tomorrow." If you want to dig a little deeper, consider the 2½-hour tour run by Robert Imber of **PS Modern Tours** (☎ 760/318-6118; psmodern tours@aol.com; reservations recommended; $75 per person, no credit cards).

④ ★ Shopping along North Palm Canyon Drive. Fans of mid-century furniture, art, and design scour boutiques like **Modern Way**

The Amigo Room at the Ace Hotel.

Tahquitz Falls.

(745 N. Palm Canyon Dr.), **Retrospect** (666 N. Palm Canyon Dr.), and **Bon Vivant** (457 N. Palm Canyon Dr.) for treasures such as Eames lounge chairs, chrome and Lucite lamps, starburst clocks, and estate jewelry. *N. Palm Canyon Dr. btwn Tacheva Dr. & Alejo Rd.*

⑤ ★★ Tahquitz Canyon. The Cahuilla people believe the canyon possesses a raw spiritual power, and named it after the guardian spirit of all shamans. The star attraction is the lovely 60-foot **Tahquitz Falls** (seasonal, as it relies on snow melt from Tahquitz Peak), which can be reached by a 2-mile round-trip hike over rocky terrain. *500 W. Mesquite (west of Palm Canyon Dr.), Palm Springs.* ☎ *760/416-7044. www.tahquitzcanyon.com. Admission $13 adults, $6 kids 6–12. Self-guided hiking 7:30am–3:30pm;* ⏱ *2½-hr. ranger-led hikes 8 & 10am, noon, & 2pm.*

⑥ ★ The Amigo Room. Duck into this hipster hangout for creative concoctions like the Figa (fig-infused vodka, Earl Grey, and honey tangerine) or the Facial (muddled cucumber and mint, vodka, and pineapple juice). *At the Ace Hotel, 701 E. Palm Canyon Dr.* ☎ *760/325-9900. www. acehotel.com/palmsprings.*

Santa Barbara

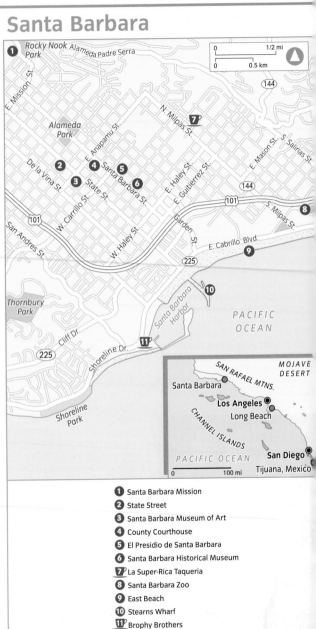

1. Santa Barbara Mission
2. State Street
3. Santa Barbara Museum of Art
4. County Courthouse
5. El Presidio de Santa Barbara
6. Santa Barbara Historical Museum
7. La Super-Rica Taqueria
8. Santa Barbara Zoo
9. East Beach
10. Stearns Wharf
11. Brophy Brothers

T he rugged Santa Ynez Mountains to the north, the sparkling
Pacific Ocean to the south, harmonious Spanish colonial revival
architecture, and a Mediterranean climate—Santa Barbara more
than lives up to its billing as the "American Riviera." A hundred miles
north of Los Angeles, the exclusive enclave is home (or second
home) to many a mega-celebrity: Oprah Winfrey, Kevin Costner, and
Michael Douglas.

① ★★★ kids **Santa Barbara
Mission.** With its stately, pink sandstone facade and twin bell towers,
the aptly nicknamed "Queen of the
Missions" occupies a verdant hill
overlooking the town and the Chan-
nel Islands in the distance. The Spanish Franciscans established the
mission in 1786 using the labor and
craftsmanship of native Chumash
Indians (whom they were trying to
convert). Over the years, the original
adobe buildings have seen substantial additions and renovations—
earthquakes in 1812 and 1925
caused serious damage. Take the
self-guided tour or the 90-minute
docent-guided tour. *2201 Laguna St.
(at Los Olivos St.).* ☎ *805/682-4149.
www.santabarbaramission.org. Self-
guided tours $5 adults, $1 kids 5–15,
free for kids 4 & under. Docent-
guided tours $8 per person; Thurs–
Fri 11am & Sat 10:30am. Daily
9am–5pm.*

② **State Street.** The town's main
drag is populated by restaurants,
loud bars, movie theaters, art galleries, and countless shops selling sou-
venir trinkets to high-end fashion.
*State St., from Victoria St. to the
beach.*

③ ★ **Santa Barbara Museum
of Art.** The small but excellent
museum boasts an eclectic permanent collection featuring classical
antiquities, 19th- and 20th-century
paintings, contemporary Latin American art, photography, and most
impressively, Asian art from India,
Tibet, China, Japan, and Southeast
Asia. *1130 State St.* ☎ *805/963-4364.
www.sbmuseart.org. Admission $9
adults; $6 seniors, students, & kids
6–17; free for kids 5 & under; free for
all Sun. Tues–Sun 11am–5pm.*

④ ★★ **County Courthouse.** Built
in 1929 in the Spanish-Moorish style,
this National Historic Landmark

The Santa Barbara Museum of Art.

For sublime views of the surrounding area, ascend the 85-foot clock tower of the County Courthouse.

features a grand archway, turrets, wrought-iron balconies, mosaic tiles, hand-carved doors, hand-painted ceilings, striking murals that illustrate the history of the land, and a grassy sunken garden. At the top of the 85-foot El Mirador clock tower, you can admire magnificent views of the mountains, the coastline, and the sea of red-tile roofs. *1100 Anacapa St., Santa Barbara.* ☎ *805/962-6464. www.santabarbaracourthouse.org. Free admission. Mon–Fri 8am–5pm, Sat–Sun 10am–4:30pm. Free guided tours Mon–Tues & Fri at 10:30am; Mon–Sat at 2pm.*

⑤ ★ El Presidio de Santa Barbara. The last of four Spanish military outposts built in California was founded on this site in 1782. Over the years only two of the presidio's buildings have survived the earthquakes and downtown expansion: El Cuartel, the second-oldest adobe building in the state, and Canedo Adobe, a remnant of the barracks. The other standing structures, including the chapel, bell tower, and padres' quarters, were fastidiously reconstructed after 30 years of research and archaeological excavations. Be sure to also check out

nearby **Casa de la Guerra** (15 E. De la Guerra St.), an adobe home built in 1820 that later served as a model of style and architecture for the city's rebuilding process. *123 E. Canon Perdido St.* ☎ *805/965-0093. www.sbthp.org. Admission (includes Casa de la Guerra) $5 adults, free for kids 16 & under. Daily 10:30am–4:30pm.*

⑥ ★ Santa Barbara Historical Museum. This first-rate museum traces the vibrant history of Santa Barbara from the early Chumash, through the Spanish explorers and Mexican settlers, American acquisition, and the ruinous 1925 earthquake. *136 E. De la Guerra St.* ☎ *805/966-1601. www.santabarbaramuseum.com. Free admission, donations appreciated. Tues–Sat 10am–5pm; Sun noon–5pm.*

⑦ ★ La Super-Rica Taqueria. Grab a couple of tasty tacos from this revered Mexican joint, a favorite of the late Julia Child. If you want to participate in the town's vigorous ongoing "best taco" debate, also try Lilly's Tacos, 310 Chapala St. (☎ 805/966-9180; www.lillystacos.com). *622 N. Milpas St.* ☎ *805/963-4940. Most items $4–$10. Cash only. Lunch & dinner Thurs–Tues.*

⑧ ★★ kids Santa Barbara Zoo. Considered one of the best small zoos in the country, this zoo

One of the many colorful characters you'll find at the Santa Barbara Zoo.

East Beach.

presents 500 animals (160 different species) on 30 acres of botanic gardens overlooking the Pacific Ocean. Exhibits include the popular Humboldt penguins and several endangered species, such as Asian elephants, snow leopards, white-handed gibbons, and western lowland gorillas. *500 Niños Dr.* ☎ *805/ 962-5339. www.sbzoo.org. Admission $12 adults, $10 seniors & kids 2–12, free for kids 1 & under. Daily 10am–5pm.*

9 ★★ **East Beach.** Santa Barbara's best all-around beach has a wide, sandy beach with volleyball courts, a rollerblading path, picnic areas, a playground, and restrooms, all hemmed in by a green lawn under swaying palm trees. It's also one of the most accessible, located across from the zoo and stretching all the way to the pier. *East of Stearns Wharf. Sunrise–10pm.*

10 ★ **kids Stearns Wharf.** The longest and oldest working wooden wharf in California is located at the very bottom of State Street (look for the statue of three dolphins), and

reels in five million visitors a year. Eat, shop, go pier fishing, or visit the **Ty Warner Sea Center,** full of interactive exhibits on marine education, the most entertaining being the live shark touch pool. *End of State St. www.stearnswharf.org. Ty Warner Sea Center, 211 Stearns Wharf.* ☎ *805/962-2526. www.sbnature. org. Admission $8 adults, $7 seniors & kids 13–17, $5 kids 2–12, free for kids 1 & under. Daily 10am–5pm.*

11 **Brophy Brothers.** It can be noisy and crowded, but you're here for the superfresh seafood, consistently voted by locals as the best in Santa Barbara. Ask for an outdoor table to savor the harbor views, but if the wait is killing you, don't hesitate to plop down at the bar. Some favorites include the clam chowder, the beer-boiled shrimp, and the garlic-baked clams. *In the Waterfront Center, 119 Harbor Way.* ☎ *805/966-4418. Reservations not accepted. Entrees $9–$19. AE, MC, V. Lunch & dinner daily.*

Santa Ynez Wine Country

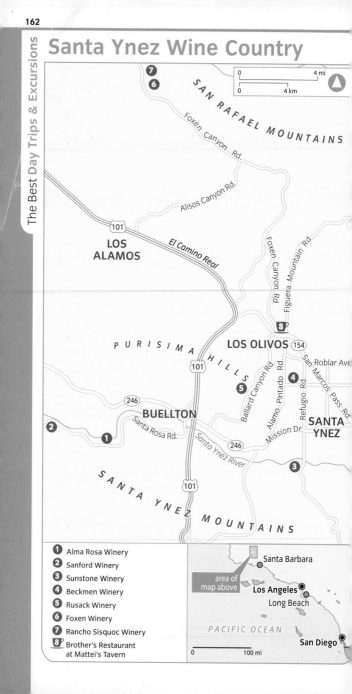

SAN RAFAEL MOUNTAINS

Foxen Canyon Rd.

Alisos Canyon Rd.

101

LOS ALAMOS

El Camino Real

Foxen Canyon Rd.

Figueroa Mountain Rd.

8

P U R I S I M A   H I L L S

101

LOS OLIVOS 154

San Roblar Ave.

4

5

Ballard Canyon Rd.

Alamo Pintado Rd.

San Marcos Pass Rd.

Refugio Rd.

246

BUELLTON

Santa Rosa Rd.

SANTA YNEZ

Mission Dr.

2

1

Santa Ynez River

246

3

101

S A N T A   Y N E Z   M O U N T A I N S

0 ——— 4 mi
0 ——— 4 km

1 Alma Rosa Winery
2 Sanford Winery
3 Sunstone Winery
4 Beckmen Winery
5 Rusack Winery
6 Foxen Winery
7 Rancho Sisquoc Winery
8 Brother's Restaurant at Mattei's Tavern

Santa Barbara

area of map above

Los Angeles
Long Beach

PACIFIC OCEAN

San Diego

0 ——— 100 mi

Thirty miles north of Santa Barbara, the Santa Ynez Valley offers an excellent wine-country getaway—rolling hills of green vineyards and golden grazing pastures, quaint restaurants, small wineries, and most importantly (perhaps surprisingly), excellent wines, particularly the difficult-to-master pinot noirs. The success of the 2004 Oscar®-nominated movie *Sideways* may have boosted this region's profile, but it's still no Napa Valley—and that's a good thing. These wineries are less crowded, more accessible, and refreshingly low-key.

Travel Tip

Don't drink and drive! If you aren't able to have a designated driver in your party, you can always practice the four S's—"swirl, smell, sip, and spit"—like a true evaluator of fine wines.

① ★ Alma Rosa Winery & Vineyards. Although pioneering vintner Richard Sanford left his namesake winery (below) in 2005, he's maintained the appealingly rustic tasting room, where *Sideways* shot a memorable scene. The new winery concentrates on organic farming and sustainable agriculture (Sanford was the first in the county to plant 100% organic vineyards) as well as food-friendly, well-balanced wines. *7250 Santa Rosa Rd., Buellton. ☎ 805/688-9090. www.almarosa winery.com. Tastings $10. Daily 11am–4:30pm.*

② ★★ Sanford Winery & Vineyards. Sample some first-rate pinot noirs and chardonnays at this winery's expansive tasting room, crafted in the California-mission style with handmade adobe bricks and local stones. The back patio provides panoramas of the estate vineyards and the Santa Rita Hills and makes a relaxing spot for a quick picnic. *5010 Santa Rosa Rd., Lompoc. ☎ 805/735-5900. www.sanford winery.com. Tastings $10 (includes souvenir glass). Daily 11am–5pm.*

③ ★ Sunstone Vineyards and Winery. Sunstone is one of the largest organic vineyards in Santa Barbara County, and its tasting room draws crowds for its old-world charm and Rhône varietals such as Viognier. With its lavender-scented courtyard and barrel-aging caves built into the hillside, the winery is designed to make visitors feel as if they've stumbled upon a country-side manor in Provence. *125 N. Refugio Rd., Santa Ynez. ☎ 805/688-9463. www.sunstonewinery.com. Tastings $10 (includes souvenir glass). Daily 10am–4pm.*

④ ★★ Beckmen Vineyards. This is a small, family-owned winery with a nifty outdoor deck and a beautiful pond ringed by gazebos, a perfect setting for splitting a bottle—the estate-grown grenache is

The barrel barn at the Sanford Winery.

A tasting at the Sunstone Winery.

excellent—between friends and taking in the rural beauty. *2670 Ontiveros Rd., Los Olivos.* ☎ *805/688-8664. www.beckmenvineyards.com. Tastings $10, reserve tastings $15. Daily 11am–5pm.*

5 ★ **Rusack Vineyards.** Tucked away in picturesque Ballard Canyon is this boutique winery that produces less than 7,000 cases a year and garners stellar reviews for its Syrahs, pinot noirs, and chardonnays. The tree-canopied deck overlooks the vineyards and the oak-dotted hills, which turn golden in the late-afternoon sun. *1819 Ballard Canyon Rd., Solvang.* ☎ *805/688-1278. www.rusack.com. Tastings $6 (includes souvenir glass). Daily 11am–5pm.*

6 ★★ **Foxen Winery & Vineyard.** Foxen offers two different wine-tasting experiences a half-mile apart: A new, modern, solar-powered tasting room presents burgundy and Rhône-style wines; the original roadside tin-roofed tasting shack has been renamed Foxen 7200 and showcases bordeaux and Cal Ital–style wines. Raves go to its pinot noirs from the Sea Smoke Vineyard in the Santa Rita Hills. *7200 & 7600 Foxen Canyon Rd., Santa Maria.* ☎ *805/937-4251. www.foxenvineyard.com. Tastings $10 (includes souvenir glass). Daily 11am–4pm.*

7 ★ **Rancho Sisquoc Winery.** Ramble down a couple miles of farm road, past the quaint, white San Ramon Chapel, a state landmark, and sample some big reds and bordeaux blends, many of which pair nicely with the local Santa Maria–style barbecue. *6600 Foxen Canyon Rd., Santa Maria.* ☎ *805/934-4332. www.ranchosisquoc.com. Tastings $8 (includes souvenir glass). Mon–Fri 10am–4pm; Fri–Sun 10am–5pm.*

8 ★★★ **Brother's Restaurant at Mattei's Tavern.** This rambling, clapboard building was built as a stagecoach stop in 1886, and it manages to retain all of its Old West history. Settle into a slow-roasted prime rib or rack of lamb, then chase it with a sinful dessert like mud pie with Kahlúa-caramel sauce. *2350 Railway Ave. (near Grand Ave. & Hwy. 154), Los Olivos.* ☎ *805/688-4820. www.matteistavern.com. Reservations recommended. Entrees $18–$44. AE, MC, V. Dinner daily.* ●

A dish at Brother's at Mattei's Tavern.

Before You Go

Tourist Office

The **Los Angeles Convention and Visitors Bureau** (L.A. INC.; ☎ 800/228-2452 or 213/624-7300; www.discoverlosangeles.com) is the city's main source for information. The bureau also provides two **walk-in visitor centers:** downtown at 685 S. Figueroa St. (Mon–Fri 9am–5pm) and in Hollywood at the Hollywood & Highland Center, 6801 Hollywood Blvd. (at Highland Ave.), Ste. 237 (daily 10am–11pm).

The Best Times to Go

In Los Angeles, as in many places, tourism peaks during **summer.** Hotel rooms and restaurant reservations are harder to come by, and top attractions tend to be packed with both visitors and locals. Although the beach communities almost always remain comfortable, summer can be stifling when daytime temperatures soar and the dreaded L.A. smog is in full effect. Moderate temperatures, fewer crowds, and lower hotel rates make travel to L.A. most enjoyable during the **winter.** From early autumn to late spring, as the smog abates, the city is at its prettiest.

Festivals & Special Events

SPRING. In mid-March to mid-May, the **California Poppy Reserve** in Antelope Valley, less than an hour's drive north of Los Angeles, comes alive in a brilliant display of red and orange. The annual **California Poppy Festival** (☎ 661/723-6077; www.poppy festival.com) blooms in late April. On weekends from late April to Memorial Day, **Renaissance Pleasure Faire** (☎ 800/52-FAIRE; www.renfair.com/socal), one of America's largest Renaissance festivals, transforms the Glen Helen Regional Park in San Bernardino into a mystical realm of knights, maidens, dragons, and fairies. Relive the days of yore, if thou wouldst, in period costume. On May 5 and the week surrounding, **Cinco de Mayo** festivities take place in El Pueblo de Los Angeles State Historic Park, Downtown (☎ 213/628-1274). Food, live music, and dancing celebrate the Mexican victory over the French Army in 1862. In the second half of May is the **Venice Art Walk** (☎ 310/392-WALK; www.venice familyclinic.org) in Venice Beach. This annual weekend event, nearing its 30th anniversary, leads art lovers on a tour through galleries, and the private home studios of more than 50 established or emerging artists.

SUMMER. In mid-June the **Playboy Jazz Festival** (☎ 213/480-3232) brings top jazz musicians to the Hollywood Bowl. Bill Cosby has presided over ceremonies since 1995. One of the largest lesbian and gay pride festivals and parades in the world, **Christopher Street West Festival & Parade** (☎ 323/969-8302; www.lapride.org) takes place in West Hollywood in the first half of June. There's food, music, dancing, general fabulousness, and then more dancing, all of which culminates in a parade down Santa Monica Boulevard on Sunday. Across 10 days in late June and early July, the well-attended **Los Angeles Film Festival** (☎ 866/345-6337; www.lafilmfest.com) showcases more than 175 American and international indies and short films. Surf's up in early August for the **International Surf Festival** (www.surffestival.org), which takes place in Hermosa Beach, Manhattan Beach, and Redondo Beach. Other contests include soccer, volleyball, running, swimming, and sand-castle building. In mid-August,

Previous page: Riding in style in Beverly Hills.

celebrate Japanese culture and heritage at the **Nisei Week Japanese Festival** (☎ 213/687-7193; www.niseiweek.org) in Little Tokyo. Festivities include parades, food, Taiko Drum performances, arts, and crafts.

FALL. One of the largest county fairs in the world, **Los Angeles County Fair** (☎ 909/623-3111; www.lacountyfair.com) takes place throughout September at the Los Angeles County Fair and Exposition Center in Pomona. Attractions include concerts, carnival rides, horse racing, food contests, arts and crafts, agricultural displays, and educational exhibitions. Over 2 consecutive long weekends in early October, the popular **Catalina Island Jazz Trax Festival** (☎ 760/323-1171; www.jazztrax.com) offers performances by contemporary jazz greats at Avalon's legendary Casino Ballroom. The **West Hollywood Halloween Costume Carnaval** (☎ 310/289-2525; www.weho.org) is one of the world's largest Halloween parties with hundreds of thousands of insanely costumed people partying all night along Santa Monica Boulevard on October 31. In early November **American Film Institute's AFI Fest** (☎ 866/AFI-FEST; www.afifest.com), going strong after 20 years, gathers some of the biggest names in the international film community to present new movies from around the globe.

WINTER. Every January 1, the world-famous **Tournament of Roses** (☎ 626/449-4100; www.tournamentofroses.com) parades down Colorado Boulevard in Pasadena with spectacular floats, precise marching bands, and colorful equestrian entries. The Rose Bowl football game plays immediately afterward. In early February, celebrate **Chinese New Year** at the **Golden Dragon Parade** in Chinatown. Dragon dancers and martial-arts masters take to the streets with two dozen floats and several marching bands. For more info, contact the Chinese Chamber of Commerce (☎ 213/617-0396; www.lagoldendragonparade.com). In mid-February the PGA Tour comes to the beautiful and historic Riviera Country Club in Pacific Palisades for the **Nissan Open.** Look for celebrity faces in the crowd. For more info, contact the Los Angeles Junior Chamber of Commerce (☎ 213/482-1311; www.lajcc.org). During the first weekend in March, the **Los Angeles Marathon** (☎ 310/444-5544; www.lamarathon.com) draws thousands of participants and a million spectators. The run starts in Downtown Los Angeles, where there's also a 5K Run/Walk.

Weather

People sometimes think of L.A. as perpetually sunny and mild, but it does have a couple of unique seasons: "June Gloom" and "the Santa Anas." "June Gloom" refers to the ocean fog that keeps the beach communities (and often the whole city) overcast into early afternoon; it's most common in June but can occur any time between March and mid-August. The "Santa Anas" are strong, hot winds that race into town from across the desert in the middle of autumn. The winds increase brush-fire danger (and, on the plus side, good offshore conditions for surfing). Aside from these minor disturbances, Los Angeles averages nearly 320 days of sunny skies per year, with an average mean temperature of 66°F (19°C). You can sunbathe throughout the year, but you'll need a wetsuit to venture into the ocean in winter, when water temps hover around 50° to 55°F (10°–13°C). In the summer and fall, the water usually warms to about 65° to 70°F (18°–21°C), which some still find to be too chilly. Los Angeles averages about 34 days of rainfall a year (usually Feb–Apr); this isn't much, but it can cause flooding when it strikes fast. Rain is extremely rare between May and November.

Useful Websites

- **theguide.latimes.com**: From the *L.A. Times*, the Guide is loaded with entertainment, nightlife, and cultural reviews, as well as specialty guides for Disney, Universal Studios, and more.

- **www.laweekly.com**: The online edition of the alternative *L.A. Weekly* paper combines listings with social commentary. It has an events calendar, arts listings, music picks, and restaurant reviews from Pulitzer Prize–winning Jonathan Gold.

- **discoverlosangeles.com**: This "official" visitors guide to the city is a comprehensive, if slightly sanitized, website that contains mini-guides and recommended itineraries. Order a free copy of the Los Angeles visitors guide or download and print your own copy.

- **losangeles.citysearch.com**: The local City Search site features movie/sports/entertainment listings, as well as user-driven recommendations and reviews.

- **www.lamag.com**: The online version of the monthly *Los Angeles* magazine offers features on local history and personalities, an events calendar, and tips on outdoor activities and where to shop and dine.

Cellphones

Most likely your phone will work fine in L.A., but to be safe, confirm with your wireless company's coverage map on its website before leaving home. It's also possible to **rent** a phone from **InTouch USA** (☎ 800/872-7626; www.intouchglobal.com). At the arrivals level of the international terminal at LAX airport, visitors can find a rental kiosk for a phone-rental company called **Trip-Tel.** Phones can be dropped off at the airport or shipped back via FedEx when you're done. For more information, call ☎ 877/TRIP-TEL or log on to www.triptel.com.

Car Rental

Los Angeles is one of the cheapest places in America to rent a car. Major national car-rental companies usually rent economy- and compact-class cars for about $40 per day and $130 per week, with unlimited mileage. All the major car-rental agencies have offices at the airport and in the larger hotels.

Getting **There**

By Plane

Five airports serve the Los Angeles area. Most visitors fly into **Los Angeles International Airport** (☎ 310/646-5252; www.lawa.org/lax), better known as LAX, which is situated oceanside, between Marina del Rey and Manhattan Beach. LAX is a convenient place to land; it's located within minutes of Santa Monica and the beaches, and not more than a half-hour from Downtown, Hollywood, and the Westside. Free shuttle buses connect the terminals and stop in front of each ticket building. Special minibuses accessible to travelers with disabilities are also available.

For some travelers, one of the area's smaller airports might be more convenient than LAX. **Bob Hope Airport** (2627 N. Hollywood Way, Burbank; ☎ 818/840-8840; www.bobhopeairport.com) is especially easy to use and is accessible to the valley, Hollywood, and Downtown L.A. Other less-than-ideal options: **Long Beach Municipal Airport** (4100 Donald Douglas Dr., Long Beach; ☎ 562/570-2600; www.lgb. org), south of LAX, is the best place to land if you're visiting Long Beach or northern Orange County and want to avoid L.A. **John Wayne Airport** (19051 Airport Way N., Anaheim; ☎ 949/252-5200; www.ocair.com) is closest to Disneyland, Knott's Berry Farm, and other Orange County attractions. **Ontario International Airport** (Terminal Way, Ontario; ☎ 909/937-2700; www.lawa.org/ont) is not a popular airport for tourists; businesspeople use it to head to San Bernardino, Riverside, and other inland communities. It can also be convenient for going to Palm Springs.

GETTING TO & FROM THE AIRPORT

By Taxi: Typical cab fares from the airport are approximately $42 to downtown, at least $35 to Hollywood, and $20 to Santa Monica, and these fares don't include the airport surcharge ($2.50), possible extra-bag fees, or tip.

By Shuttle: Many city hotels provide free shuttles for their guests; ask when you make reservations. **SuperShuttle** (☎ 800/258-3826 or 310/782-6600; www. supershuttle.com) offers regularly scheduled minivans from LAX to any location in the city. Fares range from $15 to $35 per person depending on your destination.

By Car
Los Angeles is accessible by many major highways. If you're coming

from the north, you can take the quick route along I-5 through the middle of the state, or the scenic route along the coast. To reach the beach communities and L.A.'s Westside, take I-405 south, which is notorious for heavy, slow-moving traffic; to get to Hollywood, take California 170 south to U.S. 101 south (this route is called Hollywood Fwy. the entire way); I-5 will take you along the eastern edge of Downtown and into Orange County.

If you're taking the **scenic coastal route** from the north, take U.S. 101 to I-405 or I-5, or stay on U.S. 101, following the instructions above to your destination. If you're approaching **from the east,** you'll be coming in on I-10. For Orange County, take California 57 south. I-10 continues through Downtown and terminates at the beach. If you're heading to the Westside, take I-405 north. To get to the beaches, take California 1 (PCH) north or south, depending on your destination. **From the south,** head north on I-5 at the southern end of Orange County. I-405 splits off to the west; take this road to the Westside and beach communities. Stay on I-5 to reach Downtown and Hollywood.

By Train
Amtrak (☎ 800/USA-RAIL; www. amtrakcalifornia.com) connects Los Angeles with about 500 American cities. The L.A. train terminus is **Union Station,** 800 N. Alameda (☎ 213/617-0111), on Downtown's northern edge.

Getting **Around**

By Car
L.A.'s urban sprawl is connected by an elaborate network of

well-maintained freeways, so a car is the best way to get around. The system works well to get you where you need to be, although rush-hour (roughly 6–9am and 3–7pm) traffic is often bumper-to-bumper, particularly on the congested I-405.

By Taxi

Typically, distances are long in Los Angeles, and cab fares can run high—even a short hop might cost $20. A ride costs $2.65 to begin, and then it's $2.45 per mile. It's possible to hail a cab when you're downtown, but everywhere else you'll need to order a taxi in advance from **Checker Cab** (☎ 323/654-8400), **L.A. Taxi** (☎ 213/627-7000), or **United Taxi** (☎ 213/483-7604).

By Public Transportation

It's possible, but certainly not preferable, to tour Los Angeles entirely by public transportation. The metropolis is most navigable by automobile; many areas are simply inaccessible without one. Public transport might work for you if you're in the city for only a short time, are on a very tight budget, or don't expect to be moving around a lot. The city's trains and buses are operated by the **Los Angeles County Metropolitan Transit Authority** (MTA; ☎ 213/922-2000; www.mta.net), and MTA brochures and schedules are available at every area visitor center.

By Bus: Extensive touring by bus is simply not practical; stops are too spread out, and transfers are too frequent. For short trips, buses remain an economical and environmentally correct choice. However, riding buses late at night should be avoided. The basic bus fare is $1.25 for all local lines, with transfers costing 25¢. A **Metro Day Pass** is $3 and gives you unlimited bus and rail rides all day; these can be purchased while boarding any Metro Bus (exact change is needed) or at the self-service vending machines at the Metro Rail stations. The

Downtown Area Short Hop (DASH) shuttle system operates buses throughout Downtown, Hollywood, and the Westside. Service runs every 5 to 20 minutes, depending on the time of day, and costs just 25¢. Contact the Department of Transportation (☎ 213/808-2273; www.ladottransit.com) for schedules and route information. The **Cityline** shuttle is a great way to get around West Hollywood on weekdays (9am–4pm) and Saturday (10am–7:30pm). For 50¢, it'll take you to most of the major shops and restaurants throughout WeHo (very handy if you park your car in a flat-fee lot). For more information, call ☎ 800/447-2189.

By Rail & Subway: L.A.'s subway system does not serve the entire city. The **Metro Blue Line,** an aboveground rail line, connects Downtown Los Angeles with Long Beach. Trains operate daily from 6am to 9pm; the fare is $1.25. The **Metro Red Line** begins at Union Station, the city's main train depot, and travels west underneath Wilshire Boulevard, looping north into Hollywood and the San Fernando Valley. The fare is $1.25; discount tokens are available at Metro service centers and many area convenience stores. The **Metro Purple Line** subway shares six stations with the Red Line Downtown and continues to the Mid-Wilshire area. The fare is $1.25. The **Metro Green Line** runs for 20 miles along the center of the new I-105, the Glenn Anderson (Century) Freeway, and connects Norwalk in eastern Los Angeles County to LAX. A connection with the Blue Line offers visitors access from LAX to Downtown L.A. or Long Beach. The fare is $1.25. The **Metro Gold Line** is a 14-mile link between Pasadena and Union Station in Downtown L.A. Stops include Old Pasadena, the Southwest Museum, and Chinatown. The fare is $1.50. A Metro Day Pass is $6 and weekly Metro passes are available for $20 at Metro Customer Centers and local convenience and grocery stores. For more information

on public transportation call **MTA** at ☎ 213/922-2000, or, better yet, log on to their handy website at www.mta.net.

Fast **Facts**

AREA CODES Areas west of La Cienega Boulevard, including Beverly Hills and the city's beach communities, use the **310** area code. Portions of Los Angeles County east and south of the city, including Long Beach, are in the **562** area. The San Fernando Valley has the **818** area code, while points east—including parts of Burbank, Glendale, and Pasadena—use the newly created **626** code. The Downtown business area uses **213**. All other numbers, including Griffith Park, Hollywood, and parts of West Hollywood (east of La Cienega Blvd.), use the area code **323**.

ATMS/CASHPOINTS The **Cirrus** (☎ 800/424-7787; www.mastercard.com) and **PLUS** (☎ 800/843-7587; www.visa.com) networks span the globe; look at the back of your bankcard to see which network you're on, and then call or check online for ATM locations. Find out your daily withdrawal limit before you depart.

BABYSITTERS If you're staying at one of the larger hotels, the concierge can usually recommend a reliable babysitter. If not, contact the **Baby-Sitters Guild** in Glendale (☎ 310/837-1800 or 818/552-2229), L.A.'s oldest and largest babysitting service.

BANKS Most banks are open weekdays from 9am to 5pm and sometimes Saturday mornings. Many banks have ATMs for 24-hour banking.

BUSINESS HOURS Offices are usually open weekdays from 9am to 5pm. Stores typically open between

9 and 10am and close between 5 and 6pm from Monday through Saturday. Stores in shopping complexes or malls tend to stay open late, until about 9pm, and many malls and larger department stores are open on Sundays.

DENTISTS Seek recommendations for dental services in the area by calling ☎ **1-800-DENTIST** (☎ 800/336-8422; www.1800dentist.com).

DOCTORS See "Hospital," below.

DRINKING LAWS The legal age for purchase and consumption of alcoholic beverages is 21; proof of age is required and often requested at bars, nightclubs, and restaurants, so it's always a good idea to bring ID when you go out. Do not carry open containers of alcohol in your car or any public area that isn't zoned for alcohol consumption. The police can fine you on the spot. And nothing will ruin your trip faster than getting a citation for DUI ("driving under the influence"), so don't even think about driving while intoxicated.

DRUGSTORES & PHARMACIES A **Rite-Aid** pharmacy is located in Hollywood at 6726 W. Sunset Blvd., at Highland Avenue; for the location of the store nearest to you, call ☎ 800/RITE-AID (748-3243) or go to www.riteaid.com. **Walgreens** (☎ 800/925-4733; www.walgreens.com), and **CVS** (☎ 888/607-4287; www.cvs.com) also have many locations throughout the city.

ELECTRICITY Like Canada, the United States uses 110–120 volts AC (60 cycles), compared to 220–240 volts

AC (50 cycles) in most of Europe, Australia, and New Zealand. If your small appliances use 220–240 volts, you'll need a 110-volt transformer and a plug adapter with two flat, parallel pins to operate them here. Downward converters that change 220–240 volts to 110–120 volts are difficult to find in the United States, so bring one with you.

EMBASSIES & CONSULATES All embassies are located in the nation's capital, Washington, D.C. Some consulates are located in major U.S. cities, and most nations have a mission to the United Nations in New York City. For a directory of embassies in Washington, D.C., call ☎ 202/555-1212 or log on to www.embassy.org/embassies. The embassy of **Australia** is at 1601 Massachusetts Ave. NW, Washington, DC 20036 (☎ 202/797-3000; www.austemb.org); the embassy of **Canada** is at 501 Pennsylvania Ave. NW, Washington, DC 20001 (☎ 202/682-1740; www.canadianembassy.org); the embassy of **Ireland** is at 2234 Massachusetts Ave. NW, Washington, DC 20008 (☎ 202/462-3939; www.irelandemb.org); the embassy of **New Zealand** is at 37 Observatory Circle NW, Washington, DC 20008 (☎ 202/328-4800; www.nzembassy.com/usa); the embassy of the **United Kingdom** is at 3100 Massachusetts Ave. NW, Washington, DC 20008 (☎ 202/588-7800; ukinusa.fco.gov.uk).

EMERGENCIES Call ☎ **911** to report a fire, call the police, or get an ambulance anywhere in the United States. The **Poison Control Center** can be reached at ☎ 800/222-1222, toll free from any phone. If you encounter traveler's problems, call the Los Angeles chapter of **Travelers Aid International** (☎ 310/646-2270; www.travelersaid.org), a nationwide, nonprofit, social service organization that helps travelers in difficult straits.

GAY & LESBIAN TRAVEL RESOURCES Two great resources for L.A.'s gay and lesbian visitors are the **L.A. Gay and Lesbian Center** (☎ 323/993-7400; www.laglc.org), an advocacy group; and the **West Hollywood Convention and Visitors Bureau** (☎ 800/368-6020; www.gogaywesthollywood.com), which provides info on everything from events to accommodations.

HOLIDAYS Banks, government offices, post offices, and many stores, restaurants, and museums are closed on the following legal national holidays: January 1 (New Year's Day), the third Monday in January (Martin Luther King, Jr., Day), the third Monday in February (Presidents' Day), the last Monday in May (Memorial Day), July 4th (Independence Day), the first Monday in September (Labor Day), the second Monday in October (Columbus Day), November 11 (Veterans Day/Armistice Day), the fourth Thursday in November (Thanksgiving Day), and December 25 (Christmas). The Tuesday after the first Monday in November is Election Day, a federal government holiday in presidential-election years (held every 4 years, and next in 2012).

HOSPITAL The centrally located **Cedars-Sinai Medical Center,** 8700 Beverly Blvd., Los Angeles (☎ 310/423-3277; www.csmc.edu), has a 24-hour emergency room staffed by some of the country's finest doctors.

INSURANCE The cost of travel insurance varies widely, depending on the cost and length of your trip, your age and health, and the type of trip you're taking, but expect to pay between 5% and 8% of the vacation itself. You can get estimates from various providers through **InsureMyTrip.com.** Enter your trip cost and dates, your age, and other information, for prices from more than a dozen companies. **Trip-cancellation insurance** will help retrieve your money if you have to back out of a trip or depart early, or if your travel supplier goes bankrupt. You won't get back 100% of your prepaid trip cost, but you'll be refunded a substantial portion. **TravelSafe** (☎ 888/885-7233; www.travelsafe.com) offers coverage. **Expedia.com** also offers any-reason cancellation coverage for its air-hotel packages.

Although it's not required of travelers, **health insurance** is highly recommended. International visitors should note that unlike many European countries, the U.S. does not usually offer free or low-cost medical care to its citizens or visitors. Doctors and hospitals are expensive and, in most cases, will require advance payment or proof of insurance coverage before they will render their services. Though lack of insurance may prevent you from being admitted to a hospital in non-emergencies, don't worry about being left on a street corner to die: The American way is to fix you now and bill the living daylights out of you later.

For **lost luggage** on flights within the U.S., checked baggage is covered up to $2,500 per ticketed passenger. On flights outside the U.S. (and on U.S. portions of international trips), baggage coverage is limited to approximately $9.07 per pound, up to approximately $635 per checked bag. If you plan to check items more valuable than what's covered by the standard liability, see if your homeowner's policy covers your valuables, get baggage insurance as part of your comprehensive travel-insurance package, or buy Travel Guard's "BagTrak" product. If your luggage is lost, immediately file a lost-luggage claim at the airport, detailing the luggage contents. Most airlines require that you report delayed, damaged, or lost baggage within 4 hours of arrival. The airlines are required to deliver luggage, once found, directly to your house or destination free of charge.

INTERNET ACCESS Most hotels and many cafes have wireless access. Wi-Fi hotspots are available at Starbucks, McDonald's, or FedEx Office, which also offers computer stations. You can also get online at public libraries such as the one at 161 S. Gardner St., near the Grove. Go to www.lapl.org to find more locations.

Groundwork Coffee (☎ 323/871-0107; http://lacoffee.com) provides 2 hours of free Wi-Fi and is conveniently located at 1501 Cahuenga Blvd. (at Sunset Blvd.), across the street from Amoeba Music.

In **West Hollywood,** Wi-Fi is provided for free on Santa Monica Boulevard, from La Brea to Fairfax. The signal works best outdoors, along Santa Monica Boulevard, in Plummer Park, and the Gateway Center.

MAIL Domestic rates are 28¢ for a postcard and 44¢ for a letter. For international mail, a first-class letter of up to 1 ounce costs 98¢ (75¢ to Canada and 79¢ to Mexico); a first-class postcard costs the same as a letter.

The main post office is located at 7101 S. Central Ave. (Mon–Fri 7am–7pm; Sat 7am–3:30pm). A centrally located post office is at Hollywood & Highland Center, 6801 Hollywood Blvd. (at Highland Ave.), Ste. 167 (Mon–Fri 10am–6pm). To find the one closest to you, call ☎ 800/ASK-USPS (275-8777) or go to www.usps.com.

NEWSPAPERS & MAGAZINES The *Los Angeles Times* (www.latimes.com) is a high-quality daily with strong local and national coverage. Its Sunday "Calendar" section (findlocal.lat-imes.com) is an excellent guide to entertainment. *L.A. Weekly* (www.laweekly.com), a free weekly listings magazine, is packed with information on current events around town. *Los Angeles* magazine (www.lamag.com) is a glossy, city-based monthly with great information on art, music, and outdoor adventures, as well as shopping and dining.

PARKING   There are some frustrating parts of town (particularly around restaurants after 7:30pm) where you might have to give in and use valet parking. Restaurants and nightclubs usually charge between $5 and $7. Some areas, like Santa Monica and Beverly Hills, offer self-park lots and garages near the neighborhood action; costs range from $2 to $10. Also, have plenty of quarters for meters and read posted restrictions carefully, especially in residential neighborhoods.

PASSPORTS   Always keep a copy of your passport with you when you're traveling. If your passport is lost or stolen, having a copy significantly facilitates the reissuing process at a local consulate or embassy. Keep your passport and other valuables in your room's safe or in the hotel safe. See "Embassies & Consulates," above, for more information.

POLICE   In an emergency, dial ☎ **911.** For nonemergency police matters, call ☎ 877/ASK-LAPD (275-5273). In Beverly Hills, call ☎ 310/550-4951. In West Hollywood, call ☎ 310/855-8850. In Santa Monica, call ☎ 310/458-8491.

SMOKING   California law prohibits smoking in public buildings, restaurants, sports arenas, stores, elevators, banks, offices, and even bars. Most hotels are completely nonsmoking.

TAXES   Sales tax in Los Angeles is 9.75%. Hotel tax is charged on the room tariff only (which is not subject to sales tax) and is set by the city, ranging from 12% to 17% around southern California.

TELEPHONES   For local directory assistance ("information"), dial ☎ 411; for long-distance information, dial 1, the appropriate area code, and ☎ 555-1212. Most long-distance and international calls can be dialed directly from any phone.

TIPPING   In hotels, tip **bellhops** at least $1 per bag and tip the **chamber staff** $1 to $2 per day (more if you've left a disaster area). Tip the **doorman** or **concierge** only if he or she has provided you with some specific service (for example, calling a cab for you or obtaining difficult-to-get theater tickets). Tip the **valet-parking attendant** $1 every time you get your car. In restaurants, bars, and nightclubs, **service staff** and **bartenders** expect 15% to 20% of the check, **checkroom attendants** $1 per garment, and **valet-parking attendants** $1 per vehicle. Tip **cabdrivers** 15%, **skycaps** at airports at least $1 per bag, and **hairdressers** and **barbers** 15% to 20%.

TOILETS   You won't find public toilets or "restrooms" on the streets of L.A., but they can be found in hotel lobbies, bars, restaurants, museums, department stores, railway and bus stations, and service stations. Large hotels and fast-food restaurants are often the best bets for clean facilities.

TOURIST INFORMATION   The **Los Angeles Convention and Visitors Bureau** (**L.A. INC.;** ☎ 800/366-6116 or 213/689-8822; www.discoverlosangeles.com) is the city's main source for information. The bureau provides two **walk-in visitor centers:** Downtown at 685 S. Figueroa St. (Mon–Fri 9am–5pm), and in Hollywood at the Hollywood & Highland Center, 6801 Hollywood Blvd. (daily 10am–11pm).

A Brief **History**

16,500–10,000 B.C. Humans cross over the Bering land bridge into North America around 16,500 B.C. A couple thousand years later, tribes make their way down to California.

A.D. 1542 Juan Cabrillo, a Portuguese explorer, claims southern California as the City of God for the Spanish Empire, but does not establish a settlement.

1771 Franciscan friar Junípero Serra leads the establishment of the Mission San Gabriel Arcangel near present-day San Gabriel Valley.

1781 A multicultural group of 44 settlers, under orders from Spanish governor Felipe de Neve, establish "El Pueblo de Nuestra Señora la Reina de los Angeles del Río de Porciúncula" near present-day Olvera Street.

1821 Mexico achieves its independence from the Spanish Empire and claims Los Angeles and the rest of California.

1848 After 3 years of skirmishes, the U.S.–Mexican Treaty gives California to the United States.

1850 California becomes the 31st state of the union, and the City of Los Angeles is incorporated with a population of just over 1,500.

1885 The transcontinental railroad reaches Los Angeles, and southern California experiences its first land boom.

1892 Oil is discovered in Downtown Los Angeles by Edward L. Doheny.

1903 Hollywood is incorporated. The conservative community forbids the sale of alcohol.

1911 The Nestor Film Company, Hollywood's first film studio, takes over a tavern at Sunset and Gower boulevards.

1913 After 8 years, work is complete on the Los Angeles Aqueduct, which provides the city with water from the Owens Valley 233 miles north. At the dedication ceremony, chief engineer William Mulholland says "There it is. Take it."

1914 In a barn near Hollywood and Vine, Samuel Goldwyn, Cecil B. DeMille, and Jesse Lasky make the first feature-length film, *The Squaw Man*.

1923 The city produces a quarter of the world's petroleum.

1923 A large sign that reads HOLLY-WOODLAND is erected on Mount Lee as an advertisement for a Hollywood Hills housing development.

1927 Grauman's Chinese Theatre opens in Hollywood by showing Cecil B. DeMille's *The King of Kings*.

1929 The first Academy Awards ceremony takes place in the Blossom Room of the Hollywood Roosevelt Hotel.

1932 The city hosts the Summer Olympics for the first time. Population tops one million people.

1940 A highway between Los Angeles and Pasadena opens. The success of the Arroyo Seco Parkway convinces Angelenos that an elaborate freeway system could be the solution to the region's transportation problems.

1955 Crowds start lining up at 2am on July 18 for the public opening of Disneyland.

1958 Having moved from Brooklyn, the Los Angeles Dodgers play their first game in their new hometown, in front of nearly 80,000 fans at the Los Angeles Memorial Coliseum.

1962 California replaces New York as the most populous state in the union.

1965 Race riots rage in Watts for 6 days, causing 34 deaths and $35 million in damages.

1967 Former actor Ronald Reagan is elected governor of California.

1968 Robert Kennedy is assassinated at the Ambassador Hotel shortly after declaring victory in California's Democratic primary.

1973 Tom Bradley is elected mayor and holds the office for 20 years. At the time he's only the second African American elected mayor of a major U.S. city.

1984 Los Angeles hosts the Summer Olympics for the second time.

1988 Kirk Gibson's dramatic home run wins Game 1 of the World Series, which the Dodgers go on to win in five games.

1992 Race riots sparked by the Rodney King verdict result in approximately 50 deaths, 2,000 people injured, 10,000 people arrested, and material damages estimated between $800 million and $1 billion.

1994 The 6.7 Northridge earthquake shakes the city, causing 72 deaths and an estimated $12.5 billion in damage, making it one of the costliest natural disasters in U.S. history.

1995 A jury acquits O.J. Simpson of the double homicide of Nicole Brown Simpson and Ronald Goldman.

1997 The Getty Center opens on a hilltop on the Westside.

1999–2000 Los Angeles Lakers Shaquille O'Neal and Kobe Bryant team up for the first of three NBA Championships in a row.

2001 The Academy Awards ceremony moves into its permanent residence at the Kodak Theatre in Hollywood.

2003 Former actor Arnold Schwarzenegger is elected governor of California.

2005 Antonio Villaraigosa is elected mayor of Los Angeles, the first Latino to do so since 1872.

2008 Facing a state budget shortfall of $26.3 billion, Governor Schwarzenegger furloughs state workers, raises sales tax, raises tuition at state universities, writes IOUs to contractors, and threatens to close state parks.

2009–2010 Kobe Bryant leads the Los Angeles Lakers to back-to-back NBA Championships.

Los Angeles **in Film**

Billy Wilder's *Double Indemnity* (1944)

Billy Wilder's *Sunset Boulevard* (1950)

Nicholas Ray's *Rebel Without a Cause* (1955)

Roman Polanski's *Chinatown* (1974)

Ridley Scott's *Blade Runner* (1982)

Martha Coolidge's *Valley Girl* (1983)

Garry Marshall's *Pretty Woman* (1990)

Mick Jackson's *L.A. Story* (1991)

John Singleton's *Boyz n the Hood* (1991)
Robert Altman's *The Player* (1992)
Doug Liman's *Swingers* (1996)
Curtis Hanson's *L.A. Confidential* (1997)
David Lynch's *Mulholland Drive* (2001)

Catherine Hardwicke's *Thirteen* (2003)
Taylor Hackford's *Ray* (2003)
Christopher Nolan's *Inception* (2010)

Toll-Free Numbers & Websites

Airlines

AER LINGUS
☎ 800/474-7424
☎ 3531/886-8844 in Ireland
www.aerlingus.ie

AIR CANADA
☎ 888/247-2262
www.aircanada.com

AMERICAN AIRLINES
☎ 800/433-7300
www.aa.com

BRITISH AIRWAYS
☎ 800/247-9297
☎ 0870/850-9850 in the U.K.
www.british-airways.com

CONTINENTAL AIRLINES
☎ 800/525-0280
www.continental.com

DELTA AIR LINES
☎ 800/221-1212
www.delta.com

FRONTIER AIRLINES
☎ 800/432-1359
www.frontierairlines.com

JETBLUE AIRWAYS
☎ 800/538-2583
www.jetblue.com

UNITED AIRLINES
☎ 800/241-6522
www.ual.com

US AIRWAYS
☎ 800/428-4322
www.usairways.com

VIRGIN ATLANTIC AIRWAYS
☎ 800/821-5438
☎ 0870/380-2007 in the U.K.
www.virgin-atlantic.com

Car-Rental Agencies

ALAMO
☎ 800/462-5266
www.alamo.com

AVIS
☎ 800/831-1212
www.avis.com

BUDGET
☎ 800/527-0700
www.budget.com

DOLLAR
☎ 800/800-3665
www.dollar.com

ENTERPRISE
☎ 800/261-7331
www.enterprise.com

HERTZ
☎ 800/654-3131
www.hertz.com

NATIONAL
☎ 800/227-7368
www.nationalcar.com

THRIFTY
☎ 800/847-4389
www.thrifty.com

Index

See also Accommodations and Restaurant indexes, below.

Photo **Credits**